Knowledge Creation
in Community Development

FOREWORD

Enormous changes in society in Asian countries have arisen as a result of recent economic developments—especially among ASEAN countries. These changes have brought with them numerous challenges. In order to continue stable economic growth and social development as well as to improve the quality of life, these countries need to improve domestic policies and find solutions to the many problems that their local communities are facing today. Indeed, governments have not been inactive— they have tried to enhance their capability to resolve problems of local governments and communities by promoting the decentralization of power and citizen participation in domestic policies. As yet, their efforts have not met with notable success.

This book describes a new theory that could form the basis for community development in Asia. This is Knowledge Creation Theory, developed by Professor Emeritus Ikujiro Nonaka of Hitotsubashi University. Professor Nonaka developed the theory in the course of studying Japanese companies, and it appears to be uniquely relevant to the Asian context. It is based on the idea of applying management approaches used in the business sector to community development.

A number of case studies have been conducted to test the applicability of Prof. Nonaka's theory to community development contexts in ASEAN countries including Indonesia, the Philippines, Thailand, and Vietnam as well as Japan. The SECI model, the center of Prof. Nonaka's theory, describes the process of knowledge creation and the *phronetic* leadership approach, characterized by six abilities required for a wise leader. The case studies demonstrate how the model can be used to solve various kinds of problems in local communities by advancing innovation and building local capacity, an approach that is applicable to local governments and communities in both ASEAN countries and Japan.

This book was produced in the course of the project called "Case Study and Modeling of Organization Management in Southeast Asia," conducted between March 2013 and September 2015 as a joint project of the Japan International Cooperation Agency (JICA), the Graduate School of International Corporate Strategy at Hitotsubashi University, and the National Graduate Institute for Policy Studies (GRIPS).

This study formed the basis for yet another book, *Knowledge Creation in Public Administration: A New Paradigm for Innovative Governments in Asia*, which is being published concurrently with this book. I would like to recommend reading both volumes.

This book is a pioneering work with a new approach to leadership and management in local governments and communities in Asian countries. I hope that this theory receives acceptance beyond Asia for community development worldwide.

Takashi Shiraishi
Former President
National Graduate Institute for Policy Studies
Tokyo, Japan

PREFACE

The aim of this book is to present a new paradigm of leadership and management in community development that can be used to solve social issues. It is designed to encourage better collaboration through the transformation of individual and institutional mindsets. By grounding our approach in knowledge creation theory, we hope to capture key factors and processes in changing and or creating new institutions.

Every community strives to enhance their quality of life, but that becomes more challenging in increasingly volatile and disruptive environments. The need to find new ways for communities to be more collaborative, innovative and effective in solving societal issues is a truly critical problem in both developing and developed countries. To address this, there have been movements in many parts of the world among public organizations, NPOs/NGOs, private organizations and individuals that endeavor to promote a transformation in the way people think, as well as in their actions and the way they work together to resolve societal issues. This has come to be referred to as "social innovation."

This led to the emergence of a "social innovation" movement in the late 1990s, which became widespread in the 2000s when the West faced management failures due to unethical management behaviors. Examples of this include the Enron and Worldcom scandals, the Lehman shock and the global financial crisis. Consequently, there were increasing demands for corporations to introduce corporate social responsibility (CSR) policies—that is, a company statement on their responsibilities as members of society. This provided a trigger for the private sector to undertake innovative approaches toward solving social issues by collaborating with multiple stakeholders, including public administrations at the national, regional, municipal, and community levels. This movement blurred the boundaries between private and public sectors, leading to closer collaboration. A range of research has been conducted on this movement from a variety of perspectives, including dynamic capabilities (Teece 2014), and open innovation (Chesbrough et al. 2014).

Over the same period, social entrepreneurs and social enterprises, which aim to solve social issues, have also emerged. They introduced a "business management approach" to address social issues through activities that are sustainable, if not profitable. Major characteristics of social entrepreneurs and social enterprises are that they make full use of social capital, such as love, care, and trust relationships among the people in the community, as well as the leadership capabilities of social entrepreneurs. Accordingly, research into social entrepreneurship and social enterprises from the perspective of social capital and leadership has become a major focus in these fields (Mair and Marti 2006).

We have identified a previously unexplored gap in the existing research. Little research has focused on the processes of community development from the perspective of creating new knowledge or utilizing wisdom, in order to solve social issues by encouraging people to transform their own mindsets and to collaborate and then lead the institutional transformation. Accordingly, our challenge in this book is to understand and explain the processes of community development, and consider the factors that promote or inhibit the processes, by grounding our approach in knowledge creation theory.

This challenge is based on the history of our joint projects. Following ten years of joint projects between Japan International Cooperation Agency (JICA), and Graduate School of International Corporate Strategy, Hitotsubashi University (Hitotsubashi ICS), in which government officials and staff members from ASEAN countries developed knowledge creation theory, we became confident that a knowledge creation theory on management that originates in the private sector is able to help clarify the issues that communities face and provide solutions. With this in mind, in 2013 we set up a joint project between JICA, the National Graduate Institute for Policy Studies (GRIPS), and Hitotsubashi ICS. We invited leading scholars and practitioners in public policy management and studied distinguished cases in five countries (Indonesia, Philippines, Thailand, Vietnam, and Japan). Each case study examined how communities developed and solved societal issues by promoting a transformation in the way that people work together. From the case studies, we gained insights into knowledge creation theory that show how the processes of community development can be explained, as well as the particular styles of leadership and management that initiated the transformation.

With this background in mind, we aim at achieving three specific goals in these two volumes: (1) to describe the distinguished case studies in five countries with diverse contexts as exemplars of processes for solving societal issues by changing people's and institutions' mindsets; (2) to discuss how applicable the theory is—in terms of its effectiveness in explaining the transformation processes—by reflecting on the case studies; and (3) to present the implications of the research and the practices in the public sector by grounding it in the knowledge creation theory on management. What distinguishes these two books from each other is that this volume focuses on community development, while the other volume—*Knowledge Creation in Public Administration: A New Paradigm for Innovative Governments in Asia*—examines transformation processes in public administration. In addition, the cases and discussions in this book focus more on Japan and Thailand than other countries because we have longer research records in these counties than in the other three countries, and because we think the case studies in these countries can provide good exemplars for other countries. Accordingly, this book is structured as follows:

Chapter 1 sets out the basic concepts and frameworks of knowledge creation theory on management: namely, the SECI model, the concept of *ba*, middle-up-down management, dynamic fractal organization, and phronesis (wise leadership).

From Chapter 2 to Chapters 8, ten case studies will be presented. The title, name of leading author and a brief introduction of each case study is listed below:

Chapter 2 *Collaboration on City Planning: A Lesson from Mayor Joko Widodo (2005–2011) (Indonesia)—by Anwar Sanusi, Secretary General, Ministry of Village, Development of Disadvantaged Areas and Transmigration*
This is a case study about Joko Widodo (or Jokowi)—elected the President of Indonesia in 2014—from the period between 2005 and 2011 when he was the mayor of Solo city. Mayor Jokowi established a new collaborative relationship between the city administration and the citizens by listening to the people. Jokowi's attitude toward the people's

voices became his trademark, an approach that came to be known by the Javanese word *blusukan*. He listened to the public and used this as a means of tackling public issues. This was considered an innovative approach in Indonesia at the time.

Chapter 3 *People-Centric Leadership at the Local Level: Yala Municipality, Thailand—by Orathai Kokpol, Deputy Secretary General, College of Local Government Development, King Prajadhipok's Institute*
This case study describes the process of transformation facilitated by the Mayor, Mr. Pongsak, who established a team and transformed the municipal administration to pursue people-centric value creation and innovation despite strong centralization pressures in Thailand.

Chapter 4 *Mitaka City Development: Collaborating in Harmony (Japan)—by Ayano Hirose, Assistant Professor, Department of Global Business, College of Business, Rikkyo University*
This case study examines how four mayors after WWII led city development by utilizing the knowledge of the citizens through citizen participation and collaboration.

Chapter 5 *Da Nang City Development (Vietnam)—by Nguyễn Thi Hải Hằng, Ph.D., President, Vietnam Aviation Academy*
This case study examines how Da Nang City transformed itself from a centralized and controlled city into a decentralized and independent city.

Chapter 6 *Antonio Meloto: Empowering the Filipino Poor toward Sustainable and Innovative Communities (Philippines)—by Alex B. Brillantes Jr., former Commissioner, Commission on Higher Education*
This is a case study of community development initiated by Mr. Meloto, who is an ordinary citizen but has also led the transformation of the minds of the people in communities. He has worked not only with the citizens but also the city administration, finding ways to empower poor people to improve their lives. He established an organization known as Gawad Kalinga (GK), a non-governmental organization that aims to build homes and a better quality of life for every Filipino, thereby changing the way poor people live.

Chapter 7 *Social Innovation in a Leaf-Selling Business: Irodori in Kamikatsu Town (Japan)—by Ayano Hirose, Assistant Professor, Department of Global Business, College of Business, Rikkyo University*
This case study explores the revival process of an aging rural town led by Mr. Yokoishi, an outsider who started a leaf-selling business despite strong opposition by the local people at the time of start-up.

Chapter 8 *"It Can Be Done:"* *Economic Forests and Social Entrepreneurship in Doi Tung, Thailand—by Ms. Pimpan Diskul na Ayudhya, Mae Fah Luang Foundation under Royal Patronage*
This case study is about the revival of the golden triangle on the northern border of Thailand where an NPO leader, known as Khun Chai, and his members transformed the way people lived. He did this by developing economic forests, thereby encouraging a move away from opium production.

Chapter 9 presents an overview of transformation processes in Thailand by considering how people think and act in communities to solve societal issues, and is authored and discussed by Woothisarn Tanchai, Secretary General of King Prajadhipok's Institute. It provides preliminary hypotheses on factors that can affect the transformation processes, as well examining how leadership can facilitate social innovation.

In Chapter 10—the conclusion of the book—we discuss the lessons to be learned and implications for the transformation processes of changing mindsets and facilitating the actions of the people in the community in ways that can be used to solve societal issues, from the perspective of knowledge creation theory. What makes community development unique and innovative—compared to innovation in the private sector, or innovation in the public sector in relatively larger areas—is that it involves multiple stakeholders from various organizations who may have different objectives, expectations, interests, and values in rather close and direct relationships. Ways of synthesizing this diversity and mobilizing stakeholders to collaborate and co-create new knowledge toward mutual goals will be one of the key findings and implications of this book.

As far as we are aware, this is one of the first books on community development that has transformed administration processes and led to innovation in communities. This is also one of the first books on public administration from the perspective of knowledge creation theory on management. In addition, this book contains a rare output of comparative studies by the group of leading academics and practitioners who have spearheaded reform initiatives in four East Asian countries and Japan.

This book is intended for readers who are interested in, exercising, and/or studying public administration and public policy on community development to solve social issues. The target may be students and academics in public administration and public policy management programs, as well as those in fields related to business administration and business management. In addition, municipal officials, and community leaders who are concerned with community development may benefit from this book.

Although the contexts of the cases are in the East Asian countries and Japan, knowledge creation theory on management is applicable to any part of the world. This book is the outcome of diversity and its synthesis, as well as collaboration and co-creation. We have spent over two years on this project, going through intensive workshops, dialogues, and discussions. This work could not have been accomplished without the support of representatives from Indonesia, the Philippines, Thailand, and Vietnam, as well as the support of staff members of JICA, JICA Research Institute, GRIPS, and Hitotsubashi ICS.

Our special appreciation goes first to the contributors to this book mentioned above, and the following members of this project:

Indonesia:

The late Prof. Dr. Agus Dwiyanto, former Chairman, National Institute of Public Administration (NIPA);
Prof. Sadu Wasistiono, Professor, Institute of National Governance;
Prof. Dr. Eko Prasojo, Dean, Faculty of Administrative Science, University of Indonesia;
Prof. Dr. Agus Pramusinto, Director, Department of Public Policy and Management, University of Gadjah Mada;

Philippines:

The late Dr. Cayetano W. Paderanga JR., former Chairman and Ms. Magdalena L. Mendoza, Senior Vice-President, Development Academy of the Philippines (DAP);
Prof. Eduardo Gonzalez, Professor of Center for Integrative Development Studies, University of the Philippines;

Thailand:

Dr. Borwornsak Uwanno, former Secretary General, King Prajadhipok's Institute (KPI);
Mr.Visoot Prasitsiriwongse, Deputy Secretary General, Office of the Civil Service Commission (OCSC);
Prof. Supasawad Chardchawarn, Dean, Faculty of Political Science, Thammasat University;

Mom Rajawongse Disnadda Diskul, Secretary General, The Mae Fah Luang Foundation under Royal Patronage (MFLF);

Vietnam:

Prof. Dr. Ta Ngoc Tan, former President, Dr. Ngo Huy Duc, Director, Institute of Political Science, and Dr. Bui Phuong Dinh, Director, Center of Leadership and Policy Studies, Ho Chi Minh National Academy of Politics;

Japan:

Ms. Atsuko Kikuchi, President, Japan Association for Public Human Resources Development;

Mr. Kozo Yoshida, Commissioner, National Personnel Authority (NPA);

Mr. Norio Fukuta, Director General, Human Resources Bureau, NPA;

Mr. Kuninori Matsuda, former Deputy Director General, Institute of Public Administration, NPA;

Mr. Yoichi Niiya, former Director of International Affairs Division, NPA;

Dr. Akihiko Tanaka, former President, Mr. Hiroshi Kato, Senior Vice President, Japan International Cooperation Agency (JICA);

Mr. Ichiro Tambo, former Director, and staff members of Research Program Division, JICA Research Institute;

Prof. Takashi Shiraishi, former President, Prof. Masahiro Horie, Director of Executive Development Center for Global Leadership, Prof. Hirofumi Takada, and Staff members of Research Support and International Affairs Division, National Graduate Institute for Policy Studies (GRIPS);

Prof. Kazuo Ichijo, Dean, Graduate School of International Corporate Strategy, Hitosubashi University;

Dr. Hideki Kawada, CEO of Phronetic Co., Ltd.

We hope this book will be a first but nevertheless important step toward co-creating values for society, through the partnership between people in both the private and public spheres to collaborate and innovate by unleashing our knowledge potential.

Ayano Hirose Nishihara
Assistant Professor
Department of Global Business, College of Business
Rikkyo University
Tokyo, Japan

Masaei Matsunaga
Deputy Director General
Infrastructure and Peacebuilding Department
Japan International Cooperation Agency (JICA)
Tokyo, Japan

Ikujiro Nonaka
Professor Emeritus
Hitotsubashi University
Tokyo, Japan

Kiyotaka Yokomichi
Vice President and Professor
National Graduate Institute for Policy Studies
Tokyo, Japan

REFERENCES

Chesbrough, H., W. Vanhaverbeke, and J. West. eds. 2014. *New frontiers in open innovation*. Oxford: Oxford University Press.
Mair, J., and I. Marti. 2006. Social entrepreneurship research: a source of explanation, prediction, and delight. *Journal of World Business* 41 (1), 36–44.
Teece, D. J. 2014. A dynamic capabilities-based entrepreneurial theory of the multinational enterprise. *Journal of International Business Studies* 45 (1), 8–37.

CONTENTS

EDITORS AND CONTRIBUTORS

About the Editors

Ayano Hirose Nishihara is an Assistant Professor, Department of Global Business, College of Business, Rikkyo University, and a research collaborator to Professor Emeritus Ikujiro Nonaka. She received her B.A. (Law) from Nagoya University, MBA in 2005 and DBA in 2011 from The Graduate School of International Corporate Strategy, Hitotsubashi University. Prior to her academic track, she worked as an assistant manager at NEC Corporation. Her research topics include knowledge creation at public and private organizations and communities, knowledge-creating leadership, and social innovation. Her recent publications include Nonaka, I., Hirose, A., & Takeda, Y. (2016). "Meso"—Foundations of Dynamic Capabilities: Team—Level Synthesis and Distributed Leadership as the Source of Dynamic Creativity. *Global Strategy Journal,* 6(3), 168–182.

Masaei Matsunaga is Deputy Director General of Infrastructure and Peacebuilding Department, Japan International Cooperation Agency (JICA), the core implementing body of government's cooperation programs with emerging countries. Since 1985, he has been pioneering JICA's initiatives designed for the capacity development of public organizations in emerging countries. In particular, since 2003, he has been exploring a new paradigm of development cooperation in collaboration with Prof. Ikujiro Nonaka and his colleagues, by synthesizing the mainstream ideas of development studies and unique perspectives of Japan's own development experiences. As an experienced practitioner in the field of governance in Asia, he also taught as a professor of the National Graduate Institute for Policy Studies from 2012 to 2015.

Ikujiro Nonaka is a Professor Emeritus, Hitotsubashi University, the world-renowned founder of the theory of knowledge-based management. He received his B.A. (Political Science) from Waseda University, MBA in 1968, and Ph.D. (Business Administration) in 1972 from the University of California, Berkeley. Prior to his academic track, he worked at Fuji Electric Corporation. He has won wide-ranging recognition for his work in developing the knowledge-based management theory and recently received the Lifetime Achievement Award by Thinkers50. His research interests are in the organizational knowledge creation and wise leadership in private, public, and social organizations. His recent publications include Nonaka, I., & Takeuchi, H. (2011), The wise leader, *Harvard business review, 89*(5), 58–67.

Kiyotaka Yokomichi is Vice President and Professor of National Graduate Institute for Policy Studies (GRIPS). He is a graduate of the University of Tokyo. After working for Japan's Ministry of Home Affairs, he joined the faculty of the Graduate School of Policy Science (GSPS), Saitama University in 1988. He is a leading expert on local administration and governance, with extensive research and practical experience in the area of local government reform in Japan. One of the founders of GRIPS, Professor Yokomichi now specializes in capacity development of government officials in Japan and other countries in Asia.

Contributors

Pimpan Diskul na Ayudhya Mae Fah Luang Foundation under Royal Patronage, Pathumwon, Bangkok, Thailand

Alex B. Brillantes Jr National College of Public Administration, University of the Philippines, quezon city, Philippines; Commission on Higher Education, University of the Philippines, quezon city, Philippines

Kittima Bunnag King Prajadhipok's Institute, Bangkok, Thailand

Ayano Hirose Nishihara Department of Global Business, College of Business, Rikkyo University, Tokyo, Japan

Nguyễn Hải Hằng Vietnam Aviation Academy, Ho Chi Minh, Vietnam

Orathai Kokpol King Prajadhipok's Institute, Bangkok, Thailand

Ikujiro Nonaka Hitotsubashi University, Tokyo, Japan

Lizan E. Perante-Calina National College of Public Administration, University of the Philippines, quezon city, Philippines; Philippine Society for Public Administration, University of the Philippines, quezon city, Philippines

Anwar Sanusi Ministry of Villages, Development of Disadvantages Regions, and Transmigration Republic Indonesia, Jakarta, Republic of Indonesia

Woothisarn Tanchai Department of Community Development, Faculty of Social Administration, Thammasat University, Bangkok, Thailand

Kiyotaka Yokomichi National Graduate Institute for Policy Studies, Tokyo, Japan

LIST OF FIGURES

LIST OF TABLES

LIST OF BOXES

CHAPTER 1

Introduction to the Concepts and Frameworks of Knowledge-Creating Theory

Ikujiro Nonaka and Ayano Hirose Nishihara

...all earlier pluralist societies destroyed themselves because no one took care of the common good. They abounded in communities but could not sustain community, let alone create it.
—Peter F. Drucker, The New Pluralism (1999, 1)

INTRODUCTION: WHY WE NEED A THEORY OF KNOWLEDGE CREATION

Knowledge, according to Drucker (1993, 183), is "the only meaningful resource today." Knowledge creation theory originally arose out of case studies of Japanese manufacturers in the 1980s. Since then, the scope of research has been extended to multinational firms as well as small and medium enterprises (SMEs) both inside and outside of Japan and now includes NPOs, government organizations, communities, regions, and nations. The theory

I. Nonaka (✉)
Hitotsubashi University, Tokyo, Japan
e-mail: inonaka@ics.hit-u.ac.jp

A. Hirose Nishihara
Department of Global Business, College of Business,
Rikkyo University, Tokyo, Japan
e-mail: ayano.nishihara@rikkyo.ac.jp

© The Author(s) 2018
A. Hirose Nishihara et al. (eds.), *Knowledge Creation in Community Development*, DOI 10.1007/978-3-319-57481-3_1

1

has also developed substantially by synthesizing interdisciplinary theories and concepts in philosophy, psychology, cognitive science, and neuro-science—to name a few. This has led to the emergence of a "Knowledge School," a group of scholars and practitioners—including many of the authors in this volume—who have been developing a knowledge-based theory of management that promotes sustainable innovation. Accordingly, knowledge creation theory is now able to explain organizational processes and leadership that promote knowledge creation in *any* organization, regardless of the organization's type, size, or location. This means that the twenty-first century has become an era of knowledge creators.

Based on these developments, since 2004, the Japan International Cooperation Agency (JICA) and the Graduate School of International Corporate Strategy at Hitotsubashi University (Hitotsubashi ICS) have been jointly conducting annual seminars with ASEAN government leaders on knowledge creation theory and management practices. The total accumulated number of participants now exceeds 150 from over 10 countries. The participants have been taking on the challenge of incorporating knowledge creation theory into their daily operations. Following the vision and purpose of this seminar series, JICA, GRIPS, and Hitotsubashi ICS started a joint research project in 2013, with the hypothesis that knowledge creation theory is a perfect fit for ASEAN countries, in contrast to management theories prevalent in the West.

In this chapter, we present the basic concepts and frameworks of knowledge creation theory that provide a foundation for interpreting the cases in Chaps. 2–8.

Organizational Knowledge Creation Theory

Before we go into the details of knowledge creation theory, we must point out that the theory differs from conventional theories of management in multiple ways. For example, it starts from the view that personal beliefs are established through relationships with others—that is, such beliefs are based on subjective rather than objective knowledge. The goal is to achieve value creation through practice, rather than analysis of past data. It incorporates diversity as existing in an ecosystem, which stimulates the creation of new knowledge. It is based on philosophy rather than mere economics. In short, organizational knowledge creation theory is an art rather than a science, dynamic rather than static, a process rather than a thing, a *flow* rather than a *stock*, flexible rather than rigid, practice-based rather than analysis-based, and inclusive rather than extractive.

Accordingly, one of the distinguishable differences between conventional theories on management and knowledge creation theory is evident in the definition of knowledge. Knowledge, defined as a "justified true belief" in Western philosophical traditions, has been regarded as universal, scientific, logical, and rational, following the traditions of Plato and Descartes. Considered in relation to knowledge creation theory, "explicit knowledge" can be regarded as the only form of knowledge in the West.

Here, we emphasize the importance of "tacit knowledge" over explicit knowledge, through an understanding that tacit knowledge is the foundation of all knowledge. This resonates with arguments made by Michael Polany, a Hungarian-British polymath who made substantial contributions to physical chemistry, economics, and philosophy. He articulated that all knowledge is either tacit or rooted in tacit knowledge (Polanyi 1966). We also concur with the words of Augustine the Hippo that "belief precedes knowing." Our beliefs and commitments are the sources of our knowledge, which is founded on tacit knowing. This means that knowledge is not something out there to be discovered or captured, but something we create inside ourselves.

Incorporating this understanding of knowledge, we can define knowledge as a dynamic social process of justifying personal belief toward truth, goodness, and beauty (Nonaka and Takeuchi 1995, 58). An important point here is the role of subjectivity. Our subjectivity determines our beliefs, our judgments, and our commitments. People create knowledge through interactions between themselves and with their environment. Thus, knowledge is not just something already out there waiting to be found—if it is already out there, it is merely information. Because human interactions are the source of knowledge creation, knowledge is subjective, process-relational, aesthetic, and created in practice; we view knowledge and the knowledge creation process as people-centered, action-oriented, and rooted in philosophy (Nonaka et al. 2008, 7). This is our essential understanding of knowledge.

Tacit Knowledge and Explicit Knowledge

As noted above, knowledge is often defined as a "justified true belief" in Western epistemological traditions, with a particular emphasis on the connotation associated with the term "truth." This understanding goes as far back as the ancient Greek philosopher Plato, in his examination of the development of objective thought. He insisted that unless we purify ourselves from bodily senses, we cannot come close to true knowledge (Gibbs 2005). On the other hand, Plato's apprentice, Aristotle, considered subjectivity to be an important aspect of knowing.

A good illustration of the differences between Western and Eastern thinking can be found in a drawing by Raphael in "The School of Athens." In this drawing, Plato and Aristotle are seen in the center. Plato is pointing toward the sky, representing his deductive idealism. This indicates that universal quality resides in the ultimate "forms" that exist above us. By contrast, Aristotle holds his hand over the earth. This represents his inductive pragmatism that universal qualities lie here on Earth, and our five senses are compulsory vessels that allow us to perceive such universal qualities.

While much of Western thinking has largely been rooted in Platonic ideas and passed down to contemporary scientific analytical approaches, Eastern thinking is considered to lie closer to that of Aristotle, who emphasized the importance of "belief" in what defines knowledge. This approach is predominantly analogous to that described by Polanyi (1966) above.

Polanyi's most notable contributions to the theory of knowledge lie in his insights into tacit knowledge as a process, expressing it with the use of the term "tacit *knowing*." Polanyi's framework implies the creation of knowledge but without a clear model that explains its process. Our knowledge creation theory, on the other hand, provides the stimulus for an expanded model of knowledge creation processes by incorporating insights from the humanities and social sciences, on top of Polanyi's ideas on tacit knowledge and tacit knowing.

Tacit knowing requires us to "indwell" other people and things and directly obtain unarticulated awareness inside ourselves through our five senses. One example is when we feel certain objects as parts (or an extension) of our bodies, such as when using tools, playing the piano or violin, or driving a car, we feel as if these things are a part or extension of our body, and we can use them as if we are using our own body—this is the moment when we become truly capable of using them. The extent of indwelling goes beyond people or things; it goes to the environment of which the subject is part. Thus, tacit knowledge can be considered "personal" and refers to the "person as a whole," as an individual in the environment, society, and community. In this respect, the notion of personal knowledge includes both epistemological[1] and ontological[2] aspects of its concept. "Indwelling" therefore is very critical in community settings;

we should not only understand others objectively or analytically, but also as a whole person.

Building on Michael Polany's notion of tacit knowing, in knowledge creation theory, we distinguish two types of knowledge—tacit and explicit (Fig. 1.1). Tacit knowledge is subjective experiential knowledge that cannot be expressed in words, sentences, numbers, or formulas. It is context-specific in that there are cognitive and technical skills embedded in individuals. On the other hand, explicit knowledge is objective, rational knowledge, and can be expressed clearly in writing, such as words, sentences, numbers, or formulas. Explicit knowledge is context-free. Examples include concepts, logic, theories, problem-solving methods, manuals, and databases. Although both types of knowledge present different characteristics, rather than being opposites, they coexist on a continuum, as shown in Fig. 1.1. One suitable metaphor can be provided by an iceberg, with explicit knowledge the tip of the iceberg above the water, while tacit knowledge comprises the rest of the iceberg underneath—together they comprise all knowledge.

As such, we do not intend to neglect explicit knowledge. In fact, we emphasize that we need both so that the conversion between tacit and explicit knowledge enhances both types of knowledge. What becomes important here is the need to free ourselves from the prejudice of

Tacit Knowledge
- Subjective and implicit knowledge that can not be expressed in words, sentences, or numbers.
- Direct knowledge obtained from experiences using five senses
- Commitment, beliefs, technical skills, know-how, and craft
- Personal, emotional, passion, aesthetic
- Context-specific, determined by the people, place, target
- Can be shared, developed, and extended by physical collaboration

Explicit Knowledge
- Objective and external knowledge that can be expressed in words, sentences, or numbers
- Systemized knowledge detached from specific context (context-free)
- Theory, problem-solving, manuals, or database
- Societal, organizational, rational, logical
- Can be supplemented (transfer, re-use) by ICT
- Can be shared and edited by using language or numbers

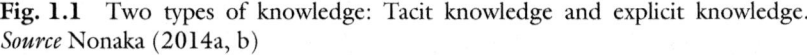

Fig. 1.1 Two types of knowledge: Tacit knowledge and explicit knowledge. *Source* Nonaka (2014a, b)

considering objective, scientific, and explicit knowledge as the only type of knowledge. We need to restore the importance of perspectives in knowledge, which will provide balance to belief and rationality, tacit and explicit, and art and science, through the notion that knowing requires commitment from each individual.

THE SECI MODEL: ORGANIZATIONAL KNOWLEDGE CREATION PROCESS

We have defined two types of knowledge—tacit and explicit—and based on this epistemological foundation, we have developed what is called the *SECI Model*, a two-by-two matrix model, which illustrates the organizational knowledge creation process. New knowledge is created in the relentless conversion between the above two types of knowledge in the context of their dialectic relationship.

The model consists of four dimensions (see Fig. 1.2): empathizing reality through actual experiences (Socialization), articulating the essence of awareness into concepts (Externalization), relating and systemizing the concepts (Combination), creating value in the form of technology, products, software, services and experiences, and embodying knowledge

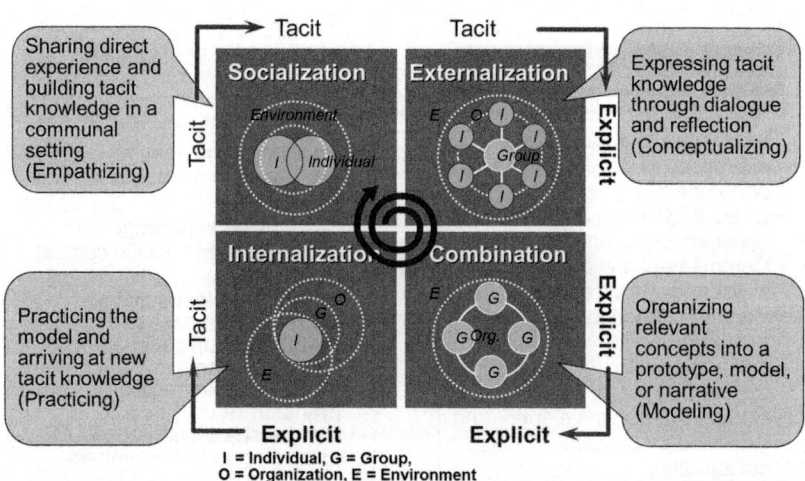

Fig. 1.2 SECI model: Organizational knowledge creation process. *Source* Nonaka (2014a, b)

(Internalization). At the same time, this stimulates the emergence of new knowledge within the organization, markets, and the environment, and results in a spiraling up reinforcement of the socialization step. As a result of the continuous and rapid spinning of the SECI spiral, a firm, a community, or a government can synthesize diverse knowledge that fosters organizational creativity and efficiency—we call this the *synthesizing capability*. Dynamic interactions between people and their environment allow new knowledge to be created organizationally. Contradictions and confrontations are synthesized in SECI spiral processes. Homogeneity, whether of people or their knowledge, can hinder dynamic interactions. This is to say that diversity matters substantially: the more diverse the organization, the broader and deeper the new knowledge.

If we use the metaphor of the second law of thermodynamics, in a closed system, entropy will increase and the potential of the organization will decrease. To increase the potential of an organization, we need open systems that maintain diversity, so that entropy will not increase as fast as in a closed system. In other words, diverse organizations can create knowledge organizationally, and by pursuing a common good, such organizations can provide society with values.

Each step of the SECI model has its own pattern of thinking and acting (Fig. 1.3). These patterns may be used as a checklist when operationalizing the SECI process in an organization, or when promoting the knowledge-creating activities of members.[3]

WISE LEADERSHIP: SIX ABILITIES OF LEADERS TO PROMOTE SECI

In times uncertainty, we need leaders with practical wisdom who will enable and drive the continuous spinning of the SECI spiral and thereby promote the creation and accumulation of organizational knowledge. We need leaders who can make balanced contextual judgments and take action at the right time—in particular, here-and-now contexts—in pursuit of the common good of the society. We call such a leaders *wise leaders* (Nonaka and Takeuchi 2011).

The concept of the wise leader was derived from Aristotle's concept of *phronesis*, but this is more than a simple revival. *Phronesis* is one of the three types of virtue that Aristotle identified in his *Nichomachean Ethics* (2002): *episteme*, *techne*, and *phronesis*. *Episteme* is a universal truth or principle that is ideal and rational as in scientific knowledge; *techne* is a

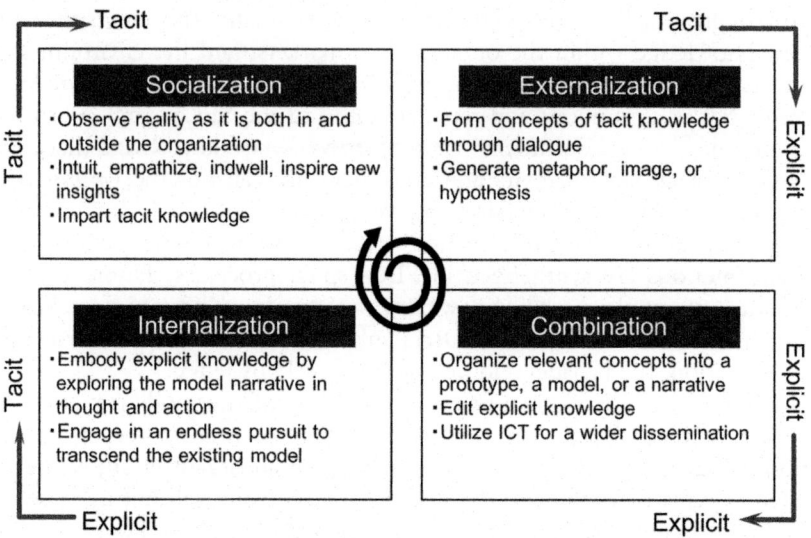

Fig. 1.3 The Dynamic triad model: The relentless upward spiral of tacit knowledge, explicit knowledge, and *Phronesis*

technological know-how or skill that enables creation of actual things, which roughly corresponds to tacit knowledge; and *phronesis* is an intellectual virtue that enables best judgments and actions in particular situations (see Nonaka et al. 2008, 53).[4] Phronesis is translated as practical wisdom, prudence, or practical reason. In this volume, we use phronesis interchangeably with "practical wisdom." In other words, *episteme* roughly corresponds to the concept of explicit knowledge, *techne* to tacit knowledge, and therefore, *phronesis* is the third type of knowledge as practical wisdom.

We define phronesis as the practical wisdom for exercising the best judgment for the common good in a particular context (Nonaka et al. 2012). It is the ability to show good judgment and to make the right decisions on actions in a particular context. This entails having the ability to synthesize the particular and the universal, as well as contemplate rationales and improvise on the spot. Finally, it requires the ability to judge what will provide the right balance within the best time frame.

The role of wise leadership is to promote the continuous spiraling of the SECI process. We present the relationship between tacit knowledge, explicit knowledge, and practical wisdom as comprising a triangular model of dynamic knowledge. The model illustrates the relentless upward spiral process of conversion between tacit knowledge and explicit knowledge, which is driven by phronesis (Nonaka et al. 2014). While the conversion between tacit and explicit knowledge itself does not clearly indicate value or direction of knowledge creation, wise leadership drives the SECI model by setting values, giving directions, and driving the process to achieve a goal. In short, the dynamic triad model of tacit knowledge, explicit knowledge, and *phronesis* indicates that value judgments are incorporated into the knowledge creation processes, and that these are necessary to interpret, grasp the essence, and create meanings out of the contexts. While tacit knowledge is closely related to ontology and explicit knowledge to epistemology, *phronesis* adds axiology—that is, the values from people's beliefs, commitments, passions, and judgments.

We have been conducting research on leaders from leading organizations who succeeded in achieving their goals—including CEOs, middle managers, and wartime leaders—and identified six common abilities (see Fig. 1.4).

The first is the ability to set good goals and make appropriate judgments on goodness. As pointed out by Aristotle, by nature, human beings want to do good things. "Good" here refers to self-sufficient

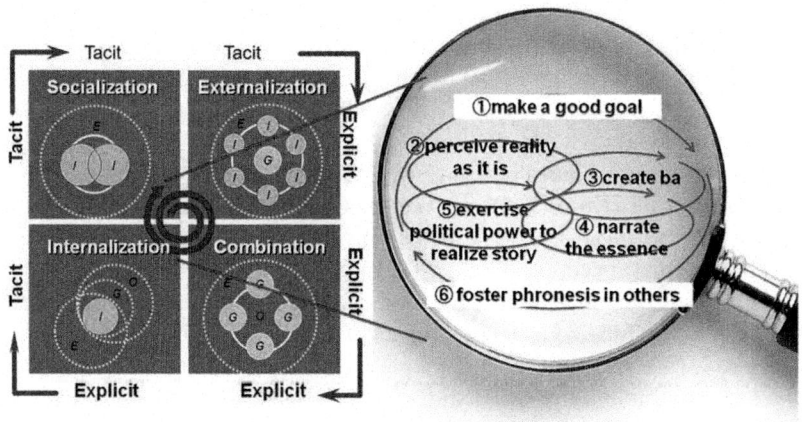

Fig. 1.4 Wise leadership: Abilities of leaders to promote SECI. *Source* Nonaka et al. (2014)

values such as happiness and self-actualization; in this sense, money is always a means of achieving good. Other aspects of "good" are artisanship and the relentless pursuit of excellence as a good in itself. The second ability is being able to perceive reality as it is. This entails the ability to quickly and correctly recognize constantly changing situations and determine what lies behind the phenomena to envision the future.

The third is the ability to create "*ba*." *Ba* is one of the key concepts in knowledge creation theory, and we therefore describe it in some detail here. This is the Japanese word for a place, space, or field. We define *ba* as a shared context in motion, in which the interaction of the people and environment occurs, and new knowledge is created. This means that *ba* connects and relates people and their knowledge, thus promoting the creation of new knowledge, by which the SECI process spirals up and new knowledge is created. In other words, knowledge needs a *ba* to be created. A leader with practical wisdom has the ability to find, locate, gather, and place appropriate personnel in a timely fashion and, with that, create a *ba* through empathy and resonance. For that, it is essential to create a *ba* that enables people to gather, sympathize, resonate, and interact with one another. It is a concept that encompasses the relationship between the people who gather in a particular context.

While always being based on the here and now, a *ba* dynamically evolves beyond time and space as the people who gather there bring and share their knowledge and experiences. One of the conditions of a good *ba* is that it is self-organizing. Those who take part in multiple *ba* can connect one *ba* with other *ba*. By connecting, linking, and relating multiple *ba*, new and diverse knowledge can be brought in, new contexts will arise, and new knowledge will be created. A formal organizational structure does not automatically create *ba*; instead, a *ba* can transcend formal organization structure. A good *ba* needs people who are committed to the *ba*. It is not necessary for it to be only a physical and real space; it can also be a virtual space.

As the participants define the boundaries of the *ba* platforms, they can connect or disconnect with other *ba* based on their movements. In order to create and activate such *ba*, leaders must understand past events, present phenomena and the context behind the changes, and have the contextualizing capacity to supplement, convert, and create new relationships to adapt to the particular context and situation. The fourth is the ability to uncover the true underlying nature of phenomena and contexts. It is the ability to grasp the essence, articulate, and conceptualize it, and create narratives by linking micro concepts to the macro context as a convincing vision and narrative for the future. To tell a good narrative, rhetorical skills are necessary. New breakthrough visions that challenge conventional knowledge are better conveyed by utilizing rhetoric tools such as paradox, metaphor, and contrast.

The fifth is the ability to exercise political power to achieve a story. It is the ability to bring people together, spur them into action, combine and synthesize the knowledge and efforts of others, and pursue a goal with shrewdness and determination. Here, we are talking about "narrative" instead of "story." The "story" is a noun-like concept that represents a complete structure, and has a beginning and an end, whereas the historical "narrative" is a verb-like concept that emphasizes the active aspect of narrating, and has the nature of making diverse developments without converging into a single story (Noe 2007).

There are six kinds of power bases: reward power, coercive power, legitimate power, referent power, expert power, and informational power (French and Raven 1959). Possessing the ability to find and use the best mix of hard and soft power depending on the context—referred to as smart power—is very critical as leader (Nye 2011).

Finally, the sixth is the ability to foster *phronesis* in others, which makes leadership organizational. It is the ability to create an organization of distributed *phronesis* by transferring wise leaders *phronetic* abilities to others. Once phronesis is fostered in every member and distributed throughout the organization, a resilient organization will be created that can respond flexibly and creatively in a variety of situations to pursue the common good of the society.

How then can we facilitate the development of *phronesis*? Since *phronesis* is a virtue of high-quality tacit knowledge, it can only be obtained through high-quality practices and reflections. Accordingly one of the bases of *phronesis* is the humanities, or liberal arts such as philosophy, history, literature, and psychology. All these help in reaching "essence of truth, goodness, and beauty." Other bases can be provided by human experience: peak and diverse experiences, direct and pure experiences, the shared experiences of exemplars, success and failure experiences, cross-cultural experiences, etc., which offer high-quality tacit knowledge. In addition, tradition and artisanship are important, because *phronesis* is about the relentless pursuit of excellence, or one's ideal of truth, goodness, and beauty. As contemporary Aristotelian philosopher Alasdair MacIntyre (1984) asserts, the ultimate practical goal is to achieve a standard of excellence for the community. Members of a community are urged to engage in the never-ending pursuit of excellence in their day-to-day lives.

As noted above, once *phronesis* is distributed through every level of an organization, such organizations are more likely to be resilient. This can be explained through by comparing organizations with fractal models. Conceptually, the fractal has evolved from the natural sciences to mean a part that can represent the whole (Mandelbrot 1983). However, each of these parts is not a complete copy of the whole. Each part contains heterogeneity, even light differences from other parts, and these can stimulate dynamic interactions between each fractal in multiple organizational layers. We call this type of organization a dynamic fractal organization.

If we could succeed in building such a dynamic fractal organization, it would encourage distributed leadership with practical wisdom or *phronesis*. In such an organization, the dynamic knowledge-triad model is the fundamental form of the fractal, and the same forms are distributed throughout the organization. In other words, multiple layers of *ba*— where the knowledge triad is occurring—are distributed and connected throughout the organization. This means that phronesis is distributed to multiple *ba* in every level and part of the organization, and in each *ba,* the SECI process spirals, making the whole organization agile and resilient to rapidly changing environments. Parts and the whole interact constantly with fluctuations. They are thus fractal but in a dynamic way.

SOLVING SOCIAL ISSUES IN COMMUNITIES: CASE STUDIES ON A NEW PARADIGM OF LEADERSHIP AND MANAGEMENT

This section takes the knowledge creation theoretical model from this chapter and considers how it could be applied. It seeks to do this through an examination of seven distinguished case studies from five countries, namely Indonesia, the Philippines, Thailand, Vietnam, and Japan. Although the contexts in each city and region are different, the ultimate goal is the same: to explore ways of improving the quality of life of citizens. The selected cases are exemplars of community development and transformation, containing good practices and processes of leadership and management. Each case study consists of two parts: narrative and analysis, with the different styles and analyses reflecting the expertise and the interests of each case writer.

Through the case studies, it may be possible to identify particular styles of leadership and management, explaining them by grounding them in knowledge creation theory. In community development, key drivers of transformation are often people from outside the community who may provide new insights, or people within the community with different points of view. Depending on the context, these outsiders or insiders can become the catalyst for transforming and stimulating a change in peoples actions and mindsets. These are people with the abilities of mavens, connectors, or salespeople—or visionaries who can lead innovation and set new trends (Gladwell 2000). Accordingly, the case studies will be divided into two sections: the first on leaders inside the community and the second on leaders from outside the community. This will allow contrast and comparison between the kinds of leaders identified in the case studies. Thus, knowledge creation theory may be useful in explaining these processes.

Leaders from inside the Community

Leaders from outside the Community

Notes

1. A branch of philosophy that investigates the origin, nature, methods, and limits of human knowledge.
2. A branch of metaphysics that studies the nature of existence or being.

3. In addition to the patterns of thinking and acting, we have prepared a list of questions for a knowledge survey based on the SECI model—the SECI survey. It includes an appraisal of phronesis, and is used in evaluating an organization's behaviors and attitudes in pursuing knowledge creation.
4. Aristotle based his concept of phronesis on Pericles, a statesman of ancient Athens. Phronesis was originally intended to describe the quality of politicians. However, for various reasons this concept was neglected for a long time and rarely addressed, even in the political science field. As scholars of philosophy and political science started to express skepticism towards objective and analytical science around the beginning of the third millennium, the concept of phronesis once again began to receive attention as a 'practice turn' in the fields of philosophy, political science, international relations and management studies (Flyvbjerg 2001; Brown 2012; Nonaka 2014a, b).

REFERENCES

Brown, C. 2012. The 'practice turn', phronesis and classical realism: Towards a phronetic international political theory? *Millennium-Journal of International Studies* 40 (3): 439–456.

Drucker, P. F. 1993. *Post-Capitalist Society.* London: Routledge.

Drucker, P.F. 1999. The new pluralism. *Leader to Leader* 14: 18–23. doi:10.1002/ltl.40619991405.

Flyvbjerg, B. 2001. *Making social science matter: Why social inquiry fails and how it can succeed again.* Cambridge: Cambridge University Press.

French, John R.P., Bertram Raven, and D. Cartwright. 1959. "The bases of social power." *Classics of organization theory 7.*

Gibbs Jr., W.R. 2005. *Embodiment and cognitive science.* New York: Cambridge University Press.

Gladwell, M. 2000. *The tipping point.* Boston: Little Brown and Co

MacIntyre, A. 1984. *After virtue.* Notre Dame, IN: University of Notre Dame Press.

Mandelbrot, Benoit B., and Roberto Pignoni. 1983. *The fractal geometry of nature,* vol. 1. New York: WH freeman.

Noe, Keiichi. 2007. *Rekishi wo tetsugaku suru* (Philosophizing history). Tokyo: Iwanami Shoten.

Nonaka, Ikujiro, Ryoko Toyama, and Toru Hirata. 2008. *Managing flow: A process theory of the knowledge-based firm.* Palgrave McMillan.

Nonaka, I. 2014a. Churchill ni Miru Kiki no Leadership [Churchill's crisis leadership]. In *Kindai Nihon no Leadership* [*Leadership in modern Japan*], ed. Ryoichi Tobe. Chikura Publishing.

Nonaka, I. 2014b. Presentation made at the second workshop on leadership and management development in Asian countries, September 29th–October 1st, 2014, at National Graduate Institute for Policy Studies (GRIPS), Tokyo.

Nonaka, I., M. Kodama, A. Hirose, and F. Kohlbacher. 2014. Dynamic fractal organizations for promoting knowledge-based transformation–A new paradigm for organizational theory. *European Management Journal* 32 (1): 137–146.

Nonaka, I., and N. Konno. 2012. *Chishiki Sozo Keiei no Principles: Kenryo Shihonshugi no Jissenron* [The grammer of knowledge creating management for prudent capitalism]. Tokyo: Tokyo Keizai.

Nonaka, I., and H. Takeuchi. 1995. *The knowledge-creating company: How Japanese companies create the dynamics of innovation*. New York: Oxford University Press.

Nonaka, I., and H. Takeuchi. 2011. The wise leader. *Harvard Business Review* 89 (5): 58–67.

Nye, Joseph S. 2011. *The future of power*. PublicAffairs.

Polanyi, M. 1966. *The tacit dimension*. Chicago: University of Chicago Press.

Authors' Biography

Ikujiro Nonaka is a Professor Emeritus, Hitotsubashi University, the world-renowned founder of the theory of knowledge-based management. He received his B.A. (Political Science) from Waseda University, MBA in 1968 and Ph.D. (Business Administration) in 1972 from the University of California, Berkeley. Prior to his academic track, he worked at Fuji Electric Corporation. He has won wide-ranging recognition for his work in developing the knowledge-based management theory, and recently received the Lifetime Achievement Award by Thinkers50. His research interests are in the organizational knowledge creation and wise leadership in private, public, and social organizations. His recent publications include: Nonaka and Takeuchi (2011). The wise leader. *Harvard Business Review, 89*(5), 58–67.

Ayano Hirose Nishihara is an Assistant Professor, Department of Global Business, College of Business, Rikkyo University, and a research collaborator to Professor Emeritus Ikujiro Nonaka. She received her B.A. (Law) from Nagoya University, MBA in 2005 and DBA in 2011 from The Graduate School of International Corporate Strategy, Hitotsubashi University. Prior to her academic track, she worked as an assistant manager at NEC Corporation. Her research topics include knowledge creation at public and private organizations and communities, knowledge-creating leadership, and social innovation. Her recent publications include Nonaka, I., Hirose, A., & Takeda, Y. (2016). "Meso"—Foundations of Dynamic Capabilities: Team—Level Synthesis and Distributed Leadership as the Source of Dynamic Creativity. *Global Strategy Journal, 6*(3), 168–182.

CHAPTER 2

Collaboration on City Planning: A Lesson from Mayor Joko Widodo (2005–2011)

Anwar Sanusi

INTRODUCTION

If a survey were conducted today to name the most outstanding figure in Indonesia, the majority of people would probably choose one particular person: Joko Widodo (known as Jokowi). Jokowi won the presidential elections in 2014, thereby becoming the first Indonesian president not to have come from the political elite or be an army general. This case study, however, primarily considers his achievements before becoming president, when he was the mayor of Solo City.

Jokowi is a former businessman from the furniture trade who later became mayor of Solo City, serving from 2005 to 2010 and part of a second term from 2010 to 2015. In 2012, he was selected by his political party, the Indonesian Democratic Party of Struggle (PDIP), to run for governor of the Special Capital Region of Jakarta (DKI Jakarta). Despite strong support for the incumbent Governor, Dr. Ir. Fauzi Bowo,

A. Sanusi (✉)
Ministry of Villages, Development of Disadvantages Regions, and Transmigration Republic Indonesia, Jakarta, Republic of Indonesia
e-mail: anwaru@rocketmail.com

© The Author(s) 2018
A. Hirose Nishihara et al. (eds.), *Knowledge Creation in Community Development*, DOI 10.1007/978-3-319-57481-3_2

by the majority of political parties that dominated the provincial legislative council, Joko Widodo was elected Governor of DKI Jakarta for the period 2012–2017. Joko Widodo was subsequently selected by five political parties as their candidate for president for the period 2014–2019 and was declared the victor on July 22, 2014, by the Indonesian General Election Commission (KPU) Indonesia for the period 2014–2019 with 53.15% of votes.

Jokowi first came to prominence as a public official as a result of his transformative approach toward street vendors in Solo City and through his development of various pro-people policies. His approach was apparent not only in the way he dealt with the issue of the street vendors (*pedagang kaki lima*, or PKL) but also in his efforts to simplify and shorten delays for those requiring public services. He also worked to promote the "Esemka" cars produced by students from Vocational Senior Secondary Education (SMK, pronounced es-em-ka) in Solo, with the goal of establishing a national automotive industry.

He projected the image of a public servant rather than a bureaucratic figure, adopting a style of leadership that was considered by many to be genuine, rather than about building an image. His leadership style also promoted participation. For example, in the debate between the presidential and vice presidential candidates on June 8, 2014, Jokowi stated his view that democracy entails listening to people's aspirations:

> This Republic belongs to all of us. What people want is to have a better standard of living, and to be more prosperous. Democracy, in my opinion, is to listen to people's aspirations and listen well. Why do we pay visits every day from one village to another or from one market to another (a practice known as blusukan)? This is because we want to listen to what they have to say. Mr. JK and I have proven it. Mr. JK resolved conflicts in Poso and Aceh through dialogue, and I resolved the issues of Tanah Abang (market relocation) and Waduk Pluit (dam normalization) through dialogue with society (Jokowi, on his Presidential campaign, June 8, 2014).

He also argued that, as leaders, the president and vice president have an obligation to implement the aspirations of the people. This approach compared favorably to the old image of the bureaucratic figure, perceived as rigid, impersonal, and dedicated to red tape.

This attitude of listening to the voice of the public as a way of understanding public issues became the trademark of Jokowi and came to be known by the Javanese word *blusukan*. This term has since become widely used, with *blusukan* recently entering the Indonesian dictionary to describe a leader's ability to grasp public aspirations directly through visiting the sites of contention. His approach since he was mayor of Solo City has thus been associated with a style of leadership that promotes participation, something he continued when he became the Governor of DKI Jakarta.

SURAKARTA: A CITY OF DIVERSE COLORS

Surakarta, or Solo as it is known locally, is located in the southern part of the Central Java provinces and is about 110 km east of Yogyakarta. The population in December 2012 was 545,653, and by December 2013, the population had increased by 18,006–563,659 people (Population and Civil Registration Service Office of Surakarta City 2013). The growth rate of Solo's population between 2000 and 2010 was 0.25%, far below the growth of the population of Central Java, at 0.46%. Yet, compared with other cities in Indonesia, the population density is relatively high, at 12,799 people/ km². This makes Surakarta city the most densely populated in Central Java and the eighth most densely populated in the country, with the 13th smallest area. The most populated district in Solo is Pasar Kliwon market, with an area only a tenth of the whole of Solo. Without control over the growth of the population, increases in density in Surakarta city are likely to continue.

Solo retains its position as the last remaining aristocratic symbol of Muslim Java and therefore is considered to be a place that preserves the "spirit of Java." According to a local newspaper, Joglo Semar (2012), Solo has a reputation for preserving traditional Javanese culture—both tangible in the form of a variety of arts and pottery, and intangible in the form of gentle, polite attitudes, and good manners. Historically, Solo City also made great contributions to the development of Islam in Indonesia and is considered a center of Islamic teaching. Many Indonesian Islamic organizations, such as the Islamic Chamber of Commerce (SDI), were started here.

The ethnic and social diversity of Solo, along with these highly cultured attitudes, has given it a sometimes-contradictory reputation. On the one hand, people respect harmony; on the other hand, things can easily turn toward chaos. People there are well known for being polite and tolerant, but they can also be radically intolerant. Thus, while relationships between the various ethnicities, cultures, and religions in

Solo are generally harmonious, there have been occasional conflicts and riots triggered by racial issues. In fact, the biggest riots since Indonesian independence in 1945 occurred in Solo in 1980 and 1998, triggered by ethnic clashes between the Javanese and ethnic Chinese communities. The first mass riots started on November 20, 1980, during the "New Order Era" following a fight in a sports school between Pipit Supriyadi, a young Javanese man, and Kicak, a young Chinese man. The fighting destroyed stores belonging to Chinese people and then spread to other cities in Central Java. At the end of the New Order regime in 1998, Solo was on fire again, but this time, the riots were caused by an economic crisis that led to public demands for President Suharto, who had ruled for 32 years, to step down (Siegel 1986, 1998). While ethnic conflicts occurred in three cities—Bandung, Solo, and Jakarta—the riots in Solo were on a much greater scale compared with the other cities.

The diversity of its socio–cultural elements mixed with the dynamics of its politics makes Solo a city that is always a barometer for the socio–political situation in Indonesia. To be mayor in such situation requires leadership that is flexible but firm.

A GLIMPSE OF JOKOWI'S LIFE

The story of Jokowi's life mirrors the experience of many Indonesians. He was born, like many other people, low down on the social and economic spectrum, on June 21, 1961, in the cheapest room of Brayat Minulyo hospital. Jokowi's family was poor and lived a nomadic life, moving from one small rented house to others by the banks of rivers. The situation at that time was not very different from today, and many people were being bulldozed off their land. Nevertheless, he was very proud of what his parents accomplished. "My parents, Notomiharjo and Sujiatmi, are great figures who know how to manage a happy family in spite of the meagerness of their lives," said Joko Widodo (Detiknews 2014).

As a child, Joko's family was forced to move because of continuous rent increases. They moved to a home on the bank of the Dawung Kidul River. Conditions were similar, but the house was smaller. Next, they moved again to the Munggur area by the Pepe River, where his parents added three more daughters to the family. The meager income that he earned from working as a village carpenter forced Notomiharjo to juggle the family finances to make ends meet, but he was able to send little Joko and his three daughters to school. After moving to the Kali

Anyar riverbank, where a large timber market was thriving, the life of the Notomiharjo family gradually began to improve. Thus, Jokowi spent his childhood and adolescence in Solo, moving from a quiet village life to a life to the bustling Gilingan market in Surakarta.

Little Joko first studied in State Elementary School 111 in Tirtoyoso, Solo, between 1968 and 1974. He continued his schooling in Solo City. For him, going to school was a luxury that had to be cherished. He saw school as "a liberating channel" from poverty. He could not afford a bike, so he walked to school instead. Step by step, little Joko (until the age of 12) observed how to cut wood and chop bamboo, and spent time gathering duck eggs that others had missed in the rice fields (Detiknews 2014).

He did not want to be dependent on his father, so he started to think about how to become a merchant. His interest in the world of business was obvious as he called out to vendors that passed by. "One day, I overexcitedly called a vendor over, not knowing what he was selling. It turned out that it was firewood. Feeling guilty, my mother had to pay for the firewood although she did not need it," said Jokowi. Those vendors inspired him to be persistent in earning a living. Since then, he became close to the world of "poor people" (wong cilik). "My childhood was my first lesson in understanding how people live. What I am doing now is the result of how I grew up. Riverbank slum areas in Surakarta taught me a lot of things: human life and hopes," said Joko Widodo (Yudha 2014; Detiknews 2014).

After completing his senior high school education in SMA Negeri 6 Solo, Jokowi furthered his studies at the University of Gadjah Mada (UGM) Yogyakarta, a university that has been very critical of government policies. Jokowi studied in the Faculty of Forestry. The reason was simple. Since he was a kid, he had been drawn to timber and bamboo, starting from small businesses with his father and relatives, as well as his community, made up of mostly carpenters and wood sellers. It seemed that wood had become a "symbol" for his life. It means that anything to do with wood seemed to be attached to his way of life (Endah 2012a, b).

After graduating, Jokowi worked for PT Kertas Kraft Aceh, a state-owned enterprise (BUMN) based in Aceh. At that time, the situation there was dangerous and growing worse due to the Aceh separatist movement (GAM). Armed conflicts frequently broke out in Aceh as GAM grew steadily stronger, often provoking and intimidating non-native people. In 1988, after 2 years working in that company, Jokowi returned to Solo to start a business as a furniture entrepreneur. Initially, Jokowi worked in a furniture company owned by his uncle, Pakde Miyono. Later, Jokowi started his own furniture company. After experiencing various ups and downs in the business, Jokowi was finally chosen as the chairman of the Indonesia Furniture Industry and Handicraft Association (Asmindo), Surakarta local commissary (Komda). This was Jokowi's entry point into the world of politics.

Jokowi actually had no ambitions of entering the political world. Calls for Jokowi to enter the political world were fostered by a paradoxical situation: Following the economic crisis that hit Indonesia in 1998, there was an increase in the dollar exchange rate against the Indonesian rupiah, which resulted in huge profits for exporters, including Jokowi. However, this situation also left many people in difficulty. Moreover, while people from outside Solo acknowledged Solo as a city of culture, many villagers who made traditional arts found it difficult to live. Jokowi said, "That was what encouraged me to initiate the establishment of an organization to protect the craftsmen and furniture entrepreneurs of Solo. The world of money took me to politics … a world that was initially far from my preference" (Endah 2012).

Jokowi oversaw the opening of the Indonesia Furniture and Handicraft Industry Association (Asmindo) branch, an organization for furniture entrepreneurs, which included furniture entrepreneurs from all over Indonesia and more than 140 craft and furniture business people in Solo. It was initiated by Jokowi in Solo on July 11, 2002, and he was elected chairman. Jokowi's activities in the organization drew the attention of politicians. In 2004, there were many rumors emanating from the board and members of the Asmindo regional commissary of Surakarta. "I heard the news that Mr. Jokowi was running for city mayor," said Jokowi, quoting an Asmindo colleague. Jokowi just laughed and confessed that he had no intention whatsoever of being mayor of Surakarta city. The income from the furniture business was a blessing for him. He claimed that he had no political ambitions. "What was more hilarious for me was that I never dealt with politics. I was never interested in joining any political party and never involved in any arena that was associated with politics and government," he said (Detiknews 2014).

One factor that did encourage Jokowi to enter politics was the falling reputation of Solo City. Although it was one of the most popular tourist destinations in Indonesia and a center of Javanese culture, it was improperly managed. There was a gloomy outlook for the city—many city areas were not well maintained, hotels had no business, and tourism potential was stagnant—and the majesty of Solo City seemed to be dying. Jokowi then thought about what development was possible and for whom (Endah 2012a, b). Entering 2005, pressure from Jokowi's business associates for him to enter politics became very strong. Officially, the Asmindo committee gave its full support for Jokowi to join the contest for mayor of Solo City. This time, he no longer laughed, but he still said no.

That remained the case until one day when Jokowi got "a spiritual call" after he prayed to God to ask for direction. Subsequently, he talked to his wife and called his children, who were studying in Singapore. His family generally opposed his decision, as stated by his oldest son, Gibran: "Why do you want to join the contest for mayor? I disagree. I would prefer you as you are now, not a public official and not involved in politics" (Detiknews 2014). Nevertheless, Jokowi had made up his mind, and his family respected his decision. The next day, he went to the Asmindo office and asked: "Who will be my running mate in the contest?" All the committee members of Asmindo responded positively.

The process gathered speed. The Asmindo team moved aggressively, as they had made thorough preparations. Jokowi chose to make his campaign as honest and as humble as possible; he did not want anything to do with money politics. "I also firmly informed my colleagues not to waste money on the campaign," said Jokowi. He decisively paired with Rudy to enter the Solo City mayoral election in 2005. Jokowi was promoted by the PDIP and the PKB. The other candidates were Ahmad Purnomo-Istar Yuliadi, promoted by the PAN, Hardono-Dipokusumo, promoted by Golkar-PD-PKS, and Slamet-Hengky, promoted by small political parties. On June 27, 2005, Jokowi-Rudy won the election with more than 37% of the votes.

That was the beginning of Jokowi's life in politics, which for him was something new and completely different from his previous activities. However, he committed himself to entering the political world by listening and seeing what the people said and did. His character as a leader was emphasized as he listened to the general public. For him, democracy meant seeing and listening to what people were directly feeling.

On taking office in his first term of office as mayor of Solo City, Jokowi inherited a very difficult situation: suboptimal government performance, high poverty and unemployment rates, and bureaucratic practices based more on rules than on a desire to deliver good public service. The bureaucracy was seen as being slow, red-tape-bound, and distant from the public. The mental shift that was needed was to change the bureaucratic culture and the mindset of the bureaucrats into a more humanistic approach. Apart from that, Jokowi also introduced a new tradition in planning the government's programs and activities by talking directly to citizens. This later became known as *blusukan*—looking at and listening directly to the facts and to public aspirations.

A number of Jokowi's legacies in Solo City (Surakarta) can be used as models for managing the best public policies, including the relocation of street vendors from Banjaransari, revitalization of traditional markets, and shortening the process of issuing ID cards.

JOKOWI'S SUCCESS STORIES

Handling Street Vendors

In 2005, when Jokowi was elected mayor of Solo City, polls showed that many people were unhappy with the number of street vendors. The number of street vendors had grown uncontrollably, with more than a thousand vendors spread across the city, leading to many social problems, including crime. The issue that drew most attention was the presence of street vendors in Banjarsari at the 45 Struggle Monument (Monumen Juang 45). They made a living from selling second-hand goods, and therefore, they named the market Klithikan (pasar Klithikan). Public officials initially ignored the vendors' practice of operating in Banjarsari without permission. This proliferation of street vendors in Solo turned the green open space at Banjarsari into a messy, dirty, and disgusting area to be avoided. At night, the location became a zone of prostitution, making local residents uneasy.

Due to this situation, there was no other alternative but to relocate the vendors. In the past, as in other Indonesian cities, the government used a repressive approach to solving this kind of problem by calling in the police and bulldozing vendors' pitches, which often led to conflict and even loss of life. While this coercive approach might initially seem efficient, it merely provided temporary relief and did not account for the problem of new unemployment, which could lead to increased social vulnerability. The question was how. It was out of the question to bulldoze them. The city hall of Surakarta had been burned down twice (1998 and 1999) due to communication breakdowns between the leaders and the people.

Jokowi tried to see the street vendors positively and felt that they needed to be empowered (Yudha 2014, 334–337). From this perspective, the street vendors were not pests to be wiped out but rather partners to work with. He believed that they were in fact the strength of the real economy and should be considered potential assets in boosting local economic development. Their persistence and their spirit in making ends meet for their families were something that the government ought to facilitate. They were also people with hearts and feelings. Therefore, a heart-to-heart approach was the one that Jokowi used to persuade them. In Javanese philosophy, it was known as "treating them as humans," or putting ourselves in their shoes. Jokowi wanted to listen to their hearts, avoid violence, and offer solutions with love.

Then, the idea emerged of organizing an open buffet for the street vendors. This idea came from Jokowi's experience in the furniture business: A good buffet usually ended up with a good business deal. The open buffet was then held, and all the street vendor associations in Banjarsari were invited to come to the event. Knowing that they were going to be relocated, the street vendors prepared themselves. They talked with the non-governmental organization that oversaw them. Banners were brought to the venue in Loji Gandrung, the mayor's official residence. But they were surprised because in fact there was no discussion whatsoever about relocating them. It was only about eating and making small talk. As Jokowi used to say, AEGH stands for "After Eating–Go Home."

A second open buffet was organized with the same agenda: to eat and make small talk. The street vendors were confused; if there were nothing important to say, why had the mayor invited them? But the open buffets were held again and again—in fact, a total of 54 banquets were held. At the 54th buffet (seven months later), Jokowi then conveyed his intention to the street vendors. Luckily, the situation was conducive to communication, and they openly aired their problems, specifically that they were afraid to lose their customers. For a solution to the relocation issue, Jokowi offered to publicize their relocation through printed mass media and local television. Jokowi also promised to put posters in strategic locations in the heart of Solo City and ordered the transportation service office to add a new bus route to the new site.

The vendors finally agreed to the program of the Surakarta city government. However, they also asked for other concessions, such as free kiosks. This request was the hardest one to meet. Fortunately, Jokowi succeeded in convincing the regional legislative council to approve the deal on one condition: The vendors must pay a daily fee of 2600 IDR/ hari. Within an 8-year period, the eight-billion IDR investment made by the city government would be returned. The street vendors were then relocated with a festival-like ceremony called *boyongan*, making them the center of public attention. All the vendors wore traditional clothes, and those that accompanied them wore traditional military uniforms. The festival was just like a 1-day royal ceremony. There were 989 vendors involved in that *boyongan* ceremony. The Monumen Juang in Banjarsari was restored to being a green open space, thus helping to improve the city's oxygen supply, and the area once again became a clean and convenient location for leisure activities.

Jokowi's success in relocating the street vendors was mostly determined by a very effective communication strategy, that is, listening to feedback from stakeholders directly related to the street vendors. Indeed, what Jokowi did seems less efficient because it took a long time—54 meetings—and required significant resources. However, the true value was in the legacy: The methods utilized by Jokowi were shown to be effective, especially in obtaining the support of street vendors and other stakeholders. Evidence for this can be seen in the sincere compliance of the street vendors in moving to a new place, and the street carnival, which received widespread media coverage. The approach catapulted Jokowi's name to the fore as an innovative mayor.

Revitalization of the Traditional Market

The other lesson that we can learn from Solo City concerns the revitalization of the traditional market. Trade and services have long been the largest sectors in Solo City, and together, they generate almost 30% of all revenues. However, prior to Jokowi's mayorship, there had been little clear management and for 40 years, and no new markets opened in the city. People were more and more reluctant to go to traditional markets, because they were muddy, slum-like, and uncomfortable, so people went to the mall instead. The negative stigma against these traditional markets can be hard to remove. However, traditional markets can play a very large role in expanding the domestic economy. Sociologically, markets are also considered an effective arena for the exchange of information between people in order to strengthen social ties. In the opinion of Jokowi, small popular economic environments with economic potential should be encouraged (Jokowi, interview by the author in Mata Najwa 2012). Jokowi described his approach as not anti-mall or supermarket, "but we as a city government should control them, limit them. Budgets should be used as much as possible to the community, especially the underprivileged" (BBC News Interview 2012).

For these reasons, traditional markets needed to be revitalized. Physically, the buildings were renovated and polished up, and by 2011, 19 of the 42 traditional Solo markets had been revitalized. In addition, traders were provided with training sessions relevant to the development of business, such as financial management, business administration, entrepreneurship, human resources, the arrangement of goods, and customer service. Traders responded well to the opportunity, including one who says his turnover increased by 41% after he attended training (*Kompas Newspaper* 2011). Prizes such as cars were given to attract the public to shop in the traditional markets. Within 3 years, revenue increased considerably—from 7 billion IDR in 2007 to 12 billion in 2008 and 19 billion in 2010. From this case, we can learn that it is possible to reorganize city management systems if there is a serious desire to do so. The most important thing is that there is political will, effective communication, and field supervision. However, there are still some problems connected with this revitalization, with some markets located quite far away from the community, reducing the number of visitors. As a result, some stalls have not been filled ("Jokowi Revitalisation for City Prostitution or Market for Prostitution" 2014).

Building Trust in Government

One of the issues perceived to be the cause of the failure of the previous relocation process was the absence of trust from the street vendors toward the city government. They lost trust following the government's frequent failure to keep their promises while never appropriately accommodating people's aspirations. In the case of the relocation of street vendors' in Banjarsari, the majority was against it due to the fact that the move would have adversely affected them. For them, the city government was not able to find a solution or appropriate alternative choices for relocation. The relocation of the Klithikan market to Semanggi was previously considered inappropriate, because it was merely a kiosk with no roof, walls, and lacked other supporting facilities and infrastructure. Moreover, the location was relatively far from downtown, and as it was also a red-light district, it was the last place that many people would want to visit.

Both the city government and the street vendors aimed to build empathy by trying to put themselves in each other's shoes. The city government built a mindset that "the street vendors are the partners of the city government"—not an enemy that must be eliminated, a sign that the city government was trying to build empathy and to respect the existence of the vendors. This was proven during the early encounter in Loji Gandrung. There was no statement from the government about the relocation plan, because they were aware that the street vendors were against it. The city government told them only after they had gotten to know one another after numerous encounters.

There was mutual respect and no prejudice during the process. The building of respect, for example, took place during the registration of the street vendors. During this process, the city government, through the staff of the Street Vendor Association Office (PPKL) and with support from the public order police squad (Satpol Pamong Praja), treated them kindly. The socialization of the street vendors was conducted directly, as the city government raised awareness of the importance of organizing them through direct communication and by treating them as partners. Furthermore, the stakeholders mutually supported one another, rather than doing the opposite. As stated by one of the radical leaders of the street vendors, who were initially strongly against the relocation plan: "... I will always understand what the city government wants, and I cherish it ..." The city government also understood the street vendors by listening and welcoming their propositions on the relocation.

There was a shared effort to exchange concerns and experiences. Various organizations provided technical assistance to them. In the initial process, SOMPIS, Solidaritas Masyarakat Pinggiran Surakarta (Solidarity for Peripheral Surakarta Society), went along with them to voice their objections to the relocation and to prepare a strategy if they failed. A series of six meetings was conducted to consolidate the rejection plan while shoring up eight related associations (Handayani 2006). When the street vendors came to an agreement on the relocation, university representatives were employed to be the facilitators in announcing their designated kiosks, as they were considered neutral. After that, the universities organized training for the vendors through a business management course.

In building trust, the government did so through an informal approach by municipal officials (the mayor, vice mayor, and head office PPKL) to vendors. The city government officials went to the street vendors' booths with no regard for their own working hours. They engaged the vendors regardless of the time of day and even came in casual clothes. As one of the society leaders stated, "... perhaps you will find it hard to believe that Mr. Rudy (the vice mayor) will come to that market early in the morning and nobody knows when he will come, and he asked 'What do you need?' I saw it myself." Whereas another vendor said, "there we met Mr. Jokowi, socializing, telling jokes, we hardly felt that we were in a face-to-face meeting with the mayor, and he was often accompanied by Mr. Bambang. At that time it was like a garden party ..." and "Mr. Jokowi often came here like a friend with no bodyguards" (Sufianty 2014). The meetings were held in an informal atmosphere, and serious issues were discussed in a relaxed manner.

All stakeholders mapped out their roles and contributions. Contributions made by the stakeholders varied depending on their resources. The city government sought to facilitate the process, the street vendors and community leaders shared opinions on the proposals during discussions, NGOs accompanied the street vendors, and universities assisted vendors during the process, and by providing technical help with building design. The budget for this activity came from the city government and the street vendors. The UNS University, Surakarta, and local officials provided technical expertise. In addition, some local officials, such as the Office of Management Vendors, Bappeda (regional development agency), and the Department of Market Management, were deeply involved in the planning, design, financing, and coordination of this initiative. The local parliament was also involved when this initiative was applied as a social strategy and a two-way consultation approach that minimizes social conflict and accommodates the voices of all stakeholders (Sufianty 2014).

The next stage was to build a shared problem solution. In accordance with the SECI model approach, this phase is understood as a phase to communicate tacit knowledge possessed by every stakeholder, especially the street vendors. With a common understanding, it will create a collective agreement. In this context, the government and vendors agreed on the crucial issues and the constraints faced by the street vendors in moving to a new location. The PKL originally filed numerous claims to overcome the obstacles posed by the new location. Among the demands that were satisfactorily resolved were: an intercity minibus route, a wider road, promotion (advertising the relocated, newly built Klitikan market for four months on local television and in print media), cooperative capital (5 million dollars per PKL), guarantees of no street vendors there, free stalls, free licenses, and a six-month payment holiday (Sufianty 2014).

The final stage requires building a shared commitment. After the learning process, the city government tried to do this through efforts to internalize the agreed-on solutions in order to maintain consistency. In the process of planning the relocation of street vendors in Banjarsari, there was a change in the attitudes of the vendors. At first, there had been a refusal to understand; then they showed a willingness to move, and even gave ideas for the move. This occurred as a result of the authentic dialogue based on trust that had been built between all parties. Reciprocal relationships are mutually adapted toward learning. Collaborative processes that occurred in planning the relocation of street vendors in Banjarsari built trust through relationships and mutual understanding. This led to joint problem-solving efforts through learning, and strengthening of commitment through adaptation. All stages occurred through face-to-face dialogue.

ANALYSIS: JOKOWI'S INNOVATION IN CITY PLANNING

Blusukan (Indonesia SECI Model)

Based on the above case study, we can see that Jokowi's leadership style in building Solo City (2005–2012) was instrumental in handling communication breakdowns within society through an alternative leadership approach that changed the style and strategy of communication. The participatory approach is in line with the phronetic leadership concept—namely a contextual leadership that exploits precision in making a decision in line with the right time and space in the framework of achieving goals (Nonaka and Takeuchi 1995). Moreover, in the framework of knowledge-based management, Jokowi's leadership can be examined through the SECI Model approach, which explores tacit as well as explicit knowledge. The main question that needs to be answered is how Jokowi's leadership can respond to various public issues to promote successful social development. The next involves considering how these various successes can be institutionalized within a more permanent policy system.

One of the authentic approaches Jokowi's utilizes in accommodating the aspirations of society is using face-to-face greetings and meeting common people, an approach known by the popular term described above: *blusukan*. This term reflects inclusive and down-to-earth political practices that break away from the formalities and rigidity of a leader who must respond to the democratic demands of society (Yudha 2014). This approach is a strategy to free that leader from a bureaucratic culture that tends to be rigid and that tends to involve only one-way communication. This bureaucratic culture thrives within a paternalistic system that always emphasizes subordinates' submission to their superiors in order to earn rewards. This constant effort to please superiors is known as the "yes-boss" culture (or known in Indonesia as ABS). Clearly, this leads to a very big gap between what the public demands and bureaucratic responses. Rather than feeling a sense of certainty that the government will act based on their real needs, people can only hope that their wishes and demands will be included in a bureaucratic agenda. Because of that, what Jokowi has done is a creative breakthrough in listening to the objective voice of society. *Blusukan* is a contrary of leadership behavior or, as Max Weber dubbed it, a characteristic of a legal, rational leader that prioritizes society as the holder of the mandate. Many leaders tend to forget their virtues and become trapped in a corrupt culture.

Jokowi's justification for *blusukan* is that it helps him discover the true condition of society, which is often obscured by a bureaucratic culture that is overly formal and opaque. By deconstructing a whole bureaucratic system that is formalistic, procedural, and confining, a more aspirational public policy can be achieved. What Jokowi has done, in Rhodes's terms, is known as governing without government (Yudha 2014). Thus, the process of building trust was achieved through the following process: building a common understanding, attaining solutions to problems, and building commitment. In terms of the SECI Model (Nonaka and Takeuchi 1995), what is being done by Jokowi can be understood as a knowledge creation process that begins with building a common understanding with key stakeholders, vendors, and NGOs.

In the context of knowledge management, what Jokowi has done is to strive to create as many arenas as possible for people to channel their aspirations through creating ba. In this case, *ba* was achieved by frequently inviting street vendors as key stakeholders to convey their ideas and propositions surrounding public issues. Many people considered them as the source of the city's problems. Although Jokowi could have used the power at his disposal, he did not do so. Instead, he preferred to use the approach of an adaptive leader, using tacit knowledge much more than explicit knowledge. This was shown by not giving directives to the street vendors or the flea market, but by listening to their creative ideas and propositions.

Jokowi's Leadership Styles

Jokowi's leadership style in addressing public issues in Surakarta provides an example of how leadership does not just rely on the authority or power to execute decisions. The coercive approach, widely used by leaders, decrees that people who break a rule should be punished. For Indonesian local government, what Jokowi does can be seen as a creative breakthrough in public policy implementation that considers the essential aspects of humanity, i.e., the need to have one's existence respected. The action of respecting others is considered an important part of Javanese values and is known as *diuwongke*, or treating people as human beings. Jokowi puts this concept into practice through recognition that other people's opinions, ideas, and experiences are likely to be different from each other. Jokowi realized that everyone has experience and if they are given an opportunity to share or communicate them, this will produce better ideas that will be more useful in solving problems, while at the same time avoiding actions that could hurt people.

When Jokowi was a mayor at Solo City, he adopted what could be seen as a phronetic leadership style. According to Nonaka and Takeuchi (1995), a phronetic leader practices moral discernment about what is good and acts on it in every situation. Judgments must be guided by the individual's values and ethics. Without a foundation of values, executives cannot decide what is good or bad. Jokowi's ability to judge goodness can be seen when he rejected a proposal from the head of local civil service police to sweep away the PKL using a coercive approach. Furthermore, he replaced the male head of the local civil service policy unit with a woman. To get closer to citizens, Jokowi changed the uniform of local civil service police from a military-style uniform to a traditional uniform, which comes across as more people-oriented and friendly.

The other character of phronetic leaders is their ability to grasp the essence of the actual situation. For Jokowi, this capacity can be seen when he saw PKL as an important sector to drive economic growth. To empower PKL in terms of economic activity, Jokowi provided them with some financial support, such as offering soft loans from local banks and reducing taxes. He also provided PKL with a proper place to run their businesses that was close to the community and comfortable. His willingness to listen to other people's opinions also contributed to the agreement between the local government officials and street vendors. Jokowi was very patient in listening to many proposals from street vendors.

To be a phronetic leader, leaders should create shared context. To establish a shared context, the leader and all the members should create a place that is convenient for sharing ideas. In Japan, a *ba* (place, space, or field) refers to the context in which relationships are forged and interactions occur. Those participating in a *ba* share information, build short-term relationships, and try to create new meaning (Nonaka and Takeuchi 1995). *Ba* in the Jokowi context is in the Loji Gandrung, the mayor's office, which in a Javanese context is usually a sacred place that not everyone can access easily. But during the Jokowi era, the office was used for public meetings involving street vendors and local officials. Street vendors could easily come to this government office and talk freely to articulate their points of view.

REFERENCES

City of Surakarta. 2013. Population and Civil Registration Service Office of Surakarta City.

Detiknews. 2014. Rabu 23 Juli 2014, 10:41 WIB Kisah Hidup Jokowi Kisah Awal Jokowi Terjun ke Dunia Politik – detikNews. http://news.detik.com/berita/2645557/kisah-awal-jokowi-terjun-ke-dunia-politik/3.

Endah, Alberthiene. 2012. Jokowi: Memimpin Kota Menyentuh Jakarta. *Metagraf,* Nov 17. http://www.goodreads.com/book/show/16165047-jokowi.

Endah, Albertine. 2012a. Jokowi Led the City by Care in Jakarta. *Metagraf.*

———. 2012b. Jokowi: Leading a City Touching Jakarta. *Detik,* \July 23.

Handayani, Suci. 2006. *Pelibatan Masyarakat Marginal dalam Perencanaan dan Penganggaran Partisipatif (sebuah pengalaman di Kota Solo)* [The Marginal people involvement on participatory planning and budgeting: Solo case study]. *Kompip.*

Jokowi. 2014. BBC Interview.

Jokowi from Solo to Betawi (Jokowi dari Solo ke Betawi). *Semar Joglo*. http://edisicetak.joglosemar.co/berita/jokowi-dari-solo-ke-betawi-69178.html. Retrieved 26 Aug 2014.

Jokowi Revitalisation for City Prostitution or Market for Prostitution. *Merdeka*, 28 Feb 2014. http://www.merdeka.com/uang/revitalisasi-jokowi-dinilai-gagal-pasar-jaditempat-prostitusi.html. Retrieved 28 Aug 2014.

Kompas Newspaper, Thursday, 3 Nov 2011. The trade vendors and unemployment, http://lipsus.kompas.com/gebrakan-jokowi-basuki/read/xml/011/11/03/23431450/Seller. Declaration of criticism. Free from Street musicians and retrieved by KPK middle manager. 31 Aug 2014.

Nonaka, Ikujiro, and Hirotaka Takeuchi. 1995. *The knowledge-creating company: How Japanese companies create the dynamics of innovation*. Oxford university press.

Siegel, James T. 1986. *Solo in the New Order: Language and Hierarchy in an Indonesian City*. Princeton, NJ: Princeton University Press.

———. Thoughts on the Violence of May 13 and 14, 1998, in Jakarta. In *Violence and the State in Suharto's Indonesia*, ed. Benedict R.O'G. Anderson, 90–123. Ithaca, NY: Cornell Southeast Asia Program Publications.

Sufianty, Ely. 2014. *Peran Kepemimpinan Dalam Proses Kolaboratif: Kasus Studi Perencanaan Relokasi Pedagang Kaki Lima Banjarsari Di Kota Surakarta* [The Role of Leadership in Collaborative Process: Case Study on Relocation Planning the Street Vendors at Surakarta City]. PhD dissertation, Institut Teknologi Bandung.

Yudha, Hanta. 2014. *Jejak para Pemimpin* [The Leadership Track]. Jakarta: PT Gramedia Pustaka Utama.

AUTHOR BIOGRAPHY

Anwar Sanusi is the Secretary General Ministry of Villages, Development of Disadvantages Regions, and Transmigration Republic Indonesia. Under the Jokowi and Jusuf Kalla Administration, this ministry plays very important role to develop Indonesia from peripheral through villages. Prior hold this position, he held several positions such a Director of Center for Development of Policy Analyst, Director of the Center for Innovation of Institutional and Human Resources Studies, and other positions related to research and development and training and education for civil servants at the National Institute of Public Administration (NIPA), Republic Indonesia. He is also a country expert for some Asian Productivity Organization Project for the some projects including *Measuring Public Sector Productivity in Selected Asian Countries*.

CHAPTER 3

People-Centric Leadership at the Local Level: Yala Municipality, Thailand

Orathai Kokpol

INTRODUCTION

Thailand has a long tradition of centralized government, and as such, initiating local innovation within this context is not an easy task. For more than a decade, decentralization has been a key objective of political and administrative reform in Thailand; yet even so, progress in implementing decentralization policies has been slow and inconsistent. The central government retains considerable power over local government. The central government has supervisory power over local government units, and many local government functions are shared with central and provincial governments. With local revenue-raising capability very limited, local governments have to rely on subsidies and grants from the central government. Despite the pressures of this centralized system, local government administrators are having to deal with increasingly complex and diversified challenges. Critical emerging issues include social and political conflicts, inequality, a deteriorating environment, and natural disasters such as severe flooding, along with calls for more innovative local policies.

O. Kokpol (✉)
King Prajadhipok's Institute, Bangkok, Thailand
e-mail: okokpol@gmail.com

© The Author(s) 2018   35
A. Hirose Nishihara et al. (eds.), *Knowledge Creation in Community Development*, DOI 10.1007/978-3-319-57481-3_3

Yala Municipality is a case in point. Over the past decade, local government has faced growing tensions in a multi-religious and multi-ethnic society. The city is situated in Yala Province, one of three restive southern provinces alongside Pattani and Narathivas. The city has faced numerous incidents of explosions, killings, and unrest, as well as the presence of military officers around the city. Security and safety are key concerns of residents. Worse still, the situation has had a negative impact on the social and economic atmosphere and engendered feelings of mistrust. Businesses are closing down, the number of visitors is declining, and residents are moving out.

Amid this crisis, Yala Municipality has worked to restore peace and economic prosperity. Various innovative projects have been introduced, including the Yala Youth Orchestra and Yala Bird City. While the work and efforts of Yala City have not put an end to violence in the city, they have shown that local government can make a difference in dealing with issues as complex as social diversity and economic development. This provides some indication that local innovation is possible, even within the centralized systems of the Thai government. The approaches developed in Yala City have been recognized around the world, and the city has won many domestic and international awards, including King Prajadhipok's Gold Award for "Excellence in Strengthening Peace and Harmony" in 2012 and the UNESCO City for Peace Award in 2002–2003. UNESCO (2016) also recognized Yala for its good practices toward the elimination of discrimination.

This case study explores the work of Mr. Pongsak Yingchoncharoen, the mayor of Yala Municipality, along with his team, in dealing with the intractable situation in southernmost Thailand between 2002 and 2013. In addition to fulfilling the role of the municipal office under the law, the mayor and the team focused their efforts on addressing the deeper needs of people in the community. This included working to hold the community together by ensuring safety and promoting harmonious relationships between residents. The self-described goal was to "make Yala a city of peace on the basis of differences."[1]

HISTORY OF THE BEAUTY OF LIVING TOGETHER IN YALA

Yala Municipality is situated at the southern tip of Thailand, bordering Malaysia. The city has an area of 19.4 km^2. In 2013, the total population was 61,507, including 29,073 men and 32,434 women.[2] A key feature of Yala is its multi-ethnic society, with many differences between cultures and religions: 55% identify as Thai or Chinese Buddhists, 43% are Muslim, while the rest are members of other religions, including Christians, Sikhs, and Hindus. There are thirty-four places of worship: twenty-four mosques, five Buddhist temples, and four Christian churches. The municipality is the economic and commercial center of the province as well as the center of government and education. Yala Municipality is also the logistic hub of the southern border provinces.

Before the outbreak of violence, Yala was considered a clean and livable city, and the city planning was recognized as the best in Thailand.[3] In addition, the city was selected by the Ministry of Public Health and the World Health Organization (WHO) in 1997 to be one of five cities in Thailand to participate in the Healthy Cities project. In spite of the differences of race and religion—Buddhist, Muslim, and Chinese—the communities shared mutual respect and had a fairly harmonious relationship for many years, with few signs of the difficulties that later emerged.

YALA AND UNREST

Although the secessionist movement in the south simmered for several decades—due to the distinct population of Muslims and for historical reasons—unrest began to escalate in 2002 in the three southernmost provinces of Narathivas, Yala, and Pattani, including some parts of Songkhla. With the expansion of secessionist movement operations, incidents of assault, incendiary bombs, and riots began to increase in these areas. While government officials were initially the only targets of assassinations, later, Buddhist monks and innocent people in the area were also attacked. Terrorist groups justified their actions by blaming the authorities for unfair arrests, the disappearances of Malay Muslims in the area, and raids on Muslim homes and Islamic schools by authorities without any prior notice.

Although the Thai government has endeavored to solve the problem by providing various resources and increasing budgets,[4] unrest and violence have persisted, affecting local lives and the operations of public officials. Violent actions such as bombings, shooting attacks, and destruction of public property and government buildings have continued. Several bomb explosions in the municipal area caused loss of life and huge damage. For example, in February 2011, a car bomb packed with explosives and oil exploded in downtown Yala resulting in 18 people being injured and setting off a large fire that caused an estimated 10 million baht in damage (Fredreickson 2011). In October the same year, more than 10 bombs rocked the heart of Yala Municipality, killing at least two people and wounding more than 40 others. In 2005, 2078 people were killed, and in response, the government passed a decree of emergency. However, the number of incidents continued to rise, reaching a high point in 2007 with 2475 events. Between 2002 and 2010, the unrest resulted in 13,085 casualties including 5469 deaths and 9653 injured. Of the total number of deaths, 4104, or 75.04%, were civilians (Panusnachee 2014).

As a result, unsafe conditions became a significaAlthough the Thai government nt drag on investments in Yala and other southern areas. The psychological impact was severe. Shops closed earlier. People were afraid to go out at night; teachers and Thai Buddhists started moving out of the area or sending their children to study elsewhere. The number of Yala residents decreased from a total of 74,718 in 2001 to 61,507 in 2013. Making matters worse, Buddhists and Muslims stayed apart, indicating divisions and mistrust in the community.

According to Isaranews Agency, since 2012, violence has steadily decreased due to the government's policy of non-violence. The approach taken by the Thai government, referred to as "From Violence to Peace," involved creating an open stage for public opinion in order to find joint solutions to the conflicts, provide opportunities for all sectors to share their problems, and suggest possible solutions. The participants involved in this activity were treated with respect with regard to dialects, identities, and multi-cultural lifestyles, including the Islamic religion. The victims of violence were also treated with fairness and equality and compensated for their losses. Although no evaluation has been made of this approach, it is widely considered to have brought about substantive positive changes in the area and the average number of incidents appears to have declined from 2.97 events per day in 2011 to 2.42 events per day in 2012, a decrease of 18.51%.[5]

Mr. Pongsak Yingchoncharoen: Mayor in the Yala Crisis

Throughout much of the crisis and violence, Mr. Pongsak Yingchoncharoen has held the office of mayor of Yala Municipality. He was first elected as mayor in 2004 and has held office for two successive terms. During his long service as mayor, he has made many distinctive contributions to the local administration.

Mr. Pongsak was born into a wealthy Chinese family in Yala on May 7, 1963. He grew up in the business area in the center of a Muslim community called Yala Old Market and was thus very familiar with members of the Muslim community. He did very well in school, and after finishing his secondary school education at a public school in Yala, he was admitted to one of the top high schools in Bangkok. He received a bachelor's degree in pharmacy from Chiang Mai University and a master's degree in business administration from the University of Queensland, Australia. During his studies at the University of Queensland, he was elected President of the Thai Student Association. Back in Thailand, he subsequently earned a master's in public administration from the National Institute of Development Administration (NIDA), Thailand.[6]

After returning from overseas, he helped out with the family business both in Yala and Pattani. During those years in Yala, he began to be more interested in public work and started working at the province's Chamber of Commerce. Later, he was invited to be on the school board at Yala Nursery School. By leading many campaigns to raise money for the construction of school buildings and facilities such as a library and computer lab, he was able to build support and gain recognition from the public.

Mr. Pongsak entered local politics for the first time as a candidate for council member in 1999, but failed to be elected. He won for the first time in 2002 in a by-election to replace a council member who had resigned from the post. The previous Yala mayor recognized his capability and assigned him to oversee work on education. When the former mayor resigned, Mr. Pongsak was elected by the council to be the mayor. He served for 1 year before winning the mayoral election for the following term in 2004. He has won the mayoral election for two successive terms and was unopposed in the latest election.

INNOVATIVE POLICIES AND PROJECTS FOR RESTORING HARMONIOUS SOCIETY IN YALA

The mayor's administration operated under the slogan of "Yala is our birth place, a place we admire and show gratitude for" (*Yala kue thinn kerd ja terd lae tan khun*). When Mr. Pongsak stepped into the mayor's chair in 2004, the local administration was very divided and lacked clear vision and was poorly organized. He told people that in the first 2 years, he was determined to seek unity within Yala society, to resolve management issues and to strengthen the local administration. He also made himself accessible to his constituents and could be reached by phone, so people always knew about every stage of progress in the area. Also, people liked to hear him talk: in interviews, local officials and others found him eloquent and persuasive. The mayor always attended the local or village meetings such as monthly community councils and mobile municipal council in person. He used these opportunities to talk not only about the work of Yala municipal office but also to share new ideas and information on regional and global issues related to the local people.

The mayor put priority on promoting collaboration between the people through a monthly community board meeting. He also launched the project "People's Council" to involve more people from every group and to let them share their wishes. The People's Council was mediated by a chairperson, and the members could share and bring up issues in the meeting. The Yala mayor responded to questions that people had submitted in advance. The academic team worked along with the People's Council to collect the results of the project in order to contribute to the development and improvement of the city. Nearly, 3000 people participated in the People's Council every month. Some municipal services were improved to address multi-cultural and religious issues. For example, the *Melayu Patani* language was included in municipal counter services and both Buddhist and Islamic traditions and festivals received support. Because of his various projects, he was dubbed "Mr. Project" by a reporter, and "The out of the box Yala mayor" due to his distinctive ways of looking at and thinking about development policy.[7]

The municipality also undertook activities to ensure public safety in Yala, including the installation of CCTV in the municipality. The municipality established community volunteers. The volunteers were people in the community who were trained in relevant skills to monitor and prevent catastrophes, and they were required to wear a uniform on duty. This would ease the burden on the police and the military by helping to cover minor areas in the municipality. Amid the violence, the mayor was committed to bringing peace to Yala through the introduction and implementation of innovative projects to restore normal life. The assurance of generosity and multi-cultural coexistence was the hope for maintaining peace in Yala.

A number of projects were developed with the goal of reducing tensions and promoting the development of trust. These included annual youth camps, the development of the Thailand Knowledge Park, the Yala City Municipality Youth Orchestra, and the Yala Bird City project. These are described in the following Sections.

1. Youth Camp and Love of Hometown: Building Youth for Peace.

Provision of public services as prescribed by law, such as garbage collection, city cleaning, citizen registration, school development, and municipal infrastructure, are the usual focus for most municipal administrations. However, the Yala mayor considered civic duty to be the foundation of the municipality and that education was a basis upon which social equality could be built. He argued that the level of education among people in the south was relatively low compared to other regions of the country. Therefore, people were more likely to be easily led and deceived. Therefore, Yala Municipality focused on plans to restore sustainable peace in the area through education, especially through the formation of a school curriculum based on a multi-cultural society. The mayor's idea was to allow people to learn about social responsibility through the development of a voluntary spirit. While love for home might be considered a universal value, it is more difficult to make people understand how important their involvement is for social development.

One innovative idea to reduce mistrust and promote reconciliation in Yala was to strengthen collaborative learning through the "Youth Camp and Love of Hometown" project. The project originated from the mayor's observation that the unrest erupting since 2004 had made local people fearful and distrustful and there was a need for reconciliation to promote social harmony. Mr. Pongsak looked first at the youth. He believed that the youth were like white sheets, easily taught but also easily tempted to join the terrorist movement or become addicted to drugs, especially for children from low-income families. "Love of Hometown" thus became a focal point of efforts to inspire young people to make their own contributions for the good of others. Participants from different backgrounds would work together on social development activities, creating local bonds and love for their hometown as well as practicing leadership roles.

This project first began in 2005 with a group of 150 youngsters aged from 15 to 20 years. The search and selection were conducted by the community committee members to find participants from different groups in the community to take part in the camp for 40 days in summer. In the second year, the camp was open to direct applications from any youngster interested in joining. However, some participants in the camp also came from the search and selection process. The youth are divided into six groups, of mixed gender, religion, community, and school. Each group is rotated through each municipal division, thus learning about the different functions of the local administration and then actually undertaking some of the work.

The youth projects integrate three facets: showing children how they can live together amid a variety of cultures and religions, the need to build awareness of social responsibility, and the importance of easing the burden of financial problems on their parents. The camp also emphasized morality and reinforced good behavior. Results at the end of the camps showed changes had occurred among participants, and that the youth had developed greater self-discipline and were able to fulfill their responsibilities. They had a better understanding of the differences in religion and backgrounds because they had learned to live and work together. Moreover, the municipal office also benefited from the help and interesting ideas gathered from the youths while undertaking their assignments. The youth camp continues to accommodate 180 youngsters a year. In addition, the youth have been encouraged to participate in the municipal administration through the establishment of a Yala Youth Council.[8]

2. Thailand Knowledge Park Yala: Sharing Knowledge of Cultural Diversity.

The mission "to create the harmony of living together on the basis of many different cultures and religions" led to the establishment of the Thailand Knowledge Park in Yala (hereinafter Yala TK Park). Yala TK Park involved the creation of a large and constantly available mutual learning space—a living library. The library was not just a place to store books. It was an area for creativity by the youth or those who love to read, consisting of books and inspiring activities to cultivate the habit of reading and motivation for life-long learning.

Yala TK Park followed the model of the first TK Park, which had opened in Bangkok. The TK Park office at that time had a policy of expanding into regional locations. The concept of the TK Park was consistent with the goals that the mayor was seeking to realize—to enrich the lives of the youth of Yala. In order to be selected, Yala Municipality had to compete against other municipalities. The process of site selection by the TK Park office included several components: the vision of leaders toward education and the importance of providing support for children's learning process, the readiness of the local administration in the fields of management and budget control, as well as an understanding of the operations of TK Park. While the situation at that time was not favorable to Yala because of unrest in the area, the crisis proved to be an opportunity. TK Park office was impressed by the good intentions for the development of the city and granted its support to Yala Municipality.

The concept of the TK Park originated in Bangkok under the administration of TK Park. The clear goals and mission of the TK Park were to build a learning center to form positive attitudes toward learning and love of reading, thinking, and acquiring knowledge among children, and to nurture innovation, enrichment of ideas, and integration of knowledge. The foundation of development is learning, and reading remains the most common form of acquiring knowledge.[9] Yala TK Park was chosen as a regional model in 2005, born out of a collaboration between TK Park, Bangkok, and Yala Municipality, and it remains the only one in the region. The park was designed to promote reading and learning among children and local people and provided a creative learning space to share common understandings in the community.

Local participation played a key role in the establishment and management of Yala TK Park. The steering committee for the establishment of the park engaged all sectors, including municipal executives and elected councils, as well as representatives from public, private, and academic sectors such as local intellectuals, teachers, students, and related government officers. In addition, the municipality created a Web site, as well as utilizing other media such as banners and newsletters, to introduce Yala TK Park to the public. Tours and activities were also arranged to promote the park as an educational setting for everyone. The management team included several committees engaged in the selection of materials to be offered in the park, including books, music, and events. For example, the youth in the community took part in the selection of materials for Yala TK Park through surveys. The collection of music in the park involved asking local intellectuals to record local music such as religious music, classical Thai music, folk songs, and modern Thai songs, representing Yala life from the past to the present.

Besides cross-sectoral participation in the area, an event—Yala Reunion—was held in Bangkok to mobilize resources and raise funds for Yala TK Park. This idea came from the mayor in an attempt to seek stronger collaboration from local people who were born and had grown up in Yala, but were living in other provinces. The event created and reinforced bonds among people originating from Yala. It brought not only funds to support activities in Yala but also generated a working network and ideas. The municipality office regularly sent newsletters to members of the network with updated information about the activities in Yala. Moreover, the management of Yala TK Park was partly funded by the Southern Border Province Administration Center (SBPAC), the central department under the Ministry of the Interior, which was established in 1981 to monitor the work of civilian government agencies and to coordinate with security forces in Thailand's troubled Malay Muslim majority provinces in the south.

Yala TK Park officially opened on February 6, 2007, with different service areas for different needs, such as a general library, children's library, internet station, multi-media room, mini-theater, dream square (a small stage for exhibitions and performances), a prayer room for Muslims, a coffee corner, and a gift shop. In addition, users have access to information similar to that provided in the service park in Bangkok—an electronic library (Digital TK), educational games, and knowledge displays. The highlights of Yala TK Park include a collection of integrated knowledge and local wisdom as well as activities for youth. During the peak of the unrest in Yala, Yala TK Park was employed as a learning space for children to come and work together. The objective was to occupy the children's free time with learning activities. This achieved the mayor's goal. The park also has activities for children to learn to live together such as camps, outreach activities, and excursions.

The results of operations over the past 7 years have been recognized by many parties, and Yala TK Park has become a major area of activities in Yala.[10] Under the administration of the mayor and his team, the management policy focused on understanding the delicacy of the local situation, including ensuring the safety of service users. Yala TK Park has created social values in a variety of dimensions among children, youth, parents, and municipal government in the three southern provinces. In view of the people in Yala, Yala TK Park has become a learning attraction and a source of Yala pride. The customers of the park are diverse, ranging from children to teachers from Islamic schools.

3. Yala City Municipality Youth Orchestra (YMO): Music as a Universal Language for Peace.

Another well-known innovation was the Yala City Municipality Youth Orchestra (hereinafter YMO), the first of its kind founded by a local government. Yala Municipality aimed to create learning activities for youth through music. The idea for YMO dates back to the year 2004 with Mayor Pongsak seeking additional activities for young people growing up in an atmosphere filled with violence. The mayor's inspiration to start the orchestra occurred during the Municipal School Sports Competition in Yala when he saw the array of brass bands from these schools. His idea was to bring young people—both Buddhists and Muslims, from 8 to 18 years of age—together to practice and play orchestral music.

However, the mayor began to realize that he lacked sufficient knowledge in this field and needed help. The mayor went to Bangkok to seek advice and assistance from Associate Prof. Dr. Sukri Charearnsuk, the Director of the College of Music at Mahidol University. While the initial obstacles seemed insurmountable, the mayor asked the professor to try, starting with training teachers from Yala. At the end of 2005, Mayor Pongsak held a Music Teachers' Conference in Yala, with participants coming from municipal, government, and private schools. The conference also included retired music teachers who were still working in the field of music education. The main objective of the conference was to build a network to help with the orchestra project before sending someone to be trained at Mahidol University.

In late 2007, the mayor got the project started with a 4.8 million baht budget to procure 109 musical instruments comprising strings, woodwind, and percussion. Nineteen trainers were invited from universities and district schools in Yala, Songkhla, and Phatthalung, to train 140 young students from various schools in the district of Yala. The municipal office invited Professor Veera, a Yala native but now working in the music department of the Faculty of Arts at Songkla Rajabhat University, to be the Director of the Training Group and Music Director of YMO. Professor Veera coordinated with music teachers in Songkhla and Phatthalung to work with the orchestra and began to recruit youngsters in Yala. Recruitment of members for YMO received a great deal of attention from people of various backgrounds, including Buddhists and Muslims.

Practice started on February 2, 2008, at the Municipal Gym Building, and the Athlete's Locker Room. During the semester, members of the orchestra were taught on Saturday and Sunday, adding more days during summer and the long breaks between semesters. The municipal office kept the public informed about the progress of the orchestra through announcements on the radio and billboards and organized performances by music teachers, with interested parents invited to experience the music firsthand. After they had practiced for three months, the municipal office invited parents to watch a performance at noon on a Saturday, with the orchestra playing four basic songs.

YMO was officially launched at a concert in celebration of His Majesty the King on December 2, 2008, at Yala Rajabhat University and on December 3, 2008, at Songkhla Tajabhat University. Music representing the charm of Yala, such as *Sanae Yala* (Yala Charm), was included in the program. Another performance of the show had to be added due to requests from local people. Since then, the municipality has organized a free annual Youth Orchestra Show for the public in honor of the King's Birthday.

Despite initial strong objections to the use of a several-million-baht budget for the foundation of an orchestra, the opposition gave way to increasing support from the public, the media, and even the private sector.[11] The mayor sought more opportunities for the orchestra to perform, such as at the "Yala Reunion" event in Bangkok, which helped to mobilize more support and financial backing from the Stock Exchange of Thailand. More recently, the Thai government has invited them to play at the government national reconciliation ceremony at the Government House in Bangkok. The orchestra also received a lot of attention from the media in Thailand and abroad, appearing in newspapers and on popular TV programs, and was subsequently contacted to perform in Singapore and Penang, Malaysia. The orchestra garnered attention not only for its performances but also because of the story of its formation, as it had been established during a period of unrest in the area; however, the orchestra represented efforts to promote harmony and unity between local people, since the members were from different backgrounds, including Buddhists, Chinese, and Muslims.

Currently, some members from the group have become professional musicians, and others have been accepted into the School of Music at the national level; other members have received support from the Yala Fund for further study. Former members have also come back to teach and coach the younger generation. In addition, the city entered into a partnership with the Music College of Mahidol University for development of musical talent, including a yearly music camp and opportunities for admission to the institution.

With the orchestra exceeding expectations, the mayor began to seek more opportunities for youth such as jobs and other income-generating opportunities.

4. Yala Bird City: Spreading Opportunity to Reduce Local Conflict

In addition to building peace through young people, another focus of activities in Yala Municipality is local economic development. Reviving the economy of Yala is one of the strategies to alleviate the conditions of conflict. Yala Municipal Office has sought more opportunities for local people by establishing the idea of a creative bird city.

Yala Municipality, in collaboration with the Barred Ground Dove Club, the private sector, and the Tourism Authority (TAT) of Thailand, has been organizing the Asian Barred Ground Dove Competition since 1986. The city has gradually become recognized as a center for bird competitions due to good management, the high standard of facilities, and judging in the competitions. The participants came not only from Yala and nearby provinces but also neighboring countries such as Malaysia, Singapore, Indonesia, Brunei Darussalam, and other ASEAN countries. The Tourism Authority of Thailand included the event on the tourism calendar it distributes worldwide. It stated that "if you want to hear the best coos from the most expensive doves, you must come to Yala."

More recently, greater attention has focused on the Red-whiskered Bulbul, with showings of this bird in small matches both in urban and various districts on a regular basis. Consequently, Yala Municipality recently began to organize competitions for the Red-whiskered Bulbul. Amid the reports of unrest in the south on TV, news of bombings in Yala changed to news that the bird competition had entered the Guinness Book of World Records for the biggest Red-whiskered Bulbul event in 2011. The competition featured more than 8000 Red-whiskered Bulbuls, resulting in greater recognition and credibility for the "bird business" in Yala and nearby provinces. Yala has become known as the city of birds, selected by the Department of Intellectual Property in the

Ministry of Commerce as an example of the creative economy and as one of 10 model businesses in Thailand.

Due to these factors, the mayor of Yala saw local economic opportunities in linking the competition to other bird-related businesses. The bird business cycle was huge and might provide new hope for Yala as well as the southern border provinces. Therefore, Yala Municipality promoted connections between bird businesses and other industries in Yala. The activities had a positive impact on business, with projects in the upstream, midstream, and downstream economy revolving throughout the year. Upstream business includes bird farms and breeding. A bird farm owner can earn from 20,000 baht to 100,000 baht for a bird with good pitch. Yala has a lot of bird farms, some as small as 10 cages to 50 cages, turning over millions of baht for people in the area. Midstream business refers to making birdcages and accessories, supplying food, nutrient supplements, and medicine, as well as worm farms and growing saba bananas. Downstream business includes racing pigeons, tea stalls, hotels, transportation, souvenirs, and OTOP bird products. The combination of art and culture has resulted in a new birdcage industry based on local designs. At tea stalls in Yala, it was very common to see a small field bird competition or to hear about bird breeding and feeding. The mayor also noticed that "bird activity has no race and religion."[12] The effects of economic stimulation creative solutions through improved the economic and tourism atmosphere of the local area. In 2013, Yala Municipality was selected again as one of the four cities with the most innovative intellectual property. The award contributed 2 million baht to Yala in order to carry out four main development activities: upstream, midstream, and downstream production, a Web site to share local wisdom about the Bird City, creation of jobs and revenue for the local people, and development of local products to meet the standards of trade both in and outside the country.

CONCLUSION: MISSION INCOMPLETE

The efforts of Yala Municipality under the leadership of Mayor Pongsak were unable to completely bring peace to the city. However, this was largely due to factors beyond the responsibility of the municipal office, and the mayor said that the situation in Yala Municipality in the last 2–3 years has significantly improved (Pongsak Yingchoncharoen, interviewed by the author). In the interview, he also said that recent bomb explosions that had occurred at four separate locations in the business center of Yala Municipality in April 2014 had shocked him and Yala residents. He said that he was tired but not without hope. As the leader, he had to show leadership. Therefore, he would not stop thinking, working, and connecting with people in order to reduce violence and restore peace in Yala by turning it into the art and music center of southern Thailand. The mayor was continuing to work on a number of projects such as the Yala School of Music to further an interest in music among people in Yala and the Thai Football Team for the World Cup to develop young sports talent and use sports as a means of reconciliation for local people. Several local economic projects, in addition to the Creative Yala Bird City, are also planned. This includes an ambitious public-private partnership project to build a modern community mall in the center of Yala.

Lessons Learned

A number of lessons can be learned from the story of Yala Municipality. These include transformative administrative processes, the applicability of the SECI model, and the importance of wise leadership.

1. Transformation of Administrative Processes

Firstly, the case of Yala reflects systematic and integrated work in dealing with the challenging situation of diversity and violence. Yala Municipality, led by the mayor, identifies the needs of the city and the people and then finds solutions. The mounting unrest in the area caused by differences of religion and culture led to an economic recession. Despite its small scope of authority, limited access to information and tiny budget, the municipal office has prioritized the needs of the local community using the following three approaches:

(a) Improving public services for all people despite their race or religion

Because of the unrest and disunity in the area, the administration of the municipality has become very sensitive to local issues, especially religious diversity. The mayor has tried to create accessible services for all groups by arranging meetings with local Buddhist and Islamic religious leaders to seek their advice on solutions, as well as providing opportunities for local people to share their ideas through the People's Council. The key activities are (1) mandating the use of the Malayu Pattani language in addition to Thai in communicating with the public because a number of Muslims in the area do not speak Thai and (2) supporting and promoting the traditions of all faiths, including Buddhist and Muslim religious ceremonies. This allows each religion to have its own cultural space.

(b) Restoring public safety

The safety of life and property is the biggest issue for the local administration. The pattern of violence such as bombings and assassinations affects all people mentally and physically. Such cases shake the community's sense of confidence in the local authority. Although control of violence primarily lies within the jurisdiction of the police and military, local government should play a supporting role. The Yala municipal office sees this role as a very important one. The installation of CCTV and a volunteer force both help to monitor the situation. The volunteer force project is known as "Pineapple Eyes."[13] Many people in the community volunteer to help patrol the alleys, easing the burden on the military and the police. The municipal office also supports the patrols by providing equipment such as radio communication devices. The protocol helps local authorities to deal with violence including explosions and fires immediately. The objective is to restore the city to normalcy as soon as possible in order to improve the morale of the public.

(c) Promoting peace and reconciliation

Thefirst and second approaches described above are not enough to promote sustainable peace since there are separate physical spaces in the community among religious groups. If the issue persists, the risk of discrimination will worsen. The municipal office tries to keep peace in Yala by building mutual confidence among all people, Buddhists and Muslims and other groups, through many projects like the Youth Camp and Love of Hometown, the Youth Orchestra Band, Yala Bird City, and Yala TK Park. These projects provide opportunities for joint activities by the two religions to learn to live together based on difference and to establish mutual understanding by forming positive images by the public.

The most important matter in establishing activities to strengthen peace lies in choosing the activities and segments of the population to be tackled. The case of Yala reflects caution in choosing the target groups and issues:

- The first target group is youth, since the young are easy to motivate or deceive. Children also face risks associated with drugs. The most sustainable development approach involves working with the youth themselves. Providing opportunities for children can result in significant impacts not just for the children but also parents. When parents see children working together, this can help to awaken awareness and motivation to build peace.
- The selection of activities to strengthen peace is based on having all parties join together. The case study in Yala includes four focal points to strengthen peace in the area. The first is "Love of Hometown," using "Love for Yala" as a common characteristic of all parties in order to live and learn together. The second is Yala TK Park and the third is the Youth Orchestra. These are helping to create pride in Yala among the youth through songs and learning activities. Music is often referred to as a universal language accessible to all religions and backgrounds and not contrary to the teaching of the Islamic religion. The fourth is Yala Bird City, aimed at reviving business in Yala divided into upstream, midstream, and downstream projects with shared interests.

2. Applicability of the SECI Model and Wise Leadership

The analysis of the knowledge creation process in the Yala case study reflects the key role played by the mayor. The following factors are important in terms of the applicability of the SECI model:

- Socialization: Each innovation has been driven by the mayor's tacit knowledge, referring to his understanding of the situation of violence and mistrust. He has insights and information and is confident that the solution to the violence in Yala Municipality lies in strengthening peace based on coexistence with difference. Such confidence derives from the fact that the mayor is originally from Yala and has served as mayor since before the beginning of the unrest in 1994, so he understands the local context very well. He was directly exposed to the two sides of the conflict in Yala. In addition, he comes from a Chinese family that lived in the Muslim community. During his tenure as mayor, he visited the scenes of unrest whenever possible. He has faced explosions himself, but survived without injury.

- Externalization: When the mayor realized the situation, he worked very hard to strengthen peace in Yala by using learning activities to teach the people to live together in harmony. The mayor always sells his ideas to his team and seeks advice from experts and other stakeholders through meetings and talks. He usually does not instruct his teams in detail, but allows them to figure things out for themselves, and then, he follows up on results.

- Combination: It is clear that the mayor and municipal staff effectively conduct innovative projects using a variety of knowledge sources to create the maximum impact for the city. For example, the establishment of Yala TK Park combined three sources of knowledge. First, the mayor had the policy of building a learning center in Yala. He committed the budget and what was needed for implementation. Second, there was the knowledge of new concepts from the library of TK Park Office, and third, the local wisdom and participation of various sectors. The mayor proposed his idea to the Yala Council, in partnership with the Thailand Knowledge Park, for the establishment of a center integrating all sources of knowledge such as educational institutions, local intellectuals, teachers, librarians, NGOs, and government agencies.

- Internalization: social innovation projects are generally short-lived. The mayor made efforts to sustain them in several ways, such as putting added value into the projects and creating a sense of ownership among the municipality team and Yala residents. The youth trained by the Youth Camp and Love of Hometown became resources in a new project called "Return Yala to Yala People." For the Youth Orchestra, in order to assure the public of its potential, the mayor introduced it to the parents after they had practiced for three months and were nearing their official launch date. This was a very successful start for the mayor thanks to the performances both in the local area and Bangkok. YMO has received tremendous support, furthering the concept of establishing a music school in Yala in the future.

Finally, the case study verifies the importance of people-centric leadership, which is equivalent to the wise leadership model. People-centric leadership refers to leaders who have the common good of the people in their hearts, and who have the ability to bring positive changes to people's lives. The leadership qualities of Mayor Pongsak are as follows:

1. Ability to make good judgments

The mayor has a clear commitment to strengthening peace and reconciliation by creating a space where people of different religions in Yala can live together. He has worked hard and put everything he has (knowledge, skill, network, and money) into achieving this goal. His decisions are guided by an inner sense of value. First is his love for his hometown. He set the working slogan of his first municipal administration as "Yala is our birthplace, a place we should admire and appreciate." That is what motivates his action to restore peace and happiness in Yala. His drive to overcome seemingly intractable obstacles is rooted in the spiritual force that drives him forward. Moreover, his capacity for judgment derives from a combination of intuition with knowledge acquired from reading, meetings with experts, and foreign experiences.

2. Ability to perceive reality as it is

The mayor has the ability to analyze situations. He has living in the area for years, both before and during the unrest. He generally has a good relationship with the people. He employed several formal and informal methods to learn and understand the local situation, including a door-to-door walking campaign, morning coffee with residents, community meetings, and the people's council. His analysis is based on making an evaluation and exploring public issues and needs and therefore reflects the reality of the area and resources.

3. Ability to create forums for the exchange of ideas

The mayor has the ability to create forums for the exchange of ideas, as evidenced by the development of innovative models such as YMO, which arose from discussions seeking collaboration and support from various sectors. He met with the Music College of Mahidol University to seek support and succeeded in having local teachers trained there. He held a music conference in Yala where he met Professor Veerasak and later invited him to become YMO's leader. Moreover, he met with the director of the Stock Exchange of Thailand and had the agency fund the project. Creating YMO was also a key element in the establishment process of the Yala TK Park.

4. Ability to articulate the essence to mobilize people

Another ability of the mayor's is to analyze important factors and use them to draw people to work together, as in "Love of Hometown." This led to the establishment of many innovative policies. He has developed outstanding projects such as the only Youth Orchestra in Thailand, which receives attention from the media and brings pride to the community. Yala Bird City achieved a Guinness World Record. Yala TK Park is the only facility of its kind outside Bangkok. The reputation of all these projects is the pride of Yala, reinforcing collaboration among local people to continue developing the community to the next stage.

5. Ability to exercise political power

The mayor's efforts to find support and cooperation from other agencies can be seen in his innovative approaches. Yala Municipality's innovation projects to strengthen peace could not succeed through the resources of the municipality alone. The Yala mayor has the ability to persuade people and organizations to work with him. Thailand Knowledge Park agreed to work with him despite the irregular situation in the area. Moreover, academic and government agencies also funded the Youth Camp project. The establishment of the YMO was supported by the Music School of Mahidol University and the Thailand Stock Market Foundation. This success comes from several factors: the mayor's ability to communicate a clear message and his reputation from previous work. His ability to communicate has helped to build support for his ideas.

6. Ability to foster phronesis in others

Mayor Pongsak has proved to be an effective recruiter of other people to help with his innovations. He always looks for smart graduates, especially those with a Yala background. He said that he is quite fortunate to have a smart, efficient, eager-to-learn team that plays an indispensable part in transforming ideas into action. Even if he does not go into the details of an idea, his assigned teams can develop it into actual practices. He enjoys getting to know experienced people and invites them to work for the municipality.

Even with the leadership capabilities of Mayor Pongsak described above, efforts to turn around the Yala Municipality remain incomplete. However, those abilities presented by Mayor Pongsak could become an exemplar to successive mayors that may lead to further changes in Yala. We hope to see further developments in Yala in the future.

NOTES

1. Interview with Pongsak Yingchoncharoen (Yala Municipal Mayor) by the author, April 2014 at Yala Municipal Office.
2. Official Statistics Registration System, Raigharn Satiti chamnuoun Prachakorn lae Bann Prajumpeeporsor B.E.2556 [Statistics of Numbers of population of the year 2013]. http://stat.bora.dopa.go.th/stat/stat-new/statTDD/views/showZoneData.php?rcode=9599&statType=1&year=56.
3. Yala City Municipality. Pung Muang [Town Planning]. http://www.yalacity.go.th/static/map.
4. From 2004–2007, the Thai government allocated a budget of 5000 million baht to solve the problem. Translated from "Larng luen senn dan sommut ... lark laai puer santisook tee youngyuen" [Unclear Border Line ... Diversity for sustainable peace]. http://www.fes-thailand.org/wb/media/Debate%20Show/Southern%20Governance_final.pdf.
5. See "Nuoy-patibatkarn satiti faitai young mai leawrai yarng tee kid" [Operation Unit says that southern violence has not worsen]. Isaranews Agency. http://www.isranews.org/south-news/stat-history/49-2009-11-17-18-22-35/7950-2012-07-29-04-37-26.html.
6. Interview with Pongsak Yingchoncharoen (Yala Municipal Mayor) by the author, April 2014 at Yala Municipal Office.
7. See: "Pongsak Yingchoncharoen: Nayok-nokkok hang Yala Sarng Santiparb duay karn Wharn Poah Yaowachon roon mai" [Pongsak Yingchoncharoen: The Out of the Box Yala Mayor who Built Peace by Cultivating the Youth]. *Thairath Online*, August 1, 2010. http://www.thairath.co.th/content/100252.
8. Interview with Municipal Officer responsible for the Youth Camp and Love of Hometown project, by author in April, at municipal office.
9. Thailand Knowledge Park: TK Story. http://www.tkpark.or.th/tha/page/story.

10. Interview with Pongsak Yingchoncharoen (Yala Municipal Mayor) and Watchalee Tuantaweel (Manager of the Yala TK Park) by the author, April 2014.
11. Pongsak Yingchoncharoen (Yala Municipal Mayor). Interview by the author, April 2014 at municipal office.
12. Interview with Pongsak Yingchoncharoen (Yala Municipal Mayor) by the author, April 2014 at Yala Municipal Office.
13. See: Yala City Municipality. n.d. "Na-yobai lae visaitas" [Policy and Vision]. http://www.yalacity.go.th/themes/default/policy.pdf.

References

Fredrickson, T. 2011. Car bomb rocks Yala. *Bangkok Post*, Feb 11. http://www.bangkokpost.com/learning/learning-from-news/221493/car-bomb-rocks-yala.
Larng luen senn dan sommut ... lark laai puer sanitsook tii yungyuen [Unclear border line ... Diversity for sustainable peace]. http://www.fes-thailand.org/wb/media/Debate%20Show/Southern%20Governance_final.pdf.
Ministry of Education. Tesaban yala sang san kijakam peur kan ruen ru kong yaowachon deng dontee klomklao jidjai klang bunyakad un ra-u na chaidan Tai [Yala municipality creating youth learning activities through music amid the unrest of southern Thailand]. http://www.moe.go.th/moe/th/news/detail.php?NewsID=8294&Key=news11.
Nuey patibatkarn santhiti fire tai ... yan mai leaw rai yang thee kid [Operation unit said the southern situation had not worsened]. Isranews, 29 July. http://www.isranews.org/isranews-all-data/isranews-data-south/item/7950-2012-07-29-04-37-26.html.
Panusnachee, Supaporn et al. 2014. Saroop Satiti hade karn kwarm mai sangn-uop in Puentee Changwat Chaidan park tai Prajum pee 2557. Deep South Incident Database (DSID). http://www.deepsouthwatch.org/node/6596.
Rattana, Suwitcha. Pongsak Yingchoncharoen Kom chad leuk online on March 6, 2010. http://www.komchadluek.net/news/detail/50906.
UNESCO. 2016. A city's good practice towards the elimination of discrimination. http://www.unesco.org/new/en/social-and-human-sciences/themes/fight-against-discrimination/coalition-of-cities/good-practices/yala/.
Yala Municipality. 2013. *Annual report of 2013*. Yala: Yala City Municipality.
———. 2013. Lao Kan Nakhon Yala [Monthly newsletters], 141, December. Yala: Yala City Municipality.
———. 2014. Lao Kan Nakhon Yala [Monthly newsletters], 142, January. Yala: Yala City Municipality.
———. 2014. Lao Kan Nakhon Yala [Monthly newsletters], 143, February. Yala: Yala City Municipality.

INTERVIEWS

Kittawat Rittirong (Yala Municipal Clerk). Interview by the author, April 2014, Yala Municipal Office.

Interview with municipal officer responsible for the Youth Camp and Love of Hometown project. Interview by the author April 2014, Yala Municipal Office.

Participants in the Youth Camp and Love of Hometown. Interview by the author, April 2014, Yala TK Park.

Pongsak Yingchoncharoen (Yala Municipal Mayor). Interview by the author, April 2014 at Yala Municipal Office.

Watchalee Tuantaweel (Manager of the Yala TK Park). Interview by the author, April 2014, Yala TK Park.

Yala Municipality. Kam-nod-karn-concert-orchestra-yao-wa-chon-tesaban-nakhon-Yala [Schedule of Yala city youth orchestra]. http://www.yala24.net/home/node/10.

AUTHOR BIOGRAPHY

Orathai Kokpol is Deputy Secretary General and Director of the College of Local Government Development of King Prajadhipok's Institute, Thailand. She also gives a lecture as an assistant professor of Public Administration at Faculty of Political Science, Thammasat University. After received her bachelor and master degree in Political Science from Thammasat University and London School of Economics and Political Science, UK, consecutively, she had her Advanced Diploma in Development Studies from Cambridge University. She received Ph.D. in Political Science concentrated on Comparative Government from University of Toronto, Canada. Her recent publication is *Urbanization: A new challenge for modern local governance* and *Policy Proposal of Innovation in the Local Government's Revenue (co-author)*.

CHAPTER 4

Mitaka City Development: Collaborating in Harmony

Ayano Hirose Nishihara

INTRODUCTION

Mitaka City in Tokyo Prefecture is widely known in Japan for collaborating with its citizens in various areas relating to their daily lives. Receiving the Intelligent Community of the Year award from the Intelligent Community Forum in 2005, brought worldwide recognition to the city. The forum noted that Mitaka had "developed a social and political culture that prizes technology and considers R&D to be of high importance. It has always been a forward-looking community and was the first city in Japan to host the field testing of the fiber-to-the-home network" (Intelligent Community Forum 2005). The acknowledgment focused on information technologies (fiber broadband communication) and their practical applications for small-office/home office businesses (SOHO); however, the chairperson also acknowledged that "in our view Mitaka demonstrates the power of collaboration, a keen understanding of how knowledge work sustains a community's economy, and a plan to

A. Hirose Nishihara (✉)
Department of Global Business, College of Business,
Rikkyo University, Tokyo, Japan
e-mail: ayano.nishihara@rikkyo.ac.jp

© The Author(s) 2018
A. Hirose Nishihara et al. (eds.), *Knowledge Creation in Community Development*, DOI 10.1007/978-3-319-57481-3_4

continue leveraging the most vital tools in the digital age" (Intelligent Community Forum 2005). In other words, the key factor behind Mitaka City's success as an intelligent community is not technology alone, but its citizens and their collaboration. The key questions then are: How did Mitaka City develop into a city of collaboration? And what are the lessons to be learned?

This case is intended to illustrate how Mitaka City became a city of citizen collaboration after World War II (WWII) and the processes and leadership involved in this transition from the viewpoint of organizational knowledge creation theory. The case will begin with an overview of Mitaka and then introduce four successive mayors—Heizaburo Suzuki, Sadao Sakamoto, Yojiro Yasuda, and Keiko Kiyohara—describing their policies, administration, and leadership styles, and how they led the city administration. Several events in which Mitaka citizens collaborated with the city administration will also be introduced.

The case of Mitaka City is a good example of social innovation; that is, co-creating social value within the networks of citizens, academia, businesses, and city staffers toward the relentless pursuit of the betterment of life. Accordingly, the case does not host a single protagonist, but deals with multiple people—often times the citizens of Mitaka—who played a leadership role in each situation.

DESCRIPTION OF MITAKA CITY AND ITS HISTORY

Mitaka City is located on the outskirts of Tokyo. It is one of several residential cities convenient to the central Tokyo area, lying just 18 km away, or a 15-min ride to Shinjuku Station along the Chūō line, one of metropolitan Tokyo's key public transport links operated by the East Japan Railway Company (JR East). As of January 2014, approximately 180,000 people reside in this community, with around 47,700 people (27%) above the age of 60 and roughly 29,900 people (17%) under 20 years old (Mitaka City 2014). About 60% of the citizens are college or university graduates, and 98% have graduated from high school. The total land area of Mitaka is 16.5 km^2 and includes several parks and farms; the city is the home of Studio Ghibli and the Ghibli Museum, the world-renowned animation producer. Approximately 90% of the total land has been designated as a residential area. Mitaka is blessed neither with natural resources nor scenic tourist attractions and does not permit the use of land for extensive industrial or commercial development. Accordingly, the majority of its residents are salaried workers with relatively high incomes who commute to central Tokyo.

With Japan's aging society, however, the number of elderly has continued to increase, while the number of newborn babies has declined. Because Mitaka did not host many industries and relied on local citizens as its major source of tax revenue, the city administration in the 1980s anticipated a decline in tax revenue due to changing demographics, presenting the city with the certainty of financial pressures in the future—a future that is no longer so far away. To cope with this problem, the city invited its citizens to play an active role in planning and executing measures to secure the future of the city.

Mitaka was once a farming village during the Meiji (1868–1912) and Taisho (1912–1926) eras. But after the Great Kanto Earthquake in 1923, many victims moved to Mitaka from central Tokyo and it gradually developed as a residential area. The population of Mitaka numbered 5000–6000 before the Great Kanto Earthquake, but rapidly increased, especially after Mitaka Station began operation in 1930 and a munitions factory opened in 1935. By 1940, the population had grown to 21,000, and in 1950, only 5 years after the end of WWII, it had risen to 55,000.

After WWII, Mitaka's population increased drastically with the building of public housing, and by 1950, Mitaka had grown from a town to a city. In 1956, Mure Condominium, only the second condominium building in Japan, constructed by the Japan Housing Corporation, was completed. From then on, many condominiums rose up in areas such as Shinkawa and Mitakadai, which stimulated population growth from 67,308 in 1955 to 124,200 in 1965, almost doubling in just 10 years. Various other infrastructures such as schools, sewers, waste processing plants, roads, social welfare halls, and libraries were built at a high pace. Mitaka is known for being the first city to achieve 100% sewerage in Japan in 1973.

Heizaburo Suzuki

The city mayor in the early 1970s, Heizaburo Suzuki, was a doctor who specialized in public health. He said, "If the city does not have sewers, then the city will be a slum, regardless of the cultural facilities it owns." In order to realize complete sewerage, he introduced the principle of beneficiaries paying for sewers and adopted a management system for the city administration similar to private company management. He remained mayor for five terms (20 years) and contributed greatly to the city's development.

Suzuki's expertise was in managing the local government and constructing the city's infrastructure, and he was able to achieve three "firsts" in Japan. The first was the establishment of a nursery for infants in 1956. He believed that "childrearing determines one's whole life." The second was the achievement of 100% sewerage in 1973, and the third was the opening of a "community center" in 1974. The introduction of the "community" concept was triggered by his visit to West Germany in the summer of 1970. He happened to visit a community center in West Germany during his one-month stay. He recalled what it was like:

> In West Germany, a community center is a place for residents to gather, communicate, enjoy and use. I learned it is a base for residents. I conducted research on the community, and upon return to Japan I did a literature search on the community. Based on my direct experience and research I adopted the concept of the community center in the second midterm financial plan issued in March 1971. (Mitaka City 1953)

Suzuki was an idealistic pragmatist who introduced rational thinking into the city administration. For example, he separated smokers and non-smokers, switched off lights during lunch breaks, outsourced some of the city's operations, and dispatched staff members for off-the-job training at private companies. All of these measures seem quite common today, but they were very unusual 40 years ago. With such advanced measures, he was sometimes rejected and criticized, but he did not particularly care; rather, he paid close attention to the citizens and staff and pursued his beliefs with a broad, penetrating projection and strong leadership. Suzuki (1989) talked about leadership as follows:

> When the mayor heads the city administration it is necessary to have full control of the operation... Leadership should be in the hands of the leader. But the leader should not be autocratic. A leader always needs to self-examine and reflect. To do so, the leader must study hard and know more about the administration. A leader should listen to his subordinates and remember there is a "silent minority" in the citizens. The leader should listen to the "voices of the voiceless" by walking around the city.

His contribution was not only in constructing city infrastructure, such as sewers and community centers, but also in establishing and disseminating the basic understanding of "citizenship" and "community" between citizens and city staff. He nurtured the next generation of leaders to ensure that innovation would continue.

SADAO SAKAMOTO

In 1975, mayor-elect Sadao Sakamoto replaced the retiring Suzuki. In the same year, he established community centers in each of the seven school districts. Community centers were constructed with citizen participation, and community regulations were established and managed by the citizens. "Community Carte," the first activity conducted by the community centers, was a "residents' council run by each community center that conducted self-diagnoses of roads, traffic, welfare, culture, and the environment in order to identify the characteristics of the ideal town to make Mitaka 'a place to live for a lifetime.'" Sakamoto was forced to tackle Mitaka's growing financial problems during his first year of office, caused mainly by the closing down of factories. Before WWII, Mitaka hosted a number of munitions factories, especially factories producing fighter airplanes. In a sense, Mitaka was already a high-tech town back then. But after WWII, as the number of residents increased, the number of problems between residents and factory owners also rose. The factory owners did not like trouble, and after 1975, they started to move out of Mitaka. This meant that Mitaka's tax revenue began to shift away from businesses to its residents.

In addition, by then the population of Mitaka had stabilized at around 160,000, and the lifestyles of the residents were changing as the quality of life improved, leisure time increased, and cultural activities expanded. Accompanying these changes was a "hardware" to "software" shift, or from infrastructure to services, in the citizens' expectations of the city administration. The "city plan" method was considered an effective means to solve this problem, because limited financial resources could be allocated effectively by prioritizing the citizens' requests and demands according to the vision of the city.

Sakamoto believed that dialogue with the citizens to reflect their voices in the city administration was the most important way to solve the issue. So he introduced the "Community Carte" workshop in which citizens walked around the community to uncover what was good and not so good about the community. The first "Community Carte" took place between 1979 and 1981, the second in 1984, and the third in 1989. The results were proposed to the Mitaka city administration and reflected in the second master plan. Sakamoto (1995) said:

> ...people expect me to reform the city administration, which is to return the administration to the hands of the citizens. Needless to say, citizens should decide what they expect from the city administration and take part in all occasions. I want to make Mitaka City a place where citizens create, which means administration by the community (247).

Alongside such citizen participation activities, Mitaka City began in 1984 to participate in the INS experiment, which was an empirical experiment to "promote information technology in the region by utilizing digital communication networks and new media in the city administration services." Mitaka provided a site for the government and companies who were conducting such experiments. Masayuki Uyama, director of the Information Promotion Department of the Mitaka city administration, recalled the impact of this experiment (Sakamoto 1995):

> The biggest impact was that the citizens and city staff participating in this experiment could actually feel and touch what we now call the "information society" and glimpse how society would evolve in the future. The "INS citizens' group" established then remains active today and continues *ba* for citizens and city staff to interact. This human network also had a significant outcome. At the same time, our participation in the experiment meant we were not resistant to new challenges later on. Not only the city staff but also our citizens enjoy participating in such experiments. I think this cycle has given Mitaka the reputation as a place for experiments by people outside the city.

Sakamoto remained mayor until 1991, greatly contributing to the opening of community centers, pursuing town management by the Community Carte, and participating in the INS experiment. During his era, the style and culture of citizen participation were established—that is, "communication and participation" between mature citizens and capable staff. However, in areas such as welfare, redevelopment of the station square, and road maintenance, progress was slow and realized only after many discussions and coordination (Sakamoto 1995, 628). Innovation and development of the city administration were delayed due to Sakamoto's indecisiveness. By then, the citizens of Mitaka had been participating in city planning for more than 30 years, but with the same routine repeated over the decades, the routine had become fixed and progress or improvements were not being made. There were frustrations and anxieties and a sense of crisis among the young eager staff.

In 1988, a few years before Sakamoto's retirement, the "Mitaka Town Management Research Association" was formed officially as a collaborative research project between Mitaka City and the International Christian University (ICU). At around the same time, young staff members eager for change gathered and established a self-organized study group called the "Trans-urbanization Research Association." It was Yojiro Yasuda, then deputy mayor and vice chairman of the Mitaka Town Management Research Association, who acquiesced to the self-organized study group. Scholars and researchers not only from ICU but other education and research organizations joined both associations, and young eager staff joined from various sections of the Mitaka city administration office. This was the starting point for Mitaka to become an "intelligent city."

The underlying issues of Mitaka were its limited land space and aging population. Ninety percent of the land in Mitaka was designated as residential area and only 5% each was allotted for commercial and manufacturing. It was projected that Mitaka would face financial difficulties in the near future due to its shrinking tax revenue, especially from the commercial and manufacturing sectors. In addition, just as in other parts of Japan, Mitaka was projecting a declining birth rate and an aging population. Many of Mitaka's residents had moved there after WWII, and the demographics of the city were somewhat skewed. This made it easy to project that many residents would age, fewer children would be born, and less tax revenue would be generated—even taxes coming from residents. These were major problems to be discussed by the "Trans-urbanization Research Association" and the "Mitaka Town Management Research Association." Both associations were eager and passionate about realizing innovation to tackle these issues.

The Trans-urbanization Research Association, or Chotoken, started with a few middle managers of the city administration who were in their late twenties and early thirties. Its representative, Takashi Kawamura, who was vice mayor of Mitaka until 2015, and four other members of the city administration formed the core. Of the 700 staff members comprising the Mitaka city administration at the time, a maximum of 120 people, mainly the young and eager with plenty of time on hand, registered to join the association, in addition to staff from nearby city offices, researchers from universities in the region, and businesspeople in Mitaka. At its maximum, 300 members were registered. Within the association, there were subcommittees on manufacturing, agriculture, business, and the like, and members with both time and the will participated in several subcommittees.

In general, study groups organized by city administration staff faced pressures from the top and were often suspended. Even if they continued, their activities were often regarded with suspicion in terms of information leaks. Even today, there is a common understanding that such self-organized study groups within a public organization are taboo. However, the Mitaka city administration at that time was stagnating, and the atmosphere within the administration leant itself to supporting such activities, particular by Deputy Mayor Yasuda. In these circumstances, the members were able to pursue their study groups freely.

Interestingly, the Chotoken was not merely a study group, but it also sought outcomes. Its goal was to promote "innovation" and to solve issues and improve practices at actual sites. There was a clear will and consensus among the participants. The members came up with various methods for pursuing solutions and formalized a procedure to have the issue-owning party make a proposal to the Chotoken, or have the beneficiary make a proposal to the owner of the issue. This procedure allowed the members to gain know-how on identifying issues, and on implementing and pursuing solutions in actual situations, skills that they would later utilize in their jobs.

The Chotoken invited professors from various universities to learn about regional business development and local governments and discuss how the local administration and community should function. They invited today's city mayor, Keiko Kiyohara, who was just then beginning her academic career as a researcher. The topics were academic in nature, but the members also wished to realize something concrete and practical. For example, they discussed the relationship between public and private. The public (i.e., the city administration) consists of a vertical relationship easily connected to power and authority; the private (i.e., citizens) comprises a more horizontal relationship that can be the source of collaboration. Usually, these two relationships are separate, but the members thought it could be fun and interesting with unexpected results if they were combined. They began to think that "collaboration" may be the way to go, and started to expand the concepts and establish methods.

Kawamura described this situation as "horizontal chain reaction expansion" (Kawamura 2007, Interview by the author).

One of the major contributions of the Chotoken was the "human network" that it established, and this network continues today. As people get older their positions and roles get higher, and as a result, the human network becomes a more important asset. Kawamura said:

> It does not matter whether someone is opposing or supporting. Many people know each other, or at least share the same ideals, and even if they oppose each other on one issue, they do not exclude the other but say, "Let's have a drink and talk it over again." People take time to listen to each other and change together to achieve the same goal. Empathy and trust that lie at the bottom are the key success factors of "collaboration" in Mitaka. (Kawamura 2007, Interview by the author)

Yojiro Yasuda

In 1991, when Yasuda became mayor taking over from the retiring Sakamoto, he told the Chotoken members that, "once you propose something, you should follow through yourself." The members were promoted to positions responsible for the issues behind their proposals. Now able to accomplish what they proposed, they struggled to realize their proposals. When stuck they sought solutions and breakthroughs. What they learned and discussed in the study groups was reflected in practice and promoted as a way to innovate within the city administration in Mitaka. With many members so busy in their jobs, and working at the same time to realize their ideals, the activities of the Chotoken gradually declined and were completely suspended in around 1998. Largely, there were two outcomes of the Chotoken: One was the development of SOHOs, and the other was a new wave of citizen collaboration. These outcomes were officially proposed to the city administration by the Mitaka Town Management Research Association, or Machiken, which became the starting point for new forms of citizen collaboration in Mitaka.

By the early 1990s, citizens in Mitaka had been participating in city planning for more than 30 years, and some harmful effects from continuing this routine for so long were becoming apparent: The same people kept participating in various planning sessions, and there were progressively fewer new participants. Clearly, it was time for change. Mayor

Yasuda said, "The citizens know better than we do. We need to ask them for their knowledge and participation. The city administration should help the activities of the citizens." His policy was to take one step further from "citizens participating in the city administration" to the "city administration collaborating with its citizens."

In 1992, the second master plan was established, with revisions drawn up in 1994 and 1996. The city administration led these plans, but it tried as much as possible to reflect the opinions and requests of the citizens. From 1996, citizen participation through workshops started to take place, and people learned how to participate in groups. Based on these circumstances, a more active citizenry was nurtured. For the third master plan in 2000, a new method of citizen participation was introduced. This was the "Mitaka Citizens' Plan 21 Conference (Plan 21)".

Plan 21 was a series of discussions among citizens who independently participated in the planning of the third master plan. The main characteristics were (1) citizens collaborated from scratch to draft the plan, (2) citizens and the city administration concluded a "partnership agreement" to clarify their roles and responsibilities (a first in Japan), and (3) different from former attempts at citizen participation, citizens operated the discussions independently, and the city administration provided only information, such as related materials, a glossary, and information by specialists in related fields, to support their activities.

The first step of Plan 21 started from the Machiken. Just like the Chotoken, it was also a *ba* for exchange and interaction between the city staff and professors and researchers from nearby universities. City staff with a special mission participated in the Machiken, and many of them also attended the Chotoken. They were eager but with problems of their own; there was also a sense of crisis among the members, including Kawamura and Uyama. The members gathered once or twice a month, held discussions with researchers and professors, and wrote articles and proposals. From their findings and research, members discussed the ideal state of citizen participation in city planning and concluded that citizens should not simply accept the plan prepared by the city administration but should independently participate in the entire planning process.

In the conclusions, the idea of "citizen participation from scratch" was proposed to the mayor from the Machiken on Christmas Day 1998, and all activities relating to the "Mitaka Citizens' Plan 21 Conference (Plan 21)" began. Before officially kicking off Plan 21, the preparation committee conducted training to nurture "citizen coordinators."

Plan 21 officially kicked off in October 1999 with a total of ten subcommittees: five subcommittees on different themes such as citizen participation, the environment, and welfare; and five subcommittees on common themes such as human rights and local government operation. Plan 21 continued discussions for almost one year, and on October 28, 2000, the "Mitaka Citizens' Plan 21" was presented. In response to this proposal, the Mitaka city administration presented the "first draft (new master plan)" and "second draft (draft of the third base plan)" to the citizens. Plan 21 conducted further discussions and presented their opinions to the city on four occasions. As a result, the plan was finalized at the end of May 2001 and presented to the assembly in June; after consideration by the special assembly committee, 14 points were revised and decided upon on September 28, 2001. There were final adjustments, and the third base plan was settled on November 28, 2001. According to the terms of validity stated in the partnership agreement, the Plan 21 process was concluded on November 30, 2001.

During the 2 years of operation, 375 citizens participated, with committee meetings held 775 times over 784 days. These 375 people came from different backgrounds and had different agendas. City staff members offered no support in facilitating the citizen discussion groups, with the exception of preparing the space, paying the costs, and providing data and a glossary on the city administration. Although the operation was a very tough job—one that no participant had experienced before—the conference proved a great success.

One of the reasons why the conference succeeded was the time and effort taken by the preparation committee to train citizen coordinators and the detailed preparation for actual operation. Yasuda commented in an interview on the "Mitaka Citizens' Plan 21 Conference Activity Results," which was issued on November 11, 2001:

> To improve the quality of citizen participation, the city administration should not move until citizens propose [something]..., this kind of patience and readiness may be most required on the administration side.

KEIKO KIYOHARA

Keiko Kiyohara, who was one of the representatives of the Mitaka Citizens' Plan 21 Conference, was elected city mayor in 2003. She was appointed the successor to Yasuda and was expected to further pursue citizen collaboration. One of her concerns after the Mitaka Citizens' Plan 21 Conference was how to listen to the voices of the silent majority. Even in Mitaka, most citizens remained silent, not just because they were uninterested in city administration, but because they did not have the chance or the time for collaboration. Kiyohara was seeking ways to encourage more citizens to participate.

In 2005, Kiyohara accepted a proposal by Sumio Yoshida, a representative from the Junior Chamber of Mitaka (Mitaka JC), to conduct an experiment on a new method of citizen participation method based on "Planungszelle (planning cell)," which originated in Germany. Mitaka JC historically had a close relationship with the mayor and city government, and Yoshida used this connection to make the proposal. The proposal was to provide solutions to concerns raised after Plan 21. The success of Plan 21 revealed two kinds of citizens in Mitaka: citizens who actively and constantly participated and citizens who never participated. To capture the voices of those citizens who never participated, the city administration recognized the need for a new method to involve them.

Planungszelle is a kind of citizens' jury system that randomly selects people from a list of registered citizens and invites them to participate in small group discussions (of five people) on either solving a problem or gathering opinions. In Germany, one *Planungszelle* program is conducted over four consecutive days and the participants are paid by the party seeking to gather data on an issue. Learning the effectiveness of this method from cases in Germany, members of the Mitaka JC proposed to Mayor Kiyohara a collaboration with the city administration to try out the method in Mitaka. Kiyohara, with her long experience and deep understanding of citizen participation, showed interest and agreed to the experiment. Mitaka City and the Mitaka JC signed a partnership agreement to host the first Machizukuri Discussions in 2006.

Based on the agreement, a preparation and execution committee was formed with 22 members from the Mitaka JC, along with six active citizens with past experience and four city administration staffers. Yoshida was appointed leader of the committee. To ensure the fairness and independence of the committee, discussions were open to the public by posting the minutes on the Web site and blog. The committee decided that the discussion theme would be "ensuring security and safety in Mitaka," which was in line with Mitaka City's policy of improving the quality of its citizens' lives. Also as a theme familiar to the invited citizens, they would be less reluctant to participate in the discussions. At the same time, to reduce the burden placed on the citizens, it was decided to run the program for one and a half days instead of the 4 days as in the case of Germany. However, the committee strictly maintained the other parts of the process: (1) inviting citizens by random selection, (2) encouraging small group discussions (five people), (3) rotating the members for each discussion, (4) paying the participants, (5) providing the participants with the necessary information before the discussions, and (6) maintaining the independence of the committee.

As it was the first time to invite citizens without any experience in citizen participation and collaboration, the members of the committee anticipated various kinds of issues. In order to properly manage their time, and at the same time come up with results, the committee members thoroughly discussed possible issues and solutions and examined any hidden issues. One concern was the possibility of unnecessary conflicts among the participants due to their lack of experience in expressing opinions and coming to a consensus. Considering the general tendencies of the typical Japanese participants, the members felt the need for some kind of rules, such as the rules shown below:

The purpose of the discussion is to come up with a consensus; try to reach a decision at the end and do not turn back.

1. Do not discuss the feasibility of the ideas.
2. Try to come up with as many ideas as possible.
3. Do not reject ideas but encourage them instead.
4. Encourage everyone in the group to speak up.
5. Understand that changing one's opinion in line with the opinions of others is acceptable.

After much intense preparation, the actual program was run for one and a half days. Out of 1000 invitations, more than 70 people accepted, in line with the acceptance level in Germany, and 50 citizens were chosen in the end. These 50 citizens formed ten groups of five people each to discuss security and safety in Mitaka over five sessions. After the discussions, the participants were asked whether this kind of discussion should continue, and every participant said yes. When asked whether they would participate again, 90% answered yes. Kiyohara observed the one-and-a-half-day session and listened to the responses of the participants and said that seeing with her own eyes the strength of the citizens' voices reconfirmed her belief that discussion is the essence of democracy.

Following the success of the Machizukuri Discussions in 2006, Mitaka City conducted another discussion in 2007 on the city's basic plan; this discussion was led once again by Yoshida. The second discussion ran even more smoothly but with much more heated talks. With these successes, the method of discussion among randomly selected citizens became known as the "Mitaka method," and similar discussions began in other cities within the Tokyo area and outlying prefectures. Yoshida became a role model and evangelist for such discussions and he willingly shared his knowledge with the other committees. Yoshida said:

> To avoid any collusion or preset plots between the administration and the interested parties, or to avoid having a few active citizens dominate, we need to listen carefully to the hidden voices of every citizen. It is the citizens who can and should make changes for a better quality of life in the community. I support the "Mitaka method" of citizen collaboration as it is currently the most effective tool to involve citizens fairly and proactively. (NPO Citizens Discussion Promotion Network 2008)

Up to this point, the Machizukuri Discussions had been successful in Mitaka, meeting the expectations of both the citizens and the city administration. Machizukuri Discussions were planned in Mitaka once again in 2008, this time with collaboration between the Ministry of Land, Infrastructure, Transport and Tourism, and Mitaka City to discuss the expansion of the highway that would cut cross Mitaka City. There is a clear transition in citizens' involvement from participation to collaboration (Fig. 4.1).

Kiyohara had once said she felt from the heart that "to respect one another" is the fundamental attitude necessary for collaboration. She also remarked that she desired everyone to feel the happiness and joy of working together. She added:

> Citizens with different opinions, different standpoints, different backgrounds, and different jobs gather to create agreements and proposals. On

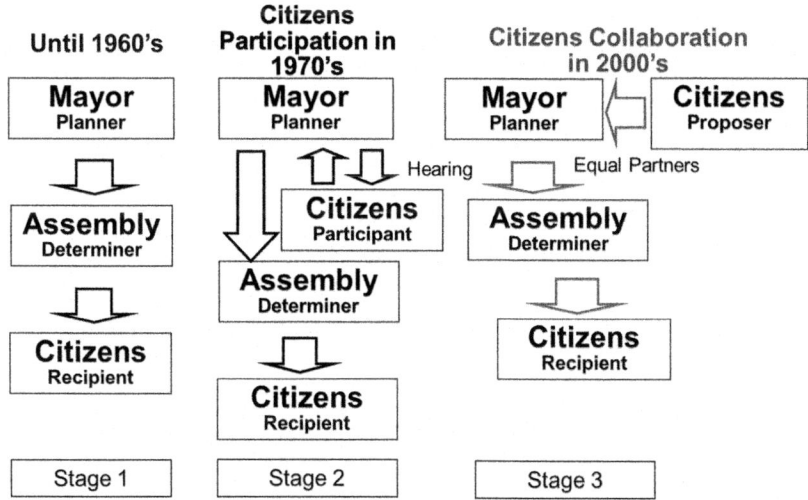

Fig. 4.1 Transformation of citizens' involvement. *Source* Uyama (2014)

such occasions I felt the need to respect others when reaching an agreement. Many people held back their egos and tried to adopt a broader viewpoint. There were "accommodations" in the process.... When there is a need for accommodation, people think very hard, and through such a process there are new findings and touching moments. (Iseki and Fujie 2005, 225–226)

Intelligent City Mitaka: Utilizing ICT to Establish New Work Styles

Aside from projects to encourage citizen participation, in order to foster new businesses in Mitaka and increase the city's tax revenue, Mayor Yasuda promoted the development of information and technology to succeed the INS experiment in 1985. He promoted digital communication infrastructure and the utilization of IT in city services. In 1996, a cable TV company was established through funding by Mitaka, which constructed a fiber optical cable network and started an internet service provider. In 1998, Mitaka established its Information and Technology Plan, which called for the revitalization of the city based on IT services. This declaration gave rise to the "SOHO CITY Mitaka Plan."

SOHO CITY Mitaka Plan

The SOHO CITY Mitaka Plan was an activity with two objectives: first to revitalize the business environment in Mitaka and the second to revitalize the city itself. It was projected that due to the rising number of retirees who not only left work at retirement age but were retiring early due to restructuring, there would be a greater number of potential entrepreneurs and SOHOs by the late 1990s. Based on this projection, the Mitaka city administration began in 1996 to research SOHOs in places like Silicon Valley. Because of the INS experiment in 1984, Mitaka had the background and infrastructure for IT among its citizenry. At the same time, there was a shared sense of crisis about the pending financial problems due to the fewer number of businesses and decreasing employment opportunities within Mitaka City. Based on these circumstances, Mitaka decided to adopt SOHOs as a means to utilize its limited land space and surplus human resources, and to revitalize businesses without affecting the environment.

The Mitaka city administration conducted a questionnaire for 200 SOHO-type workers when conceptualizing the basic plan, and the idea came to light that "SOHOs cannot grow by themselves," so the city placed the human network at the center and decided to form a council. In the same questionnaire, SOHOs were asked about soft support specific to them, such as "supporting entrepreneurs," "introducing jobs," and "providing financial support," but at the same time, SOHOs faced the same issues as ordinary small businesses, such as "lack of sales personnel," "lack of development," and "issues in cash flow management." It was then decided that the plan would emphasize the creation of business opportunities, and for that, the council would provide a system to support SOHO incubation and office spaces to start up new businesses. In addition, in order to support the daily activities of SOHOs, the council would place SOHO coordinators to support their needs. Thus, the SOHO CITY Mitaka Council was established in 1998, and in the same year, the SOHO Pilot Office was opened (SOHO City n.d.).

Mitaka Town Management Organization

In 1999, the Mitaka Town Management Organization (MTMO) was established as a SOHO incubator. Since its establishment, MTMO's eight facilities have become home to more than 100 SOHO businesses.

MTMO provides business-matching programs and venture investment, as well as other financial services, to encourage business start-ups and growth. MTMO hosts the annual SOHO festival, where SOHOs from various parts of Japan gather and introduce their businesses in search of business partners and new business opportunities. The SOHOs incubated thus far include NPO Senior SOHO Salon Mitaka (n.d.), established in 1999 as a platform for seniors living in Mitaka to promote their participation in business activities in the region by providing IT training and various work opportunities. In 1999, Senior SOHO was entrusted by the Ministry of Economy, Trade and Industry's "Senior Venture Support Business," and in 2003, awarded the Nikkei Shimbun Nikkei Regional Information Award.

Another SOHO supports childrearing mothers. The NPO "Convini for Raising Kids" was established to release mothers from the isolation of raising children by creating an environment where mothers can enjoy nurturing their children. It hosts activities such as mothers' circles, sharing information about childrearing, supporting mothers who wish to return to work as a means of self-actualization, among others. Another example is SOHO Venture College, founded through the collaboration of MTMO and Mitaka Network University with the aim of supporting venture start-ups in Mitaka by providing seminars on basic business knowledge and business practices. Mitaka Network University is a business aimed at utilizing the knowledge assets in private, academic, industry, and public sectors to revitalize the town and create new business opportunities. By utilizing the knowledge assets and latest information and technology owned by academic institutions, it provides *ba* and occasions where citizens meet and collaborate with people from academic institutions, corporations, city administrations, and so on. It aims to be a new type of university where the needs and wants of education are matched in the region. This seminar also offers simulation exercises to help entrepreneurs prepare for starting their own business. The lecturers are experienced in business people who have started SOHOs or other venture businesses. The contents of the classes include theory and simulations on how to start a business, business plan simulation, financing, and accounting. After finishing the course, participants are fully supported by MTMO on their actual start-up and business operation.

Takamasa Maeda, chairman of MTMO, who has evaluated more than 100 SOHOs accepted by the SOHO Incubation Office, said:

If you are at retirement age, you have been a worker for nearly for 40 years. You can revive yourself as a CEO by starting up a SOHO. You will be able to live your own life, full of new purpose, interest and joy. Use your experience to plan your own business. Do not be satisfied by simply learning techniques or knowledge; you need to share what you have learned. Once you start doing this, you will continue to improve… If you are no longer interested in the things you started after you retired, it is because you are not sharing the obtained skills or know-how; in other words, you are not communicating or interacting with others. To live the second stage of your life happily, it is important to have the mindset "for people and for society."

Town of Tomorrow Mitaka Project

In 2002, following the e-Japan initiatives of the Japanese government, the "Town of Tomorrow Mitaka Project" was announced. The aim of the project was to conduct various experiments utilizing ICT technologies, transforming Mitaka into a model city exhibiting new initiatives, such as connecting homes and schools with broadband, networking school classes with wireless and IPv6 networks, and facilitating on-line tax petitions and payments. The project also aimed to experiment with battery-powered community transportation, recycling kitchen refuse, and supporting the elderly and childrearing, which are closely related to the quality of everyday life. The project followed the policy of "town management for a better environment and better welfare," which was set by citizens in the third master plan in Plan 21.

The project set a promotion committee led by Takamasa Maeda, the chairman of MTMO, with members ranging from 31 business leaders, including IBM, NTT, and SECOM, 12 researchers, academics from eight universities, and representatives from NPOs and other organizations. The project members formed subcommittees on various topics to investigate and execute individual projects. To ensure fairness and feasibility, individual projects were screened by the evaluation/judgment committee led by Keiko Kiyohara and then the dean of Media Science, Tokyo University of Technology.

The project was completed in March 2006 as originally planned, leaving the results of more than ten experiments in schools, the city administration, hospitals, and home caregiving. The project led to the establishment of Mitaka Network University, which gave citizens more opportunities for lifelong education. Citizens, academic institutions, businesses, and the city government gained confidence that ICT would contribute to the quality of citizens' lives. The new mayor, Keiko Kiyohara, when she succeeded the retiring Yasuda in April 2003, set the policy toward promoting collaboration between citizens, academic institutions, businesses, and the city government. She explained her intentions as follows:

> I want Mitaka to be a "magnet" of encounters. I want people to have encounters in Mitaka. What we can prepare is the first occasion. Then people can come and encounter again and again. It could be one on one, but when you meet a number of people then there is always linkage. I think linkage is what is important .... I think it is important for Mitaka to send out messages. In that sense, Mitaka's goal is to become a "context city". (Iseki and Fujie 2005, 211–212)

Intelligent Community

On June 14, 2005, the Intelligent Community Forum (ICF) announced the recipients of the 2005 awards, naming Mitaka as the 2005 Intelligent Community of the Year (Mitaka City 2005). ICF noted several reasons for the award, including that Mitaka has always been a forward-looking community and has developed a social and political culture that prizes technology and considers R&D of high importance. ICF also noted that Mitaka displays exemplary characteristics in citizen collaboration, which is critical for intelligent community development. Mitaka has been the hometown for research and development for business, academic, and government institutions, hosting research centers for Dentsu and IBM Japan as well as hosting the ICU and Kyorin University. The city was also acknowledged by ICF as the worldwide hub for the production of *anime* cartoons, hosting Mitaka Forest Museum Ghibli in collaboration with Studio Ghibli.

The chairman of ICF, John G. Jung, said in the press release:

> This little-known suburb of Tokyo is the story of the importance of broadband in creating the jobs of tomorrow. Mitaka was evaluated along with more well-known, world-class intelligent cities, including our 1999 Intelligent Community of the Year, Singapore; Toronto, Canada; and Sunderland in the UK, which is the only community in history to be named to ICF's Top Seven list for four consecutive years. While these

communities are remarkable, in our view Mitaka demonstrates the power of collaboration, a keen understanding of how knowledge work sustains a community's economy, and a plan to continue leveraging the most vital tools in the Digital Age. We hope other communities seeking to transform themselves will look to Mitaka and our other six communities, as examples. (Intelligent Community Forum 2005)

In May 2007, Mitaka City announced its basic policy on promoting the adoption of ICT technologies by the year 2010. This policy set a new direction for ICT in the daily lives of the citizens following the results of the past experiments since INS in 1984. The basic policy stated that with the adoption of ICT technology, a ubiquitous community would be created to allow "anytime, anywhere, for anyone" to enjoy the convenience, quality, and joy of living, which is the ultimate goal of the initiative. The city set five focus areas:

(1) Secure and safe living environments
(2) Revitalized local communities
(3) Attractive child education and lifelong education
(4) Openness of information and convenient use of the city administration
(5) Construction of infrastructure for a ubiquitous community

This initiative was not just the city following the policy of the Japanese government, but rather, Mitaka using the initiative to further promote the city's fundamental policy of "town management for a better environment and better welfare." Kiyohara combined ICT with collaboration, which she referred to as *kyodo* in Japanese, and placed the citizens at the center of innovation. In Kiyohara's keynote speech at the ICT seminar held at Mitaka Network University on February 1, 2007, she made the following remarks:

What I wish to emphasize is that people are living their lives. ICT can only be useful when people with warm hearts and lives actually exist. It is not about ICT taking over or us controlling ICT. ICT may be used to resolve conflicts between people, or, may be used to worsen the conflicts. Because we live our lives we cannot avoid conflict when we interact. What we experienced in Mitaka was not always simple and neat. They were the results of hard labor with sweat and tears. We even faced some embarrassing situations. But such experiences have helped us move forward. (Kiyohara 2007)

LESSONS TO BE LEARNED

Mitaka's case is often regarded as "special," that citizen collaboration as in Mitaka can only happen in Mitaka. We think this is half right and half wrong. It is right because all the events happened as they did because they happened in Mitaka. In other words, all events are context specific, dependent on particular situations and particular participants. However, it is wrong to say that citizen collaboration can only happen in Mitaka. It can happen in other places, but in other ways because of the different contexts.

What then are the lessons to be learned from the case of Mitaka? We do not want to over-generalize and would rather list the key episodes relating to the knowledge creation theory that may be duplicated in a different context.

(1) SECI and *Ba*

Let us look at the Mitaka case from the theory of organizational knowledge creation. The first step of the process of knowledge creation in the SECI process is socialization, where people share their tacit knowledge while interacting with each other through direct experiences. In the case of Mitaka City, we saw that active citizens and many of the young energetic staff of the city administration could do this naturally, while non-active citizens could do this only after given the opportunity in the Machizukuri Discussions. Led by the shared intention to solve here-now issues, participants collaborated in the each step of the SECI process. The participants engaged in various relationships in multiple *ba* proactively, voluntarily, and autonomously, creating an unintended chain reaction among the participants.

We can see this in the case of the eager young city staff that joined the Chotoken and Machiken and led the innovation of the city administration, where the current mayor Keiko Kiyohara and current vice mayor Takashi Kawamura distinguished themselves. We can also see this in the case of Sumio Yoshida and the Mitaka JC in their promotion of the *Planungszelle* (planning cell) random selection of citizens to participate in town management discussions. Yoshida changed the way of citizen participation not only in Mitaka but also in other cities in Japan. When the activities first started, they probably never dreamed of the magnitude of the impact on themselves and the community. While they interact, they exchange experiences and knowledge, and establish shared values that support the continued spiral of the SECI process, which further expands to the new participants, creating the organic configuration *ba* in the knowledge eco-system.

(2) Wise leadership in citizen collaboration

Leaders in the social context, especially in communities, are not like traditional leaders in politics or administrations who stand on their power to control people; they are not like charismatic business leaders who stand out to press for change, revolution, or revival by managing, controlling, and leading people. Leaders in the social context do not conform to closed systems or organizations; but rather, they base their values and criteria on the shared values and ethics of the community, as well as their own practical wisdom built upon their experiences, and take the most appropriate actions on particular occasions in particular contexts. Such leaders collaborate with human networks built upon their personal magnetism and respect and are able to act on their influence. In the social context, leadership does not focus on one person; it is through relationships that people take turns in the leadership role according to the context and their expertise. With the ability to create *ba* based on shared social capital, any citizen can become a leader, which means leadership in the social context is distributed and collective.

Malcom Gladwell (2006) points out in his book "The Tipping Point" that when small changes lead to a big change, three kinds of people are necessary: connectors, mavens, and salespeople. Citizens who have the ability to create *ba* and become a leader have the characteristics of all three. They can find, empathize, and connect people with similar intentions, purpose, and passion. They select the necessary information gained through dialogue and practice. They know who knows what and who knows who, and can access the right person at the right time. And they do not reject or neglect people in public, even during confrontations; rather, they trust and collaborate with others to synthesize conflicts. These types of people act as a hub and connect multiple people at multiple *ba*, both inside and outside of Mitaka City. It is a chain reaction of active citizens creating new active citizens. The Machizukuri Discussions were aimed at inviting non-active citizens into this chain reaction. How the distributed leadership of citizens can be nurtured through new initiatives is an issue requiring further research.

(3) Mitaka as a fractal organization

As analyzed, unintended reactions of the participants' collaboration emerge through various kinds of relationships and multiple *ba* and are never stable but always changing as they reflect the values and intentions of the participants. Such *ba* may be restated as "publicness" or "commonness," which appears in between the public and the private. Generally, the word "public" is used as an antonym to "private," meaning civic, communal, common, national, and social. When the word "private" is focused on individual/personal rights and interests, the word "public" stands as a power to limit or control the "private," and thus, the focus on communal or common aspects would disappear. To synthesize the conflict between public and private, the common or "publicness" should be distinguished. "Publicness" or "common" is *ba* where both the private and the public bring in the "here-now" issues and try to solve them based on past experiences and knowledge assets for a better future in collaboration and co-creation.

Since around 2000, more NPOs, volunteers, and local administrations have begun taking action to cope with issues arising from conflicts between the private and the public in order to realize the common good, as in the case of Mitaka. While collaborating and co-creating in various activities in multiple *ba*, participants impart their values and establish relationships through sharing knowledge and experiences and determine the "common good" of the particular community. If values are not sufficiently shared, and respect and trust are not well established between the participants, the path to the common good will be lost and *ba* may fall prey to chaos. To avoid this scenario, sharing experiences and creating new knowledge through the SECI process can help build trust relationships.

In other words, one *ba* is a fractal, and as one *ba* connects to another *ba*, which is also a fractal, multiple layers of *ba* eventually expand into a self-organizing ecosystem. The ecosystem should look like it has its own life or own purpose, and that life and purpose can be tacitly shared among each part of the whole. Such phenomena are the key factors that make Mitaka resilient.

There are many more episodes that were not told in this case, episodes in elementary and junior high school education, in lifelong learning, and in community libraries, to name a few. In Mitaka, new values for society are co-created as people collaborate in multiple *ba*, and as such continue to expand within and beyond the boundary of Mitaka City. Just as Mayor Kiyohara once said, it is a context city that works as a magnet of encounters.

REFERENCES

Convini for Raising Kids. n.d. http://www.kosodate.or.jp/.
Gladwell, Malcolm. 2006. *The tipping point: How little things can make a big difference.* Little Brown.
Intelligent Community Forum. 2005. http://www.intelligentcommunity.org/mitaka.
Iseki, T., and T. Fujie. 2005. [*Era of Social Management: Social Methodologies on Establishing Relationships and Problem Solving*] [*Social Management no Jidai: Kankei Zukuri to Kadai Kaiketsu no Shakaiteki Gihou*]. Tokyo: Daiichi Houki Kabushikigaisha.
Kawamura, Takashi. 2007. Group interview with Takashi Kawamura and other city staff on Feb 6, 2007.
Kiyohara, K. 2006. [*New Age of Local Administration of Mitaka: Policy for the 21st Century*] *Mitakaga Tsukuru Jichitai Shinjidai: 21 Seiki wo Hiraku Seisaku no Katachi.* Tokyo: Kabushiki Geisha Gyousei.
Kiyohara, Keiko 2007. Presentation at the ICT seminar held at Mitaka Network University on Feb 1, 2007.
Mitaka City. 1953. Mitaka City Bulletin (Koho Mitaka), Nov 3, 1953 issue.
Mitaka Citizens' Plan 21 Conference. 2001. How we want Mitaka to Be: Activity Report of the Mitaka Citizens' Plan 21 Conference [Konna Mitaka ni Shitai: Mitaka Shimin Plan 21 Kaigi katsudou houkokusho]. Tokyo: Mitaka Shimin Plan 21 Kaigi.
NPO Citizens Discussion. 2008 Setsuritsu Shuisho [Prospectus]. NPO Citizens Discussion Promotion Network (blog), October 23. http://pz-supports.asablo.jp/blog/2007/10/23/1866979.
NPO Senior SOHO Salon Mitaka. n.d. Tokyo: Mitaka City. http://www.svsoho.gr.jp/.
Sakamoto, S. 1995. Jiden Fuusetsu wo Koete [An Autobiography Beyond the Wind and Snow].
SOHO CITY Mitaka webpage. SOHO CITY Mitaka Plan Overview of the Plan. http://www.sohocity.jp/sisaku.html.

SOHO Venture College website. http://www.mitaka.ne.jp/tmo/business/svc/index.html.

Suzuki, H. 1989. *Hi-nouritsu Gyousei heno Chousen Challenging Inefficient Local Administration.* Jichisencho, Tokyo.: Daiichi Houki Kabushikigaisha.

Uyama, Masayuki (2014). Presentation made at The Second Workshop on Leadership and Management Development in Asian Countries, September 29th–October 1st, 2014 at National Graduate Institute for Policy Studies (GRIPS) Tokyo.

AUTHOR BIOGRAPHY

Ayano Hirose Nishihara An Assistant Professor, Department of Global Business, College of Business, Rikkyo University, and a research collaborator to Professor Emeritus Ikujiro Nonaka. She received her B.A. (Law) from Nagoya University, MBA in 2005 and DBA in 2011 from The Graduate School of International Corporate Strategy, Hitotsubashi University. Prior to her academic track, she worked as an assistant manager at NEC Corporation. Her research topics include knowledge creation at public and private organizations and communities, knowledge-creating leadership, and social innovation. Her recent publications include Nonaka, I., Hirose, A., and Takeda, Y. (2016). "Meso"—Foundations of Dynamic Capabilities: Team—Level Synthesis and Distributed Leadership as the Source of Dynamic Creativity. *Global Strategy Journal, 6*(3), 168–182.

CHAPTER 5

Da Nang City Development

Nguyễn Hải Hằng

INTRODUCTION

Vietnam is in a critical transformation stage, moving toward common international standards and pursuing active integration into the global community. Since efforts toward reform began in 1986, Vietnam has made great progress, yet significant weaknesses remain, especially in terms of public management. Strong and dynamic governance at all government levels would unquestionably facilitate the development of the country. In Vietnam, steps to promote innovation (or reform) in public administration began some 10 years ago. However, this has produced only limited results, especially at the local government level where all policies of the Vietnam Central Communist Party as well as those of the Vietnam Central Government are implemented. Good policies are useless pieces of paper if they are not implemented in ways that will create benefits for the country's citizens. Thus, an operational level of administration—local government—needs to play a crucial role in strengthening the citizens' belief in the leadership of the Vietnam Communist Party. There is an urgent need for reform/innovation in managing local government, as many issues were exposed during the last decade. This points to an urgent need to explore different solutions that will boost

N.H. Hằng (✉)
Vietnam Aviation Academy, Ho Chi Minh, Vietnam
e-mail: hangnh@vaa.edu.vn

© The Author(s) 2018
A. Hirose Nishihara et al. (eds.), *Knowledge Creation in Community Development*, DOI 10.1007/978-3-319-57481-3_5

and reinforce innovation toward higher levels of effectiveness and efficiency, and facilitate reform at the local government level. Lessons learnt from best practices could be a considerable help in working toward a rule-of-law society in a state "by people, for people" as determined by the Communist Party of Vietnam.

LOCAL GOVERNMENT IN VIETNAM
AND PUBLIC ADMINISTRATION REFORM

Vietnam has 64 provinces and cities, including five central-level cities: Ha Noi, Ho Chi Minh, Hai Phong, Da Nang, and Can Tho. Of these cities, Ha Noi and Ho Chi Minh are classified as special cities, while the other three are classified as first level cities. Under the national government, there are 64 local governments in Vietnam, which have the same three-layered structure according to the Law on Organization of People's Councils (HDND) and People's Committees (UBND) issued in 2003. Consequently, local governments are structured and function following a uniform legal regime, regardless of the huge differences between metropolitan cities (such as Ho Chi Minh) and rural provinces.

The roles and responsibilities of People's Councils and People's Committees are set out in the newly revised Constitution, including greater autonomy for local government. However, specific adjustments based on localized needs and characteristics of different localities or communities have not been developed yet.

In order to identify an appropriate model for the centrally controlled cities, in November 2008, the National Assembly Resolution number 26/2008/QH12 was issued to initiate a program to experiment with the abrogation of People's Councils at district/urban district/ward levels across ten provinces and central-controlled cities, including Da Nang. This pilot program is ongoing, drawing lessons and experiences for incorporation into the draft Law on Local Government organization. This has been discussed at the 8th meeting of the National Assembly XIII in November 2014 and will be decided upon during the coming meeting in 2015.

From 1986, Vietnam carried out *Doi Moi* (which means "renewal" or "innovation" in all aspects (political, economic, and social) (Stern 1987; Thayer 1987). Old-fashioned public administration had exposed many weaknesses, leading to a strong push for the reform of administration. In Vietnam, the public administration system plays a very important role as it is integrated into the political system. Public administration is a dynamic part of the state machine. This shows advantages and disadvantages, strengths, and weaknesses of the state in all its activities, especially at the local governmental level, where most of the policies of the country are implemented, and government interacts more closely with the people. In 2001, the Public Administrative Reform Master Program (PAR) of Vietnam was launched. Its objectives have been adjusted to meet the requirements of the development of the national economy and society. The most updated PAR (for the period 2011–2020) is presented in the Government Resolution No. 30c/NĐ-CP dated November 8, 2011, in which the following main objectives are specified:

- Development of a free-market economic socialist-oriented system.
- Development of an equal and transparent business environment.
- Development of a state administrative system that is transparent, modern, effective, and efficient.
- Ensure democracy for the people; it is the right of the people.
- Development of civil and public servants with the competence to meet with the requirement to serve the people and promote the development of the country.

Public Administration Reform in Vietnam is an ambitious program that seeks to implement "rule-by-law" within a centralized, state-managed framework. During the past 10 years, some local governments including Da Nang City were selected for the pilot stage with the idea that supports for local, "bottom-up" reform initiatives could help obtain and sustain the reform.

TRANSFORMATION OF DA NANG CITY

Da Nang is a coastal city, situated right in the middle of Vietnam. It lies on the North–South communications axis of land (National Highway 1A), rail, sea, and air routes. Da Nang borders Thua Thien-Hue Province in the North, Quang Nam Province in the South and the West, and the Eastern Sea. Da Nang comprises six urban districts—Hai Chau, Cam Le, Thanh Khe, Lien Chieu, Ngu Hanh Son, and Son Tra; one rural district—Hoa Vang; and one island district—Hoang Sa. The total area is 1283.42 km² and the population is 951,572.

In the middle of the sixteenth century, Da Nang was only a small port for goods in transit and ship repair. It gradually developed into a commercial port, replacing Hoi An in the early eighteenth century, to become the largest commercial port in the central region. Local small-scale industries, including shipbuilding, preliminary processing of agricultural, forestry and fishery products, trade, and services, prospered accordingly. In 1889, under the French colonial administration, Da Nang was renamed "Tourane" and placed under the control of the Governor-General of Indochina. In the early twentieth century, Tourane was developed based on a European model, which focused on social infrastructure and manufacturing technology. Various economic activities took shape and thrived, such as agricultural production, small-scale industries, export product processing (tea, food, beverages, alcohol, fish sauce, dried fish, etc.), ship building and repairs, and services. Together with Hai Phong and Sai Gon, Tourane became an important trading center of the country.

In March 1965, when the South Vietnamese Government was under the direction of the USA, US Marines set up a big military complex in Da Nang. The city was defined as a centrally governed city in 1967, after which time, Da Nang became a political, military, and cultural center for the South Vietnamese Government and the US military. Military bases and infrastructure such as an airport, ports, warehouses, roads, public works, communication stations, and banks were constructed. Industries flourished, resulting in industrial zones supplanting handicraft workshops. For example, Hoa Khanh Industrial Zone was used for oxygen, acetylene and detergent production, as well as textile industries. However, the devastating war forced thousands of rural people flee to refugee camps. Urban slums appeared, social evils increased, and production came to a standstill.

In 1975, after the war, Vietnam gained complete independence and after being united, Da Nang (at that time a provincial city of Quang Nam-Da Nang Province) began to overcome the severe legacy of the war. As with other cities in Vietnam, Da Nang's rehabilitation and development achieved some results, especially after the renewal in 1986, but it was still a poorly developed provincial city. The outdated governance mechanisms slowed the development of the city, and without repairs, its infrastructure became run-down. Da Nang at this time was just a temporary stopover on the way from northern to southern Vietnam.

On July 6, 1996, the tenth session of the 9th National Assembly of the Socialist Republic of Vietnam adopted a resolution separating Quang

Nam-Da Nang Province into two: Quang Nam Province and Da Nang City. It became a municipality under the direct control of the central government. The new city of Da Nang consisted of the previous Da Nang, Hoa Vang Rural District, and Hoang Sa Island District.

THE ACHIEVEMENTS OF DA NANG'S REFORM

One clear symbol of change in Da Nang City is the construction of new bridges to connect the two sides of the Han River. Before 1996, Han River comprised a demarcation line between the developed center and the "remote" parts of the city. Under the policy framework of the Urban Construction Plan of Da Nang to 2025, the Han River Bridge—the only swing bridge in Vietnam—was built on March 29, 2000. This initiative marked the transformative development of Da Nang City, on its way to becoming an economic hub of the central and central highland regions. Since then, there have been several other bridges crossing the Han River. Each of them has its own story and special characteristics that have contributed to enhancing the city's image. It took 7 years for Da Nang to become a first level city. In order to achieve this, certain standards needed to be met relating to the environment, population density, infrastructure, service quality, as well as management capacity of the local government.

Da Nang has consistently outpaced Viet Nam's national average growth rate—often nearly doubling it—for the past 20 years (Thanh Vo 2016). Da Nang has been restructuring the economy based on its own strength—the advantages of its location. Da Nang has been prioritizing the development of the service sector in which tourism is the spearhead industry. As the result, GDP per capita surged from 6.9 million in 2000 to 40 million in 2010 (Vietnam Trade Promotion Agency 2013). According to the Vietnam Provincial Competitiveness Index 2013 (PCI 2013), conducted within the framework of the ongoing collaboration between the Vietnam Chamber of Commerce and Industry (VCCI) and the U.S. Agency for International Development (USAID), the city has again topped the ranking of cities and provinces of Vietnam.

With the goal of achieving sustainable development, Da Nang has implemented various social policies that have received support and high levels of involvement by citizens. This has helped to establish a sound living environment and turn Da Nang into a green and smart city as well as a place worth investing and living in. The following sections provide an overview of some specific achievements.

1. The modernized urban infrastructure system

During the period between 1997 and the present, Da Nang's infrastructure has changed profoundly. The traffic system, water and electric supplies, and telecommunication systems have been upgraded to meet the demands of people and to facilitate the development of the city, including

- Seven big bridges crossing Han River have been constructed.
- More than 600 additional roads have been built and all streets inside and outside of Da Nang have been upgraded.
- Almost all slums have disappeared.
- Da Nang International Airport was renovated, and direct flights now enter from Japan, Korea, Singapore, Taiwan, and other Asian countries.
- A municipal public wireless network has been set up, now covering all areas of the city.
- By May 2012, Da Nang had achieved almost all objectives in the final phase of the program of Urban Construction Plan of Da Nang to 2025.

2. Solving social problems and improving the living quality of citizens

The Da Nang local government has been a leader in solving social problems. Until 2000, statistics revealed that there were 85 households suffering from hunger and 9769 households (up to 46,300 people) living in poverty in the city. One thousand seventy children aged 6–14 and 1589 adults needed to improve their literacy. Beside those, there were more than 1000 wandering beggars and many people who used drugs. In order to tackle these issues and reach special groups of citizens, many meaningful social programs were launched from 2000 called the "Five No": no hunger, no illiteracy, no beggars in the city, no drug addicts in the communities, and no murder for money (Decision number 129/2000/QĐ-UB dated 28th December 2000). The "Five No" program was declared to be completed its first stage in 2005 and followed by the "Three Have" program.[1] The objectives of the "Three Have" part of the program are: Every citizen should have a house to live in, every citizen of working age should have a job for earning a living, and all citizens have the right to enjoy a better living environment—a civilized and humane living style regarding behaviors and socializing, a protected environment. If the program "Five No" aims to solve the remaining social problems and ensure social security, the "Three Have" program is the commitment to a better life for all citizens. Various policies were passed and implemented pursuing these challenging objectives. At first, there was doubt that this might be the city's leader paying "lip service," because achieving the goals seemed impossible as the city resources were always limited. However, in 2005, the city declared that all of the objectives "No" had largely been achieved beyond all expectations, and decided to continue with a second stage of the "Five No" with "Three Have" program, making Da Nang the only city in Vietnam that has been able to deal with these social issues successfully (CCCO Danang 2015: Preliminary Resilient Assessment Report Danang City).

Nearly, 10,000 houses and places of accommodation for low-income people have been built and distributed to citizens of the city. A city bureaucrat working in a job exchange agency stated that the important aspect "is not only finding jobs for the unemployed people, it is also the issue of matching vacancies with the abilities and expectation of people." During the period from 2005 to 2008, there were more than 1000 projects offering funding for business households, creating 5000–6000 jobs. One of the most ambitious plans of Da Nang City is still to reduce the unemployment rate to 0%. The city administration is looking for more effective ways to achieve that goal in the future. The third "Have" comprises the most demanding objective as the changes relate to human beings: the innovation lies in the culture, the habits, and the behaviors of people. The theme of 2009 was the "Year of Civilized and Urban Living" as the commitment of all city members to wage a war against the problems of pavement encroachment, trading on the streets, traffic law trespassing, family violence, and motorbike racing, among others.

At present, the "Five No" and "Three Have" programs of Da Nang are still being carried out and have become part of Da Nang's identity. Many citizens talk of their home city with profound pride.

3. High-quality human resources for sustainable local development

Many local governments in Vietnam have been issuing favorable policies for a high quality of human resources since 2000, but Da Nang has been the most successful pioneer in attracting and facilitating talented experts and highly educated people. The Center for Developing High Quality Human Resources was established under the local government and specializes in attracting and training high-quality people for local governmental agencies, as well as for universities and institutes and other organizations. The city has created suitable policies to attract better-qualified people to Da Nang, especially people that have graduated from university in more advanced countries.

As a result, over 10 years (2000–2010), the city has received more than 900 experts and highly educated and talented people. The issue is not only one of attracting talent, but more importantly, allocating them to appropriate positions and organizations where they can work and contribute to the development of the city as well as of themselves, so that those who have been recruited can stay and consider Da Nang their hometown. By the end of 2010, a survey conducted by Da Nang Institute for Socio-Economic Development confirmed the success of these policies: 100% of the organizations were satisfied with the performance of the recruits they had been allocated, and 87% of bureaucrats (recruited in the framework of talented experts/graduates programs) showed satisfaction with their job assignments and the facilitating working environment.

The city's top leaders understood the important role of bureaucrats as the forefront of implementing policies. The party secretary, in a speech to the city's bureaucrats on February 24, 2012, stated that, *"It would be very difficult to find a bureaucrat who is talented, ambitious, and caring for people ..."*. Various policies were implemented in order to support bureaucrats to ensure at least the minimum level of living standards were met for the city's citizens. On the other hand, their performances are evaluated strictly. Da Nang is also one of the very few local governments applying a competitive principle for promoting high-ranking executive officials (leaders) in public organizations. There have been more than 70 leading positions appointed accordingly.

Da Nang is still on the way to reform and innovation. The theme of 2014 is the "Year of Business" to promote improvement in the business environment of the city and to facilitate business development in this period of severe economic recession. The city government has requested the entire city's administrative system to join hands in solving business problems, supporting businesses to develop their production and overcome the current economic downturn. In the 2014 "Year of Businesses," Da Nang proposed seven specific action programs to address business difficulties. First of all, the city will prioritize city funding in support of business innovation in technology, trade promotion, training human resources, administrative procedures reform, and other matters. Accordingly, Da Nang City People's Committee established a credit guarantee fund of approximately VND150 billion to support enterprises with flagship products, export products such as seafood, footwear, textiles, and other products. Ms. Bich Chinh, the Deputy Director of the Da Nang Planning and Investment Department said:

> We determine this year to be the one for business so as to be more focused, more drastic and more specific. It means that we will focus on administrative reform, reviewing administrative procedures, finding out inappropriate regulations and services which negatively impacted on business activities for further reform (Voice of Vietnam, Friday 28 March 2014).

The year of 2014 marked drastic administrative reforms in Da Nang when the Public Administration Building was inaugurated and put into operation. In this 37-floor building, all leaders and local governmental bureaus/organizations are working and sharing various resources. Citizens and visitors can get the public services they need easily with the "one door policy" of the city government. It is strongly believed that the city will top the provincial-level public administration reform index again in 2014 as it did in 2013 (PCI 2013). In spite of these changes, Da Nang is still on its way to becoming a modern, civilized, and humanistic city.

CASE ANALYSIS

The ultimate objective of this research is to uncover ways of applying knowledge-based theory for local development in Vietnam, drawing from the experience of successful Japanese cases. Adopting a knowledge-based view as described in Chap. 1, and taking into account the differences in the countries' contexts, the case of Da Nang City was selected for analysis.

1. Mobilizing the stakeholders' power for local development

Da Nang has successfully done many things that could not be done in other places in Vietnam. And the root of this change is, as President Ho Chi Minh (1945/ 2002, 212) said: *"Dễ trăm lần không dân cũng chịu, khó vạn lần dân liệu cũng xong*" [meaning, "Even just an easy thing cannot be done without people. Only if people have consensus and wish to do a very difficult thing will it be done completely"]. The Han River Swing Bridge was the first impressive evidence of phronetic leadership and provides a lesson on total resource mobilization from the local stakeholders. The investment required for construction of the bridge was more than VND100 billion, of which the contributions from the city's stakeholders' own money comprised about 30%. This kind of generous contribution from the people in Vietnam has been seen in the past during wartime. The bridge was a victory of the innovators against the inertia of the old bureaucracy of the bulky governmental system.

More than 90,000 households were impacted by the construction of the new Han River bridges and roads. The majority of these households needed to be relocated, while the rest needed to reduce the size of their current houses. There was a period of time when the whole city looked like a huge construction site. But there were no "hot spots" or significant problems of legal action. Compared to other areas in Vietnam where land-related cases are usually very heated and account for about 70–80% of cases, the approaches in Da Nang might therefore be considered successful. The city government took the responsibility of balancing the benefits of all related parties (i.e., the city, citizens, organizations, and investors) to make a decision on compensation solutions in every case. This approach was considered an innovation because at that time, in other places than Da Nang, investors were responsible for direct negotiations with people for land compensation (stipulated in the Decree 84/2007/NĐ-CP issued on 25th May 2007). In principle, only when more than 80% of the households agree can a project be implemented. Consequently, thousands of meetings between all levels of local government agencies with stakeholders were conducted. Talking with citizens to understand people's needs and circumstances to arrive at a social consensus was the first priority of the city administrative organizations. In reality, there have been no cases in Da Nang where the ratio of citizen agreement was lower than 80%.

Applying this method, Da Nang has been successful in implementing the city infrastructure renovation plan: thousands of kilometers of roads, alleys, pavements, sewers, and power lines with total investment of hundreds of billions in Vietnamese dong, of which approximately 36% was spontaneously contributed by the city's citizens. Da Nang citizens have not only collaborated well with the city government but also donated family land as well as their own savings, "*Because we believe ...*" they said. The citizens' belief has become the motivation for their collaboration with the city government in all other social programs. Citizens are playing an active role in the "Five No, Three Yes" programs. Social associations, enterprises, NGOs, donators as well as ordinary citizens have been taking part in solving problems. For example, in order to achieve the objective "No wandering beggars on the street," as the issue is a sensitive social issue, the city perceived that it would not only be solved by decisive administrative action such as abandoning or punishing the beggars but also by "soft solutions." The Social Sponsor Center has been opened for all beggars in the city, where they can be provided with food, newspapers, and even televisions. There were beggars who were not in an extremely poor situation who wished to return back home after a few days at the center. Those people were requested to sign a commitment letter not to return to begging after the meeting with the official in charge who explained to them about the policies of the city dealing with begging issues. Other beggars who really need help can stay in the center and receive support from the city until they can find a solution for themselves.

In a city such as Da Nang, beggars and street vendors are a headache as they are not criminals. They need to be supported instead of being arrested or punished while the resources of the city government are always limited. The city called for collaboration from all citizens in the campaign to reduce the number of beggars and street vendors. A hotline was also set up so that people could call anytime to inform the officials when they identified beggars or vendors on the streets. The beggars then were invited to the Social Support Center. The city leaders held talks with people who provide motorbike and bicycle services to encourage them in collaborating with the officials in charge. Slowly and persistently, through collaboration with the citizens and other stakeholders, formerly impossible things have become possible in Da Nang. Collaborating with the city government has become the "habit" or "style" of Da Nang's citizens.

In terms of policy making, Da Nang City Government decided to use the advantage of its strategic location to turn the city into an economic and cultural hub of the central region and the highland area. In the master plan, Da Nang gave the first priority to developing tourism as a key industry. The city's main objective was to make Da Nang a destination, not just a stopover place for tourists. To achieve this objective, the city government developed and implemented a system of policies aimed at: (1) attracting strong investors in tourism to build resorts, hotels, etcetera, and (2) upgrading the living environment and the security level of the city, making the city a green city, as well as a friendly and hospitable destination. As a result, Da Nang is now one of the most popular destinations not only for domestic tourists but also for international tourists. The city has been named the most valued living place in Vietnam. In 2014, it topped the list of TripAdvisor's "destinations on the rise".

The involvement of stakeholders in the policy-making process is different from case to case as presented in Fig. 5.1. This figure shows the stages of the citizens' collaboration in the policymaking process at local government in Japanese cases. In the case of Da Nang, even though the involvement of stakeholders in managing the city has been highlighted, the role of stakeholders in the policymaking process is still limited.

It was observed that at the Vietnamese local government level, citizen participation in the policy-making process was around about the second stage, even though the structure of local government is not exactly

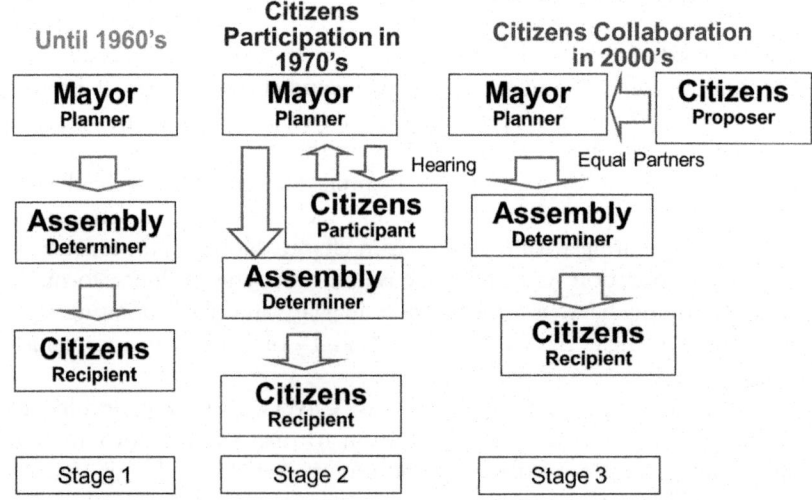

Fig. 5.1 Utilizing the knowledge of citizens: Successful cases of evolving policymaking process in Mitaka. *Source* Uyama (2014)

the same (in Vietnam, local governmental leaders are the Provincial Communist Party Secretary, the Chairman of the People's Committee, and the Chairman of the People's Council) and the level of autonomy assigned to the local government in Vietnam is quite different.

In this research, state-level policies were not mentioned, as they are normally formulated by national strategists. At the local government level (province, city, district, town...), as autonomy has been promoted by the national government and policies are more pragmatic, the participation of stakeholders is likely to improve the quality and effectiveness of the policies. In the case of Da Nang, success came from the effort of the top city leaders to socialize with the citizens and other stakeholders during the policy implementation stage: talking to the ordinary people, communicating with businesses to understand their difficulties and their expectations, then actively responding by supportive adjustment policies, as seen in the SECI model (from *Socialization* to *Externalization* and *Combination*). As the participation of the stakeholders was still limited, the *Externalization* step was sometimes not well conducted. Tacit knowledge through dialogue and reflection was not well articulated. As a consequence, the *Combination* occurred at a low level. The whole process of knowledge creation was barely moving. The analysis revealed that even though Da Nang has achieved a lot by having effective policies for local development over the last 15 years, according to the knowledge-based management theory, there is still a lot of room for the city to improve its performance in terms of knowledge creation for long-term development as the most valuable resource. In other words, the tacit knowledge of stakeholders has still not been used to any great extent.

Socialization with stakeholders to share and create tacit knowledge through direct experience is not new to Vietnamese bureaucrats, but is just being expressed in a different way. "*Lấy dân làm gốc*" (meaning "people are the foundation") is the basic principle of all Vietnam Communist party members. President Ho Chi Minh also taught that Communist Party members must live close to the people; what is good for the people should be done, what is not good for the people should never be done. Da Nang is more successful than other places in mobilizing the stakeholders' power for local development based on this principle. And as a result, citizens' beliefs were shared and consolidated. With a strong belief in the Communist Party's leadership, citizens can actively collaborate with the city government in the city government management. Without being aware of knowledge-based management theory, what was observed in Da Nang proved that people do act toward the common good in accordance with their beliefs. The Da Nang City Government was successful to a certain extent because it could lead its people for the common good of the community and develop the city based on local values. It also shows that when the local government knows how to mobilize the collaboration of the stakeholders/citizens, it can create great impetus for local development. Knowledge-based management theory could help the local government to set up a methodology to practice a strong knowledge-creating process and be able to profit effectively from the knowledge available in the community.

Knowledge-based management theory states that a knowledge creation process (SECI model) needs *ba* to happen (Nonaka and Konno 1998). The role of the city government is to create a good *ba* to facilitate knowledge creation processes (*Socialization–Externalization–Combination–Internalization*), and to respond positively by considering its results as the base for local policies. The participants of all stakeholders such as citizens, businesses, academics, NPOs, and bureaucrats in *ba* are crucial for the city to benefit from tacit knowledge creation. The participation and collaboration between stakeholders/citizens and local government must be designed, nurtured, and developed for a long time through consistent policies aimed at the social common good. People need to be trusted and encouraged to contribute their knowledge and their efforts to the development of their homeland.

2. Role of middle management bureaucrats

Thanks to the effective human resource development policies over the last 15 years, the city government has many competent bureaucrats. Talented young people were recruited and trained for specific positions in the public system. The promotion policy was competitiveness-based for the city's bureau's leader position, and Da Nang was the first local government to introduce this kind of promotion policy. The city also recognized that the competence of the leaders of the commune level (the third layer in the local governmental structure) was still below what is required. A special training program was conducted to improve their capabilities and to create a source of competent leaders for the positions in Communist party and the People's Committee chairman for the communes. Thus, Da Nang City Government has built up a strong team of civil servants from the commune levels up to the leading positions of the city bureaus. They are now bringing into play their roles in the development of the city.

Bureaucrats at Da Nang established a club for young bureaucrats based on the ideas of the city leader. The key members were middle management level officials from different bureaus (offices) and assigned by the Home Affairs Bureau. Here, they can share their explicit and tacit knowledge both virtually (through on-line forums) and face-to-face (off-line activities). While the total number of bureaucrats in Da Nang is more than 1500 and more than 40% of them are under 40 years old, only 164 people are registered as members of this club. Members were classified into three different groups: economic science, technology science, and humanistic and social science. The club conducted research and made proposals to the city government. Many ideas received approval to be implemented in Da Nang. Another primary objective of the club was to create a study environment for young bureaucrats who would like to improve their knowledge and skills. They therefore organized training courses for the members as well as supported the most competent members in getting scholarships for further education both in Vietnam and abroad. From a knowledge-based view, to some extent, this club could be considered a type of *ba* for bureaucrats sharing their knowledge (both tacit and explicit), strengthening the network for better collaboration, although there were still many limitations.

Another interesting initiative of Da Nang's bureaucrats was the idea to create another channel for interacting with the citizens on a social media network: an open Facebook group called "Urban Administration," which people could freely access, and send requests, comments, or share any kind of information with the purpose of making Da Nang green, clean, comfortable and beautiful. At the moment, this open group has 10,769 members with more joining daily. The administrators of the page are cross-bureau city middle management officials, and the active members are journalists, ordinary citizens, small business households, bureaucrats, etcetera, depending on the issues discussed. The issues discussed and shared on the page are varied: information about a badly damaged road, a streetlight that is not working, or an unsafe place for tourists, or why the city's leaders decided to implement certain policies and the advantages and disadvantages that people see and feel. The spontaneous responses from administrators are key to keeping the page live. As the administrators come from different sections of the public management bureaus in Da Nang, they work voluntarily as coordinators for fixing the problems. In reply to the question: "Why do you think you should participate in the page 'Urban management'?" most interviewees answered that it is the citizens' responsibility: "… if you want to live in a good place, you must contribute/you must help the city government …"

One of the key members, when asked the question: "Why do you do it?" said, "We think we should do something more effectively… it's voluntary work, it created more works [sic] for us as the administrators, and also a lot of works [sic] for other people … Sometimes we got complaints from other bureaucrats when we pushed them too much. But luckily, we got a lot of support from the city leaders. We believe that what we have done is right…" The key member also confirmed that many proposals gathered from the citizens' opinions received positive responses from the public management system and this provided the motivation for the page's members to stay active. The support from the city government was not only in the material resources but the encouragement and the unwritten agreement between the city leaders and the top leaders of the city bureaus/organizations accepting the group's activities and allowing their subordinates to participate in the group. This Facebook group page can be considered as a virtual *ba*, but focuses more on Socialization (in the SECI model) and receiving information for solving problems rather than on knowledge creation. From the comments of the members, it appears that Externalization and Combination were sometimes exercised, but this was not done in a systematic manner.

However, the above-mentioned activities provide examples illustrating the fact that even without being aware or supported by any scientific theories, when the focus is on the common good, this can become an engine for innovative thinking and an initiative of the people. They will act upon a belief in the common good. What was observed in Da Nang once again confirmed that the strength and initiatives of the middle management bureaucrats are important factors that can be decisive in ensuring the effectiveness of a policy. These are positive signals that if the city government can adopt a knowledge-based management theory into the city's management and build up a long-term strategy accordingly, these initiatives will become a strong engine for city development like in Da Nang, which already has a strong batch of bureaucrats at all levels.

A finding from the successful cases in Japan was that autonomy and independence are needed for bureaucrats to develop competence and to contribute successfully in the knowledge creation process. *Ba* is effective if it is created as a self-organizing space, without interference from political leaders. This characteristic of good *ba* may explain the limitations of the club for young officials, in that this led to difficulties in spreading their impact to the majority of city bureaucrats. Support from and facilitation by political leaders is always necessary for good *ba*, but too much interference could limit the knowledge creation process, as members would not speak freely, and as a result, tacit knowledge may not be shared. The supportive and open-minded attitudes from political leaders should involve much more than just administrative interference.

Another finding was that a trigger event can activate initiatives for innovation/reform among bureaucrats and recognition of problems by the leaders as well as by the community. Even though bureaucrats may act based on their own intrinsic values for the common good, the transformation in mindset of the bureaucrats is still stronger if there is a distinctive trigger event and encouragement from the leaders. According to knowledge-based theory, a management system needs to be designed with the purpose of facilitating a continuous knowledge creation process within an organization. During the start-up phase, when the focus on common good is still "under construction", relying only on tacit transformation mode is not enough to ensure long-term sustainability. The support of an explicit mode (rules, regulations, code of conduct, etc.) is also necessary.

The case study in Japan also revealed that the endogenous learning ability of the bureaucrats based on the tacit knowledge of the stakeholders can be decisive in the sustainability of local reform/innovation. A decline in citizen satisfaction in regard to the city administration was observed in Da Nang, including a disagreement between citizens and businesses on the proposal to demolish the Con market in order to construct a modern shopping mall, as well as the slow implementation of policies for households affected by urban development projects. In response to the question: *"How do you feel about the effectiveness of the local government now in comparison with what it was before?"* most interviewees answered that it was lower (70–80%). The symptom was recognized by the Secretary of Da Nang Communist party Tran Tho at the meeting of the People's Committee on 10–12 December 2014: *"... If we don't keep trying our best, we may not to be ranked at the top position in PAR next year."* Sharing and learning about tacit knowledge endogenously and continuously from stakeholders can help bureaucrats develop competence in dealing with the occurring issues and thus may be the only way to sustain reform and innovation in an organization.

3. Lessons to be learned

This case study has presented an analysis of Da Nang City in Vietnam, exploring how KM should be adopted in city management for local development, and how this could be applied in the future. Even though there are still many arguments about Da Nang's development, nobody can deny the transformational socio-economic achievements of Da Nang. The city's key actors have not been aware of KM theory, but some of the management techniques practiced by them can be classified as initiatives toward KM. The case study has shown that KM is a must for good management, and it can be practiced if the leaders and bureaucrats strongly commit to its implementation. The findings from this study have shown some useful implications for local government management in Vietnam:

1. Effective development policies for local areas must be built on the tacit knowledge of stakeholders/citizens about local values. The role of the city government is to create a good *ba* to facilitate a knowledge creation process *(Socialization–Externalization–Combination–Internalization)*, and use the results as a base for local policies. Local values should define the differences in local development. Triggering local values by developing tacit knowledge of stakeholders/citizens would generate strong power by mobilizing the highest commitment from all stakeholders and creating harmony in the community in sharing responsibility for local development.

2. Participation by and collaboration between stakeholders/citizens and local government needs to be nurtured and developed by consistent policies aimed at promoting the common social goods. People need to be trusted and encouraged to contribute their knowledge and their efforts to the development of their homeland.

3. The strength and initiatives of middle management bureaucrats are important factors that are decisive in the effectiveness of a policy. Autonomy and independence within the legal framework are needed for bureaucrats to develop their competence and to contribute well in the knowledge creation process. *Ba* is only effective for knowledge creation if it is created as a self-organizing space, without political leaders interfering. And even though initiatives for innovation/reform by bureaucrats can provide an important intrinsic push, the transformation in mindset of the bureaucrats is more robust if there is a distinctive trigger event, and when there

is encouragement not only from the leader but also from the community. In other words, the local management system should be designed scientifically and focused consistently to facilitate the knowledge creation process of the organization as well as to develop the competence of its human resources.

4. Local reform/innovation cannot be sustained unless the endogenous learning ability of the <u>bureaucrats is based and built on the tacit knowledge of stakeholders. The SECI process needs to</u> be routinely practiced at all levels (organizational and individual) to ensure that the endogenous learning process is continuously going on to nurture the innovation spirit of the organization.

5. Applying KM in managing local government is very challenging as it relates to changes in the human mindset and the operation of a huge system, in which many stakeholders are evolving. The implications gained from this exploratory analysis need to be further investigated empirically with the objective of proposing the most effective guidance for KM initiatives for the public sector of Vietnam.

NOTE

1. http://www.danang.gov.vn/portal/page/portal/danang/chuyen_de/dbgt_asxh/thanh_pho_3_co/gioi_thieu.

REFERENCES

Cai Cach Hanh Chinh Da Nang: 'Sang nam xuong đung nhi thi roi doi' [Administrative Reform of Da Nang: We Might be Downgraded to the Second Position Next Year]. 2014. *Infonet,* October 9. http://infonet.vn/cai-cach-hanh-chinh-da-nang-sang-nam-xuong-dung-nhi-thi-roi-doi-post146925.info.

Central City Makes Headway in Development. 2006. *Voice of Vietnam,* April 24. http://english.vov.vn/society/central-city-makes-headway-in-development-35651.vov.

Da Nang: A Beautiful City on the Coast of the East Sea. 2011. *Vietnam Pictorial,* March 14, 2011. http://vietnam.vnanet.vn/vnp/en-us/13/20996/local-development/da-nang-%E2%80%93-a-beautiful-city-on-the-coast-of-the-east-sea.html.

Da Nang: A Look Back at 10 Years of Development. 2013. *VietnamPlus,* July 28. http://en.vietnamplus.vn/Home/Da-Nang-A-look-back-at-10-years-of-development/20137/37181.vnplus.

Da Nang: Chi Trong cay mot nha may bia? [Da Nang: Relying on Only One Beverage Factory]. 2014. *Infonet*, October 9. http://infonet.vn/da-nang-chi-trong-cay-mot-nha-may-bia-post146810.info.

Danang City. 2010. 'Three Have' Program. Danang City Portal, April 27. http://www.danang.gov.vn/portal/page/portal/danang/chuyen_de/dbgt_asxh/thanh_pho_3_co/gioi_thieu.

Da Nang chọn năm 2014 là "Nam Doanh Nghiep" [Da Nang Chooses 2014 to be 'The Year of Businesses']. 2014. Vov, March 28. http://vov.vn/Kinh-te/Da-Nang-duoc-chon-lam-Nam-doanh-nghiep/317918.vov. http://www.pcivietnam.org/diem-tin/da-nang-chon-nam-2014-la-%E2%80%9Cnam-doanh-nghiep%E2%80%9D-a302.html.

Da Nang: Giam doc so xay dung khong biet co bao nhieu diem ngap ung [Da Nang: Director of the City Construction Department Doesn't Know How Many Flooding Places are in the City]. 2014. Infonet, November 29. http://infonet.vn/da-nang-giam-doc-so-xay-dung-khong-biet-co-bao-nhieu-diem-ngap-ung-post152474.info.

Da Nang: Giam sat viec thuc hien cac van de nong cam ket voi cu tri. [Da Nang: Surpervising the Implementation of the "Hot" Issues, Committed to the Citizens]. 2014. *Infonet*, October 8. http://infonet.vn/da-nang-giam-sat-viec-thuc-hien-cac-van-de-nong-cam-ket-voi-cu-tri-post146855.info.

Da Nang Khong Xin Tien ma xin co che thi Diem [Da Nang Doesn't Request Money but the Trial Mechanism]. 2011. *Infonet*, November 26. http://infonet.vn/da-nang-khong-xin-tien-ma-xin-co-che-thi-diem-post152235.info.

Da Nang: Lanh dao so xay dung chia nhau ve quan huyen lang nghe dan. [Da Nang: Leaders of the City Construction Department go to Distrists, Wards, to Listen to People]. 2014. *Infonet*, October 5. http://infonet.vn/da-nang-lanh-dao-so-xay-dung-chia-nhau-ve-quan-huyen-lang-nghe-dan-post146704.info.

Da Nang: Tre hen ho so phai xin loi cong dan to chuc bang van ban [Da Nang: Public Servant must Send the Public Letter of Apology to the People if they Delay in Returning Documents]. 2014. *Infonet*, October 8. http://infonet.vn/da-nang-tre-hen-ho-so-phai-xin-loi-cong-dan-to-chuc-bang-van-ban-post152284.info.

Da Nang voi bai hoc than dan an dan va dong thuan xa hoi trong xay dung va phat trien. [Da Nang with the Lesson of Being Close to People and Creating the Harmony in the Society for Development] *Vusta*, June 29. http://www.vusta.vn/vi/news/Trao-doi-Thao-luan/Da-Nang-voi-bai-hoc-than-dan-an-dan-va-dong-thuan-xa-hoi-trong-xay-dung-va-phat-trien-38803.html.

Malesky, E. 2013. PCI2013: The Vietnam Provincial Competitiveness Index. USAID/Vietnam: Hanoi. http://eng.pcivietnam.org/tailieu/PCIReport_2013_EN.pdf.

Minh, Ho Chi. 1945/ 2002. *Completed Selected Works.* Vol 12. National Politics Publishing.

Nonaka, I. 1991. The knowledge creating company. *Harvard Business Review* 69 (6): 96–104.

Nonaka, I. 1994. A dynamic theory of organizational knowledge creation. *Organization Science* 5 (1): 14–37.

Nonaka, I., and H. Takeuchi. 1995. *The Knowledge-Creating Company: How Japanese Companies Create the Dynamics of Innovation.* New York: Oxford University Press.

Nonaka, I., and N. Konno. 1998. The concept of "Ba": Building a foundation for knowledge creation. *California Management Review* 40 (3): 40–54.

Steering Committee for Respose to Climate Change and Sea Level Rise. 2015. Preliminary Resilience Assessment Report. Standing Office of Da Nang. http://ccco.danang.gov.vn/104/default.aspx.

Stern, L. 1987. The Vietnamese Communist Party in 1986: Party Reform Initiatives, the Scramble towards Economic Revitalization and the Road to the Sixth National Congress. *Southeast Asian Affairs Institute of Southeast Asian Studies.* 14 (1): 345–363.

Thanh, Vo. 2016. Danang–The Key Driver and Powerhouse of the Central and Central Highland. GAIN report number: VM5085. USDA.

Thayer, C. 1987. Vietnam's sixth party congress: An Overview. *Contemporary Southeast Asia Institute of Southeast Asian Studies.* 9 (1): 12–22.

Uyama, Masayuki. 2014. Presentation made at The Second Workshop on Leadership and Management Development in Asian Countries, September 29th–October 1st, 2014 at National Graduate Institute for Policy Studies (GRIPS) Tokyo.

Vietnam Trade Promotion Agency. 2013. Socio-economic Achieverments of Danang afters 15 years Becoming a City Directly Under the Central Government. *Vietnam Trade Promotion Agency,* July 3. http://www.vietrade.gov.vn/en/index.php?option=com_content&view=article&id=2070:the-socio-economic-achieverments-of-danang-afters-15-years-becoming-a-city-directly-under-the-central-government-1997–2012-&catid=20:news&Itemid=287.

AUTHOR BIOGRAPHY

Nguyen Thi Hai Hang is the President of Vietnam Aviation Academy (VAA), the only state-owned organization in the national educational system of Vietnam specialized in aviation. Knowledge management has been her principle research topic since she started her PhD program in 2008. She has been working in various functions in the aviation sector of Vietnam since 1995: specialist in Planning and Investment at the Civil Aviation Authority of Vietnam, project manager, project coordinator for ODA projects in aviation, instructor at the Civil Aviation Training Center, course developer, lecturer/researcher, Dean of the Air Transport Faculty, and President of VAA since December 2015.

CHAPTER 6

Antonio Meloto: Empowering the Filipino Poor Toward Sustainable and Innovative Communities

Alex B. Brillantes Jr and Lizan E. Perante-Calina

INTRODUCTION

"My power lies in not desiring power." This is one of the most quotable remarks of Mr. Antonio Palermo Meloto, one of the more influential and, indeed, powerful men in the Philippines today. "A leadership that does not seek power, in the process becomes more powerful." This has indeed been the guiding principle of Meloto, a private individual whose only

A.B. Brillantes Jr (✉) · L.E. Perante-Calina
National College of Public Administration, University of the Philippines,
quezon city, Philippines
e-mail: alex.brillantes2014@gmail.com

L.E. Perante-Calina
e-mail: lizanpcalina@gmail.com

A.B. Brillantes Jr
Commission on Higher Education, University of the Philippines, quezon
city, Philippines

L.E. Perante-Calina
Philippine Society for Public Administration, University of the Philippines,
quezon city, Philippines

© The Author(s) 2018
A. Hirose Nishihara et al. (eds.), *Knowledge Creation in Community
Development*, DOI 10.1007/978-3-319-57481-3_6

dream is to build homes for the poor toward sustainable and empowered communities. His vision is a Philippines freed from poverty by 2024.

The Philippines is a country where poverty is a major problem. This was especially true in the 1990s, when the incidence of poverty was dramatically higher than its neighbors in the region. Extreme poverty is a social ill, and fighting it is a struggle, particularly if the effort comes from a private individual. Creating social innovations for the poor takes a lot of inspiration and care. The efforts Meloto made to lift the poor out of their state of deprivation is perhaps one of the most laudable efforts to emerge in the Philippines between the late 1990s and today.

Known to many as "Tito Tony" (Uncle Tony), Meloto's two-decade immersion in poor Filipino communities led him to transform squalid local communities into livable and sustainable ones. It was the realization of what is now known as the Gawad Kalinga (GK)—a non-governmental organization that aims to build homes and a better quality of life for every Filipino. Gawad Kalinga, which means "to give care," has affected people's lives and built a network of Filipino communities made up of rich and poor alike, along with the educated and less educated, the young and the old, leaders and followers, Muslims and Christians, and academics as well as the business sector. Together, they made GK an accepted framework for development in the country.

CHALLENGES IN COMMUNITY TRANSFORMATION

Tito Tony was raised by a modest family in Bacolod City, Negros Occidental. Although his native land was known as the home of the elite, sugar barons, and the landed, Meloto was born poor. He recalls that they had "no property, except for the 700 square-meter lot in Alunan Street owned by their maternal grandfather, Fidel Palermo" (Ong 2006). At an early age, he was exposed to a poor community near the shoreline, where the way of life was one of abject poverty. Born on January 17, 1950, Meloto was second to youngest in a family of six. Many times in his younger days, he dreamed of faraway places and better times. "Although the rich were never unkind to them personally, he felt the social wounds of rejection and the insecurity of being born without pedigree" (Ong 2006).

Meloto was determined to get a good education in spite of being poor. Although he was physically weak and had a damaged eye, he was supposedly blessed with a photographic memory that helped him excel at school. During his elementary and high school days, he earned the highest honors, graduating at the top of his class. These achievements led Meloto to a full scholarship from Ateneo de Manila. Aside from being an academic excellence awardee, he was also active in the school's extracurricular activities, where he received the Most Outstanding Student of the Year award from the Rotary Club. Prior to his admission to Ateneo de Manila, where he earned a degree in economics, he won an American Field Service scholarship from the United States at the age of 16 and spent a year of his high school education at De Anza High School in Richmond, Virginia. His experience in De Anza was significant, as he was able to see "how people of different nationalities can live together as equals in worth and dignity." Even as a boy Meloto saw education as a way for people to "escape poverty" (Ong 2006). After obtaining a degree in economics, he worked for private firms and was appointed as Senior Vice President for Procter & Gamble. His business career soared high, but he chose to sever his ties with large private international corporations and became a lay missionary to serve the poor. The difficulties and challenges he encountered further strengthened him.

As a devout Christian, Meloto's mission in life is to help the poor—in other words, being his brother's keeper. His first immersion in a poor community started in 1995, when he took a leap in the dark in Phase Nine of Bagong Silang in Quezon City, a place considered a den of thieves, drug addicts, prostitutes, or, as he describes it, a place of underworld characters, a university of criminals, and a burrow for them to hide and rest. The residents live in shacks and shanties, with no formal education, no regular jobs, and no special skills. The place has an unwritten rule: "Enter at your own risk." "Even the priest, 'Bombay,' (money lenders) or Mormon missionaries would not dare to enter Bagong Silang," Meloto says. It was his first venture into a realm where he wanted to blend into feel people's misery, rejection, and desolation.

Meloto, originally inspired by a strong Christian faith "in action," demonstrates how the achievement of a utopia (the massive struggle against extreme poverty) can evolve into a peaceful national movement with no political or religious attachments. "I figured that, to make a difference, I had to be different. The more people I cared for, the more leaders of state and market I engaged in honest and noble endeavors, the more support I got for the cause, so I would gain moral ascendancy by not putting a price tag on my soul" (Meloto 2009).

He wanted to adopt the community by living with them and learning to love them. This may have seemed like a foolish idea, but to understand the depth and immensity of poverty in the slums, according to Meloto, one has to take risks in order to learn and experience good research, as it were. Accordingly, Meloto writes:

> Risking is learning, experience is research, I thought gallantly as I surveyed my surroundings to reinforce my crazy foray into the unfamiliar. I was bored with living life vicariously, with reading other people's ideas and passively learning from people's mistakes. I had to feel of their pain—my own affinity with their helplessness and frustrations; my own insight into their dreams and aspirations, if they had any left. I had to discover their innate capacities and potentials for myself, and perhaps prescribe some answers as to why they were poor and how they could possibly get out of poverty. No one had shown me why and how and where, or if there was any model community where those in extreme poverty have become "un-poor" or at least less poor". (Meloto 2009, 33)

Meloto learned from experience that transforming communities was challenging and difficult, to say the least. The residents of Bagong Silang were diverse and varied, coming from different regions of the country. Most of them were victims of forced evacuations and demolitions, and almost half of the residents had been in prison. In short, it is a place of criminals and neglected, abandoned individuals. Having them in one place is dangerous and life threatening.

Meloto's boldness in finding a way to help these people in the slums cannot be understated. He risked his life, living with them with no assurance that he would be able to get out alive. Nevertheless, he shepherded them to a better life. "I discovered that there was evidence of life—of goodness and hope, not the dumpsite of human misery or the grim object of fear that I had always known it to be. All it took was for me to be there with the people, even just for a day at a time" (Meloto 2009, 33).

Meloto continues his journey with nothing but his compassion for the needy and unwanted. Initially without any assistance or intervention from the government, he found a way to be part of the solution. Meloto emphasized that, "what was needed was a new look at old problems, so as to break free from the bureaucratic cycle of recurring mistakes and to put an end to blaming every administration for the shortcomings of past leaders" (Meloto 2009, 43).

For Meloto, who has neither political power nor business capital, his only hope is his trust in God—he believes that real power lies in not wanting it. Meloto demonstrates that community self-help, cooperation and solidarity, unity and integrity of faith, and practical reason can lead to the transformation of people, communities, and leaders from different spheres of life". In order to sustain his noble cause of helping the poor, he collaborated with civic clubs, mainstream catholic organizations, universities (moving beyond the classroom and into the community), big businesses, and political leaders. Together, Meloto and the volunteers pursue their noble cause.

Setting up Gawad Kalinga (GK)

Given this context, Meloto was moved to organize a social program called Gawad Kalinga (GK), a social movement that builds sustainable communities with particular focus on housing, land ownership, education, health, and values. Put succinctly, GK, which means to "give care," is a social movement for nation building that transforms poverty-stricken areas into livable and sustainable communities. As a non-governmental organization, it aims to build homes and a better quality of life for every Filipino, as dreamed of by Meloto.

As the founding Chairman of Gawad Kalinga, his dream of building communities was indeed a phenomenon, which "started not just a project but a journey" (Meloto, cited by Graham 2014, 1). Volunteerism and the spirit of *bayanihan* (cooperation) were the buzzwords. When GK began its journey, thousands of volunteers from different sectors—academia, business, and government—freely joined together to build the first community for 43 families in the biggest slum in Manila. Today, GK has over 2000 communities across the country, living with restored dignity, quality of life, and sustainable livelihoods. Under Meloto's leadership, GK has undertaken many social innovations to be proud of, all of which demonstrate social values, social entrepreneurship, and social justice.

Meloto, in his commitment to help the poor, has reaffirmed in many speeches that the reason why we are poor is that "we keep leaving the poor behind." And leaving the poor behind means losing human capital—both intellectual and talent capital (Meloto, cited by Graham 2014, 1). Meloto argues that, "we are graduating job seekers not business owners, not wealth creators, and not job generators." Our education is also an education of disconnection—disconnected from the land, from the poor, and from the elite schools. The best places to look are the State Universities, which can help sustain economic growth and create social entrepreneurs in the countryside. State universities are connectors that have intellectual capital in the rural areas.

It is in this context that Meloto stressed the need for Gawad Kalinga and its stakeholders to have a strong sense of social justice, being an important element in building the economy—land for the landless, homes for the homeless, and food for the hungry. As pointed out in this case study, Gawad Kalinga's first step in its development road map was "Building Communities: GK Roadmap to End Poverty". The aim was the restoration of human dignity of the poorest of the poor by providing them with land, home, potable water, and sanitation, and by mitigating hunger. In the whole process of liberation, sustainable growth and peace cannot be attained as long as there is poverty around us. A country cannot be globally competitive if the impoverished remain.

> Accordingly, Meloto stressed that he must learn to work with other people's initiatives to achieve connectivity, solidarity, and scale. His ability to use political power is vital in his role as a leader. Meloto and the GK model have become an accepted framework for development in the Phillippines, contributing significantly to the achievement of the country's Millennium Development Goals (MDGs). This framework went global when it was used to build houses for the poor in Cambodia, Indonesia, and Papua New Guinea with support from people around the world—the United States, Canada, Australia, and Europe. "Seen through the lens of public administration, Gawad Kalinga may be described as a distinctly Filipino invention that effectively delivers basic services to Filipinos living in poverty by engaging cooperation between government, business, and civil society". (Brillantes and Fernandez 2008, 283)

Based on this philosophy, Gawad Kalinga and Meloto worked hard to provide land for more than a million families through land banking, and through partnering with local governments. Utilizing land banking, GK was the first to build homes for the victims of typhoon Yolanda in 2013. Meloto presented a new way of looking at old problems—that is, to stop blaming the bureaucracy. Gawad Kalinga was his answer to old bureaucratic problems, which consisted of continuous interactions between individuals, among groups and organizations, and again back to individuals. The GK model, as shown in Fig. 6.1, illustrates how to end poverty for five million families by 2024. This is the knowledge vision of Meloto and Gawad Kalinga.

This is the vision articulated by Meloto and Gawad Kalinga toward the common good, with the objectives of restoring the dignity of the poorest of the poor, empowering the poor and the communities in which they live, and making the poor productive as stewards of resources. By achieving these objectives, continuous dialogue and practices, as well as creation of new knowledge, can occur through what is referred to as *ba* (GK communities) toward nation-building and citizen-driven change. The Meloto and the GK development framework are an indigenous model engaged in several component programs: 1) shelter and site development (GK Tatag), 2) community health (Gawad Kalusugan), 3) education/child and youth development (Sibol, Sagip at

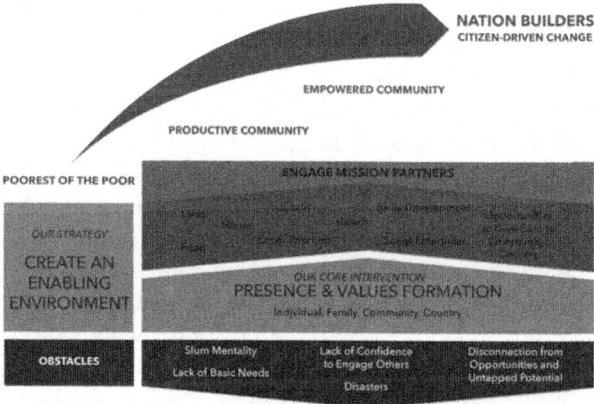

Fig. 6.1 Building Communities—The GK Roadmap to End Poverty begins with dignity restoration and includes community empowerment, access to mainstream opportunities and basic services, and eventually to character building and good citizenship. Gawad Kalinga is there to guide the poor throughout the many stages of their journey out of poverty, taking them from the level of the poorest of the poor to becoming the empowered poor, the productive poor, and eventually the new middle class. *Source* "Our Model." Mandaluyong City: Gawad Kalinga Community Development Foundation. http://www.gk1world.com/our-model

Siga), 4) productivity/livelihood (Kapitbahayan), 5) culture and tourism (Mabuhay), and 6) environment (Gawad Kalinga). Meloto's ability to create *ba* is manifested by the rapidly growing number of organized communities in the country living where people can live high-quality, dignified, and sustainable lives. Global headquarters were also established in Africa, Australia, Cambodia, Canada, Europe, Indonesia, and Papua New Guinea, with the Philippines as the central hub. Meloto and the Gawad Kalinga made remarkable efforts in helping the Philippines to attain the eight Millennium Development Goals by 2015. The seven components programs and the eight MDG goals are in harmony.

Meloto's immersion in a poor community brought remarkable changes to the lives of thousands of poor Filipinos. Meloto said that "for so long, we've looked at ourselves as second-class citizens of the world because we've seen our 20 million poor as ignorant, hopeless, and helpless citizens, worthy only as objects of charity" (Thomas 2014, 120) but with his journey with the poor, Meloto established that he has a significant role to play in lifting these people out of poverty through values formation and education.

Known as the "builder of dreams," Meloto's two-decade journey with poor Filipino people resulted in the creation of the GK community, which may be described "as a distinctly Filipino invention that effectively delivers basic services to the poorest citizens by engaging cooperation among government, business, and civil society, and the poor themselves" (Brillantes, cited by Graham 2014, 101). Building houses for the poor was not Meloto's only main intention but the added value to it was that Meloto and Gawad Kalinga have introduced social innovations for the common good. Significantly, Meloto has inspired not only millions of Filipinos but also people all over the world who now adhere to his internationally known social innovation platform, Gawad Kalinga. "As a transforming leader of Gawad Kalinga, a housing and community development movement, Meloto, his ideas, and personal example stand out and compel attention and active response from people in various walks of life".

Transformational Leader: Making a Difference as an Ordinary Citizen

Over the years, Meloto has introduced many remarkable social innovations that inspired poor communities to find high-quality, sustainable, and decent ways of living and raised their social status. Meloto and his team have built around 200,000 houses and made 2000 communities along with GK's 250 employees, 20,000 regular volunteers from all over the world, and more than 500 major corporations collaborating with them (Rebelo 2011). These communities were not only given the opportunity to have their own homes but they were also inspired to create a sustainable neighborhood to aid in ending poverty for five million families in 2024. Values formation, education, and social entrepreneurship are among the key components of Meloto's leadership. Through GK, Meloto introduced the Development Roadmap in three stages as described in Table 6.1.

In his quest to make a difference as a leader in a private capacity, he pointed out that "politics in the country is not about heroic sacrifice, but about wielding power; not about citizenship but about authority; not about ordinary citizens like me, but about our rulers." So, the missing ingredient in the country's development, he stressed, is power from the people. With this in mind, Meloto wondered how he could collaborate

Table 6.1 Gawad Kalinga's development road map 2003–2024

Target	Aim
2003–2010: Social justice	Challenging and inspiring everyone to go beyond charity and become their brother's keeper in order to heal the wounds of injustice in the country. This has opened the door to major streams of generosity through donations of land and resources to build homes for the homeless, a dream realized through the heroic response of volunteers from all sectors of society
2011–2017: Social artistry	The designer phase, called "Social Artistry," invites greater expertise, science and technology to grow a holistic model for development. Major innovations will be pursued through stronger collaboration with credible and distinguished institutions and individuals. By engaging them to use GK communities as convergence points and social laboratories, this will concretely and permanently improve the quality of life of the poorest of the poor and allow them to attain their maximum potential
2018–2024: Social progress	This phase envisions a new standard of living to take a permanent foothold in the life of the nation. This will be achieved only by working on the scale and sustainability of what has been established earlier—the spirit, the science, and the structure. By this time, a new generation of empowered, productive citizens will have emerged, who have lived through an exciting time of change—moving from poverty to prosperity, from shame to honor, from third-world to first-world and from second-class to first-class citizens of the world

Source http://www.gk1world.com/gk-2024-roadmap

with government leaders and the business sector to support the voices of the poor and to sustain the cause of building the dreams of the poor for social justice, social artistry, and social progress.

Leadership does matter—especially in addressing the country's basic problems of massive poverty and endemic corruption. Leadership is a passport to development. "Leadership is essential for all types of organizations and is the key to performance in ensuring that the organization operates at its maximum effectiveness" (Brillantes 2013). Gawad Kalinga, through Meloto, has demonstrated a leadership that motivates and transforms people for the greater good. "As a transforming leader of Gawad Kalinga, a housing and community development movement, Meloto and his ideas and personal example stand out and compel attention and an active response from people in various walks of life".

During the 10th anniversary of GK, seven learning points were raised: "1) that poverty is a behavioral problem with economic consequences; 2) that poverty is man-made and hence can be unmade; 3) that there are many generous people who are just looking for ways to help; 4) that it is important to match passion and spirit with science and systems; 5) that the poor are not just beneficiaries—they are GK's partners; 6) that lasting and sustainable peace is possible; and 7) that caring and sharing is universal, and people are willing to give the best for the least" (Rebelo 2011). With these learning points, Meloto and the GK continue to inspire and create innovations for three main reasons, which he emphasized during his speech at the Skoll Awards Ceremony in Europe: "1) We wanted to dream big for small people; 2) We decided to give the best of ourselves to the least of our people; and 3) We wanted to build a better and safer world for the next generation."

Meloto taught GK communities the skills of becoming social entrepreneurs through the establishment of the company Gandang Kalikasan, Inc (GKI), especially through its Human Nature brand—a fast growing pro-Philippines, pro-poor, and pro-environment natural and organic consumer brand. Another social innovation platform is the Gawad Kalinga Enchanted Farm, which helps local farmers create wealth in the countryside and develop an enterprise by making use of the natural resources of the country. The goal of the GK Enchanted Farm is to build a farm village university, to become the Philippino version of Silicon Valley for social entrepreneurship, and the Disneyland for social tourism—thus providing a means of rising out of poverty.

As founder of Gawad Kalinga, Meloto's leadership shows ingenuity and generosity. "The leadership here enjoys the public's trust. We are nonpartisan but we always like to work with national and local leaders who believe in the vision of Gawad Kalinga, which is simple: To bring the Philippines out of the Third World; to make it a First World nation" (Orejas 2008) This shows that Meloto shuns politics despite his collaboration with politicians. Meloto has proved that Gawad Kalinga, which was founded on trust, is "a working model of development that can be complemented with research, training, and extension work" (Brillantes and Fernandez 2008, 288). In research conducted by various student groups, the Civic Welfare Training Service (CWTS) students of the University of the Philippines School of Economics in particular presented their findings on "how GK is transforming people's lifestyles, arousing hope and aspirations, resulting in greater self-reliance (lower, if not zero, incidence of scavenging and mendicancy among GK residents), disciplined habits (lower spending on vices such as alcohol and gambling and greater spending on food), and improved health (less incidence of disease, less spending on medicines)" (Brillantes and Fernandez 2008, 288).

Meloto's way of leadership is inclusive as well as transformational: "One who is selfless, yet determined; one who is deeply spiritual, yet non-judgmental; one who leads by example" are the guiding principles that have moved Meloto to inspire people from all walks of life to build communities for the poor. An army of volunteers, particularly the young, trust his good judgment and his quest to reduce poverty in the country and transform the lives of poor Filipino people to find high-quality, sustainable, and decent ways of living. As a leader, he constantly places importance on the people behind him by recognizing their sacrifices, especially those who believe in his noble cause. Convincing people to join him without monetary reward is not easy, but together with Luis Oquinena (GK Executive Director), Issa Cuevas-Santos (IT Department Leader), and the ragtag team of hope weavers and dream builders, he was able to further the good cause.

The decades of hard work and the dedication of Meloto and his team toward lifting the poor out of poverty have gained local and international recognition by respectable institutions. He has received the following accolades: the 2012 Skoll Award for Social Entrepreneurship, 2011 Nikkei Asia Awards, 2010 Ernst & Young's Social Entrepreneur of the Year Philippines, 2010 Asia CEO Awards, 2010 Schwab Foundation for Social Entrepreneurship, 2010 Reader's Digest Asia Philippines' Most Trusted, 2009 Asia-Pacific Economic Cooperation, 2009 Hilton Humanitarian Award Finalist, 2006 Ramon Magsaysay Award for Community Leadership, 2006 Gawad Haydee Yorac Awardee, 2006 The Outstanding Filipino Award (TOFIL) for Community Service, 2006 Filipino of the Year (*Philippine Daily Inquirer*), and the 2003 Ateneo Ozanam Award. He was also invited to the 2011 Economic Forum.

ANALYSIS: MELOTO'S LEADERSHIP AND TRANSFORMATION PROCESSES

This case study has focused on the leadership and management style of Antonio Palermo Meloto, a private individual who was able to build communities for a global Filipino nation. Meloto was able to empower the poor through value formation, education, and social entrepreneurship toward a sustainable and livable community in the spirit of caring and sharing. This case study delves into how Meloto helped the administration to transform in ways that brought poor and rich alike together to work for one common cause.

MELOTO'S LEADERSHIP AND VISION

Meloto has established a leadership style that works best in the Philippines, and which has effectively reduced poverty in the country. As a private individual and founder of Gawad Kalinga, he plays a significant role in delivering innovations through collaboration with various sectors of society. In the process of collaborating with poor communities, he has been able to illustrate the process of creating new knowledge through continuous immersion with the communities for more than two decades, where he discovered that there is great potential in the slums only if they are considered part of the development process. As he embraced Bagong Silang as his second family, he was able to perceive the reality faced by the underprivileged. By empathizing with them Meloto led the rebirth of a new community of people.

Meloto's leadership and management approach in the process of introducing innovations is guided by his principles that one's love for one's country has to go beyond politics or profit. He argues that, "What this country needed was a truly honest leader. I am not a partisan; I am an ordinary citizen who is not blinded by party loyalties. The future of the country is not only dependent on the top leaders (referring to the politicians) but it is also really in every citizen, especially the young and the poor. Lifting the poor out of poverty means expanding the market and making it more sustainable". Meloto stressed that he has the responsibility to promote good citizenship, as well as good governance. He considers that both should be advanced by everyone, as these two concepts go together. The focus should also be on nurturing new leaders among the young, as they are the people with the spirit of innovation. The country has a young population to educate and train, and, given their skills and potentials, they will be the country's greatest asset and human resource.[1]

Meloto summarizes his leadership and management principles as follows:

> First, I must not desire power or profit for myself. I must not seek any public office or engage in business for personal gain. Second, I must discover power in the powerless. Democracy is about people power. Nation building is about being a leader of people. Third, I must have a big dream for even the smallest citizen. No one will pay attention to us unless we have a big idea embraced by many. Government and business will listen if we have the members. It was a numbers game for them—numbers of voters and consumers. The poor and the youth will give us the numbers. Fourth, I must build that dream on the ground for everyone to see and believe, build, share and tell. Convince people that change is possible. Finally, I must learn to work with other people's initiatives to achieve connectivity, solidarity and scale. (Meloto 2009)

What drives the entire dynamic process is the leadership capability of Meloto, with his practical wisdom to choose the right course of action in complex situations. Based on experience as evidenced by Meloto's work with Gawad Kalinga, we may conclude that he has demonstrated phronetic leadership. For example, his ability to make judgment on "goodness" is evidenced by his love of country, which goes beyond politics or profit. His embrace of the most unwanted and troubled communities in the country, putting them at the center of development is exceptional—something that makes Meloto different from other leaders. His ability to grasp the essence stems from his actual experience and research while living with poor communities. He was able to see things as they are in the community and feel the reality of being deprived. He did not think for the poor—rather he thinks as one of them. Meloto desires to discover power in the powerless, as democracy is about people power and nation building is about being a builder of people.

With Meloto's knowledge on the state of poverty in the country, not to mention his exposure to depressed areas during his younger years, he articulated the essence of his noble cause around the world, as he does not desire power or profit for himself. Despite his popularity, the thought of seeking public office or engaging in business for personal advantage was never part of his agenda.

Seen through the lens of the theory of the knowledge-based view of the firm, Meloto's way of fostering phronesis is grounded in his principle that "he must build that dream on the ground for everyone to see and believe, build, share and tell. Convince that change is possible." During the first phase of GK (2003–2010), he successfully promoted social justice by providing land for the homeless. "In seven years, we proved that landowners will share their land if we show them that there's value here not only for the poor but also for them". It is through land sharing that the physical environment of ugly shanties is transformed into a peaceful and orderly community, where economic activity is present. Over the years, Meloto and his team have made a strong commitment under the following tenets of *Padugo, Tataya Ako* (I commit to bleed for the mission), *Una sa Serbisyo, Huli sa Benepisyo* (I commit to serve, rather than to be served), *Para sa Diyos at Para sa Bayan* (I commit to love God and my country), *Bayanihan* (I commit to challenge the impossible in solidarity with others), *Walang Iwanan* (I commit to leave no one behind). Toward this end, Meloto continues his journey as his brother's keeper through social innovations toward the common good.

It is within the above context that we bring in our own analysis of the leadership style of Tony Meloto, viewed from the theoretical platform of Professor Nonaka—the SECI Model and the Wise Leader. We found it useful and informative to make our point of departure the Governance Reform Framework (GRF) we developed at the University of the Philippines National College of Public Administration and Governance (Brillantes and Fernandez 2008; Brillantes et al. 2014). Our own GRF underscored, among other things, the imperative to focus on and recognize the key role of leadership in designing reform interventions. Our GRF identified the other areas of reform in addition to leadership: (1) institutions, processes, and procedures, (2) changing values, mindsets, and paradigms, (3) citizen engagement (claimholders), and (4) communication. The reform interventions are all driven by a common vision. Figure 6.2 shows the suggested Framework for Governance and Reform. The following is a discussion of each of these elements.

(1) Leadership

Leadership is the key to performance in ensuring that the organization operates at its maximum effectiveness. Effective leaders are able to mobilize collaborative forces of the public and private sectors at the national and local levels. A number of features are necessary for good governance and a responsive public administration, including efficiency, effectiveness, accountability, and transparency—all of which are translated into reality by effective leadership (Brillantes 2013). Leadership, as one of the areas for reform, goes along with other components that have to be reinforced by the duty bearers (leadership) and claimholders (citizens) operating within the context of an enabling environment.

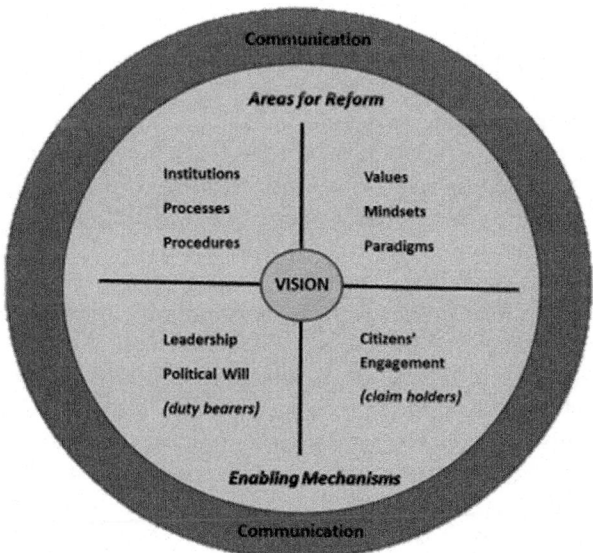

Fig. 6.2 Framework for Governance. *Source* Brillantes, Fernandez, and Perante-Calina 2013

(2) Reforming institutions, structures, processes, and procedures

The increasing distrust and bureaucratic maladies that could weaken the bureaucracy have been behind various pushes for reforms in governance, particularly in institutions, structures, processes, and procedures. Bureaucratic and political corruption, often referred to as "trust deficits" in the politico-administrative system, create negative consequences (i.e., weak institutions, lack of professionalism, poor quality of programs, projects and services, and ineffective and unaccountable administration). Accordingly, Fukuyama (2004) argues that state building is one of the most important issues for the world community because weak or failed states are the world's most serious problems. "Nation building is the creation of new government institutions and the strengthening of existing ones. It is a response to promote the governance of weak states, improve their democratic legitimacy, and strengthen self-sustaining institutions; thus, the imperative for reform in institutions," he added. Reforming institutions includes reforms in processes and procedures and improvement of structures (Brillantes 2013).

(3) Reforming values and behavior

Changing mindsets is one of the most challenging aspects of reform, but, at the same time, it is imperative in restoring trust in the government. "Changing mindsets as well as behavior is difficult in general, especially in a country where there is still a strong overlap of traditional social systems with modernization efforts" (Brillantes 2013). As pointed out by Pant (2007, 82), reforming values and mindsets refers to the molding of individual and collective perspectives or paradigms of public officials in line with the demand of the changing context. It is also called reforming the "culture." In the case of the Philippines, reforming mindsets and behavior will surely be a long process. It involves the presence of equally important imperatives for reform, such as political will, reformed institutions, and an engaged citizenry. Unless citizens participate, then we cannot say that there is acceptance in any reform effort (Brillantes 2013). It is in this context that it is important to build capacity by designing and implementing a network of capacity-building institutions and developing a performance mindset among national and local governments, such as performance indicators for civil servants, performance indicators for local governments, performance management systems, and a seal of "good housekeeping."

(4) Enabling mechanisms for leadership

Leadership *really* matters. As one area for reform, leadership is an important handle not only for elected officials but also for bureaucrats. "Leadership is key in terms of restoring or sustaining accountable, responsible, and inclusive governance. Leaders with integrity who are not afraid of public scrutiny are indispensable. Effective leadership is central to effective and sustainable implementation, thus it plays a vital role in the success or failure of the government" (Brillantes 2013). As pointed out by Kotter (1996), the key to successful organization is "leadership, leadership, and still more leadership." It is in this aspect that leadership by example may lead to restoring values, changing mindsets, and streamlining of processes and procedures toward the establishment of strong institutions. "Many times, political will refers to the right political support. Innovative leadership is crucial in reforming public administration and tackling corruption" (Brillantes 2013).

(5) Enabling mechanisms: Citizen engagement

Citizen participation in government activities is imperative in a democratic country like the Philippines. As the government engages the citizens in policy-making processes, their participation is imperative for reforms to be successfully implemented. According to Meskell (2009, 1; as cited by Brillantes 2013), they (government) know that, for democracy to flourish, citizens must take an active part in public life, sharing their ideas and opening their minds to the opinions of others, and taking ownership of the well-being of the country.

(6) Communication, an Indispensable Fifth Dimension for Effective Governance Reform

Communication is synonymous with socialization, as described in the SECI Model, which should be seen as a vital component of good governance. The dysfunctionalities in the Philippine bureaucracy, particularly regarding the myriad issues such as concerns and challenges in accountability, continue to trouble the Filipino people. For the past several decades, issues of corruption and inefficiency in the delivery of government services have been the focal point of reform initiatives as there is a high demand for reform.

Further, Meloto also highlights the five things to do toward building a culture of good governance and good citizenship: (1) Take the high road. Go for integrity and honor above money and power; (2) serve the greater good; (3) seek the highest interest of the lowest and the weakest; (4) raise the bar of excellence in public service; and (5) love this country with all your heart and value the privilege of being Filipino.

Meloto's introduction of Gawad Kalinga to the country can be considered as an excellent paradigm for good governance that, incidentally, also incorporates the areas included in our GRF. Good governance revolves around the values of transparency, accountability, participation, the rule of law, equity and social justice, and sustainability and continuity, while "GK revolves around the values of *bayanihan* (becoming a hero to one another and addressing the root cause of poverty—not simply a lack of money but an absence of shared values, sense of community and higher purpose)" (Brillantes and Fernandez 2008, 288). The Gawad Kalinga development model has been adopted by various sectors, which describe it as a good governance framework.

Being a radical optimist, Meloto believes that the country will be out of poverty by 2024 through its "build philosophy," which showcases two very Filipino and Christian qualities: *Kalinga* (to care) and *bayanihan* (spirit of cooperation). A decade from now, the slum communities of the country will be replaced by decent housing brightly painted in the colors of hope. In achieving this, Meloto emphasizes innovation as a key factor, by posing the following questions: "(1) Is it doable? (2) Is it visible? (3) Is it quantifiable? (4) Is it sustainable? (5) Is it replicable? (6) Does it lead to better social inclusion?".

MELOTO'S PHRONETIC LEADERSHIP FOUNDED ON TRUST

As shown in this case study, Meloto has demonstrated phronetic leadership. According to the knowledge-based view, phronesis consists of six abilities: 1) the ability to make a judgment on "goodness," 2) the ability to grasp the essence, 3) the ability to create *ba*, 4) the ability to articulate the essence, 5) the ability to use political power, and 6) the ability to foster phronesis in others (Hirose 2013). Table 6.2 shows beyond doubt that Meloto is a phronetic leader.

Table 6.2 Meloto as a phronetic leader

Meloto as a Phronetic Leader	
Ability to make judgment on goodness	This is evidenced by his love for the country, which goes beyond politics or profit
Ability to grasp the essence	His ability to grasp the essence stems from his actual experience and research while living with poor communities. He did not think *for* the poor but he thought *as* one of them
Ability to create *ba*	This is manifested by the rapidly growing number of transformed communities—from squalid to high-quality, dignified, and sustainable ones
Ability to articulate the essence	Meloto's tacit and explicit knowledge on the state of poverty and his actual experience for more than two decades with poor communities enabled him to perfectly articulate the essence of his noble cause around the world
Ability to use political power	He learned to work with other people's initiatives to achieve connectivity, solidarity, and scale
Ability to foster **phronesis** in others	Based on his leadership principle that "one who is selfless yet determined; one who is deeply spiritual yet non-judgmental; and, one who leads by example" reflects his being a phronetic leader

Succinctly, the case study recounts and communicates exemplary practices from the third sector, showing that in governance, the engagement of private individuals plays a significant role in defining the interlocking responsibilities of different actors in achieving sustainable development. "Essentially, good governance comes down to four key factors: structures, leadership, values, and engagement" (Brillantes, cited by Thomas 2014, 101). The values formation approach by GK as described by Brillantes (2014, as cited by Thomas 101) is important as love for one's neighbor, charity, and selfless leadership are fundamental aspects of sustainable communities.

As such, the true essence and philosophy of Meloto's leadership are founded on trust. Given his r achievements in terms of driving social innovations—from building homes and communities for the poorest of the poor to empowering them through education, restoring their dignity, and teaching them entrepreneurial skills, Meloto has indeed transformed thousands of poor Filipinos toward a better life. But what drives him to continuously sustain his true intentions is his principle that "a leadership that does not seek power in the process becomes more powerful" (Meloto 2009). He even emphasized that "the more people he cared for, the more leaders of State and market he engaged in honest and noble endeavors, the more support he gets for the cause, and that he would gain moral ascendancy by not putting a price tag on his soul" (Meloto 2009). Another striking leadership trait of Meloto is his being inclusive as he inspires people to be creative and innovative. "One who is selfless yet determined, one who is deeply spiritual, yet non-judgmental; and, one who leads by example" is one of the leadership principles that make him different from other leaders. He also highlights the five things to do toward building a culture of good governance and good citizenship:

1. Take the high road. Go for integrity and honor above money and power.
2. Serve the greater good.
3. Seek the highest interest of the lowest and the weakest.
4. Raise the bar of excellence in public service.
5. Love this country with all your heart and value the privilege of being Filipino.

It is worthwhile to note that Meloto started Gawad Kalinga as an individual commitment that is value-driven. The concept of *padugo* (self-sacrifice) was one of the initial steps Meloto employed until he gained the trust of the poor community. The case study illustrates that in Meloto's continuous interaction with poor communities, new knowledge was created, commonly shared by individuals, among groups and organization, and again back to individuals. The Meloto and Gawad Kalinga demonstrate that socialization with the poor is one of the best strategies to truly feel their pain. The processes involved in building communities for the poor are not an easy task. It takes a lot of inspiration to do the same. Meloto remarked that "I had to have a feel for their pain—my own affinity with their helplessness and frustrations; my own insight into their dreams and aspirations, if they had any left." To do this, one has to take risks in order to learn as "risking is learning, research is experience" (Meloto 2009).

The ability and sincerity of Meloto to feel the pain of his people and his affinity with the poor have been the source of his moral ascendancy to launch a massive movement for social transformation that has now been recognized globally. As a result, he has been offered the opportunity to run for political office, or even become a member of the government's Cabinet. Through it all, he has managed to remain above the partisan political fray, and resist the temptation to accept any powerful position in government, and that is where Meloto's power lies.

The magnanimous contributions and global milestones that Meloto and Gawad Kalinga have initiated in building strong communities, changing mindsets, encouraging active citizen participation, and providing effective communication strategies cannot be understated. As he shuns politics and continues working for the good of the country, Meloto as a phronetic leader and a devout Christian always emphasized that love for country is the key to the realization of every Filipino's dreams and aspirations toward good citizenship, good governance, and an improved economy.

NOTE

1. This portion is taken from the speech delivered during the closing program of the 2014 International Conference of the Philippine Society for Public Administration with the theme "Public Administration Governance Reforms and Innovations" last February 9–11, 2014 at the Water Front Hotel in Davao City. More than three hundred international and local delegates attended from different sectors—academia, business, civil society and international organizations, participated in the conference.

REFERENCES

Brillantes, Alex B., Jr. 2014. Accountable, Responsive and Inclusive Governance. Presentation at the National Workshop of Governance Stakeholders, Crowne Plaza, Ortigas Center, Mandaluyong City on Mar. 4 2013.

Brillantes, A.B., M. Fernandez, and L. Perante-Calina. 2013. Governance Reform Framework. Presentation at the 2013 making reform happen (MRH) policy workshop in Southeast Asia and Korea, public sector reform since the late 1990s. Center for International Development, Korea Development Institute and Korea Research Institute, University of New South Wales. Siem Reap, Cambodia.

Brillantes, Alex B., Jr., and Maricel T. Fernandez. 2008. Is there a Philippine Public Administration? Or better still, for whom is Philippine Public Administration? *Philippine Journal of Public Administration* 52 (2–40): 245–307.

Fukuyama, Francis. 2004. *Building: Governance and world order in the 21st century.* Cornell University Press.

Graham, Thomas. 2014. *The genius of the poor, a journey with Gawad Kalinga*. Mandaluyong City, Philippines: Kawad Kalinga Community Development Foundation.

Kotter, John P. 1996. *Leading change*. Boston, MA: Harvard Business School Press.

Meloto, Antonio P. 2009. *Antonio Meloto: Builder of dreams*. Mandaluyong City, Philippines: Kawad Kalinga Community Development Foundation.

Nonaka, Ikujiro, and Ayano Hirose. 2013. *Social innovation: Creating new knowledge for new social value*. Tokyo: Graduate School of International Corporate Strategy, Hitotsubashi University.

Ong, Charlson L. 2006. Antonio Meloto Biography, Ramon Magsaysay Award Foundation-Awardees.

Orejas, Tonette. 2008. Gawad Kalinga takes Panlilio as Partner in Lifting Poor. *Philippine Daily Inquirer*, June 1 2006.

Pant, Dinesh. 2007. Revolutionizing the mindsets: Roles and challenges for management development institutions in governance reform context. *Administration and Management Review* 19 (2): 77–96.

Rebelo, Jose Antonio M. 2011. Tony Meloto: I am a Radical Optimist. *World Mission Magazine*, July. http://www.gk1world.com/i-am-a-radical-optimist.

Authors' Biography

Alex Bello Brillantes, Jr. Ph.D. is Professor of Public Administration at the National College of Public Administration and Governance of the University of the Philippines. He is on secondment as Commissioner to the Commission on Higher Education. Brillantes earlier served as Executive Director of the Local Government Academy of the Department of Interior and Local Government and President of the Philippine Society for Public Administration. He obtained his PhD and MA from the University of Hawaii, and MPA and AB from the University of the Philippines. His areas of expertise are in governance, institutions, development administration, local governance, and higher education.

Lizan E. Perante-Calina DPA is a university lecturer at the National College of Public Administration and Governance, University of the Philippines (UP-NPCAG) where she obtained her Doctor of Public Administration in 2016. She is also a lecturer at the Center for Local and Regional Governance of UP-NCPAG, Executive Director of the Philippine Society for Public Administration, and Associate Editor of the Philippine Governance Digest. She is connected with the Legislative Research Service, Reference and Research Bureau House of Representatives. Her recent publication is entitled Citizen's Charter: An Assessment of Contributions to Frontline Service Delivery.

CHAPTER 7

Social Innovation by a Leaf-Selling Business: Irodori in Kamikatsu Town

Ayano Hirose Nishihara

INTRODUCTION

Kamikatsu Town is a small village with an aging population situated in the mountains of Tokushima Prefecture on Shikoku Island in the southwest part of Japan. Roughly, 1800 people reside in the village, with more than 50% of the total population over the age of 65 (as of January 1, 2014). However, the success story of this village has captured attention in and outside of Japan since the early 2000s. TV programs and a movie have been made about the village's revival, in addition to numerous news articles, reports, case studies, and books. Visitors eager to learn from its success call in from around the world. The success of Kamikatsu comes from "Irodori," a company that sells decorative leaves for Japanese traditional dishes. Today Kamikatsu is known as the "town of miracles," revitalized by selling leaves.

But this was not always the case in Kamikatsu. Back in the 1980s, the aging and declining number of residents as well as increasing competition from imports saw production of the town's major product, lumber, begin

A. Hirose Nishihara (✉)
Department of Global Business, College of Business, Rikkyo University, Tokyo, Japan
e-mail: ayano.nishihara@rikkyo.ac.jp

© The Author(s) 2018
A. Hirose Nishihara et al. (eds.), *Knowledge Creation in Community Development*, DOI 10.1007/978-3-319-57481-3_7

to dwindle. The town's other major product, mandarin oranges, was also severely damaged in 1981 by unseasonably cold weather and was unable to recover for years afterward. Many elderly residents had very little to do but complain or drink. It was the 20-year-old Tomoji Yokoishi who came to Kamikatsu and initiated the changes that made the miracle possible.

Yokoishi has spent nearly 30 years in Kamikatsu since first arriving as a young man in 1979. Kamikatsu Town was already a small aging village, but after his arrival, the lives of the townspeople began to change dramatically. Instead of complaining and drinking, many residents were now busy selling leaves, working in the business begun by Yokoishi in 1986. The questions then are: How did the miracle happen? How was it made possible? And what are the lessons to be learned?

This case is intended to illustrate how Kamikatsu became the "town of miracles" and the processes and leadership involved from the viewpoint of the organizational knowledge creation theory. The case will begin with an overview of the town and then describe the events and processes of how the leaf-selling business was developed by Tomoji Yokoishi. It focuses on Tomoji Yokoishi as the main protagonist who initiated and led the business; the elderly residents are also main characters because they were the ones who cultivated the leaves and co-created new value for the town.

Description of Kamikatsu Town and Tomoji Yokoishi

Kamikatsu is a small village with 1823 residents. The percentage of residents over 65 years old stands at 50.3%, a figure well exceeding the national average of 26.1%. It was called an "unsustainable village" or "disappearing village" due to its increasing number of elderly and declining number of young people. Already by the 1980s, Kamikatsu faced a decreasing overall population with the number of elderly on the rise. Its population continued to decrease from its peak of 6000 residents.

It was not easy to live in Kamikatsu. With the village situated in the mountains, land use is limited; villagers cultivated *tanada*, or small-scale terraced rice fields. Many villagers also worked in the lumber industry or cultivated mandarin oranges. Although seasonal change in Kamikatsu is distinct, with the mountain leaves taking on the colors of autumn, it also means that temperature fluctuations are quite large. Fig. 7.1

In 1979, just 2 years before an unusual cold snap hit Kamikatsu, Tomoji Yokoishi, at the age of 20, began working at the Farmers'

Fig. 7.1 Kamikatsu Town. *Source* Kamikatsu Town webpage (www.kamikatsu.jp)

Cooperative (*Nokyo*) in Kamikatsu Town. He had recently graduated from Tokushima Prefecture College of Agriculture, hoping to become a local government employee following the advice from his father, who worked for the Tokushima prefectural government. However, the local government had no plans to hire an agricultural expert in the year Yokoishi graduated. But like the proverb "when one door shuts, another opens," just then a letter arrived asking him to take a position at the *Nokyo* in Kamikatsu, which was looking for a young willing person to revive the town. Yokoishi with his outstanding appeal was given the chance; in fact, he was well known for his handsome looks and involvement in various activities while at college. With the *Nokyo* suffering financial difficulties, the town paid Yokoishi's salary as a *Nokyo* employee. It was a special arrangement for Yokoishi right from the beginning, but Yokoishi was not aware of this at the time. His real plan, as well as his father's, was to stay for a few years and then apply for a local government position, ensuring young Yokoishi a stable and promising life.

But being invited by the *Nokyo* and getting along with the local people were two different issues. As an outsider, many local people simply rejected him. Yokoishi was told to his face that, "a young fellow like you from the outside won't understand anything about this town. I'll kick you out" (Nakajima 2008, 121); or he was asked by the farmers, "What can you do for us?" "How much money can you get for us?" (Yoshioshi 2007, 23). Yokoishi, who hated to lose, promised himself that someday the locals would take back their words. To fulfill his promise, Yokoishi committed himself to finding a way to generate income and cash for the townspeople and to help the town overcome its serious financial problems. By doing something good for the town and its people, he believed he would gain their appreciation and change their opinion about this young outsider.

For the first 2 years, Yokoishi tried to memorize the "who's who" of the townspeople, hoping to become acquainted with them. He walked around the town every day and listened to what was said. He was surprised to find elderly men who had lost their work and source of income gathered at the *Nokyo* or town hall, drinking from the morning and complaining continuously. And the elderly women were even worse. In the late 1970s and early 1980s, most country women were housewives living with their mothers-in-law or daughters-in-law; they either complained about their daughters- or mothers-in-law or told tales about their neighbors. Yokoishi wondered, "why are the elderly always talking ill of other people?" and soon realized that "it's because they have nothing else to do." He came to believe that "being busy is good for both the pocket book and the mind" (Yoshioshi 2007, 25). With this belief, Yokoishi started working on plans to increase the incomes and jobs of the townspeople.

CHALLENGING NEW PRODUCTS

As a member of the *Nokyo*, Yokoishi's challenge was to introduce new agricultural products that could bring revenue to the town. Lumber used to be one of Kamikatsu's major products until the 1970s, but due to the decline in youth and the increase in imported lumber products, the industry grew sluggish and many people lost their jobs. People gradually shifted from lumber or rice cultivation to the cultivation of mandarin oranges, but this crop was also under pricing pressure from cheap imported fruits like bananas and oranges. What made the situation worse, the mandarin orange trees were severely damaged or destroyed by unseasonably cold weather in 1981, and eventually, the farmers had to give up the mandarin cultivation and find other income sources. The town faced a severe financial crisis and was in serious need of other income sources only a few years after Yokoishi arrived in Kamikatsu.

In 1982, Yokoishi introduced the cultivation of spinach and spring onions in the summer, products once only consumed in town. He gathered the farmers' vegetables every day and sold them at the wholesale market. In the winter, he instructed them to produce dried sweet potatoes, a widely favored sweet during the winter season. Watching the trends and listening to the needs at the wholesale market, Yokoishi discovered an increasing demand for green onions and instructed the farmers to cultivate them. More used to earning income from lumber and mandarin oranges, the farmers were surprised to learn they could earn money in much shorter cycles; lumber and oranges took years to harvest while vegetables took only a few months. However, this also meant that sales revenues were seasonal and lower in amount compared with revenues earned from lumber and oranges. To stabilize and increase their income, Yokoishi had to think of other agricultural products that could be harvested throughout the year.

In 1984, Yokoishi introduced shitake mushroom cultivation. Sales revenue from shitake mushrooms provided a stable income that was higher. But there was one problem: Only the younger and stronger men could handle shitake cultivation because the mushrooms grew on log-beds so heavy that the elderly and women could not handle them. Knowing that the elderly and women were the unhappiest in general, and the ones most prone to complaining, Yokoishi had to think of other products that could be cultivated and easily handled by these people. He wanted to create jobs to keep them busy and fulfilled.

Let's Sell Leaves: An Idea Strikes
Yokoishi but Nobody Follows at First

In 1986, when at a sushi restaurant in Osaka while on a business trip, Yokoishi was struck with an "aha!" idea. Next to his table were three young women chatting over their plates of sushi. There was a red maple leaf on each plate, and Yokoishi heard one woman say, "What a pretty leaf. I'll take it home as a souvenir." (Yoshioshi 2007, 51). He watched her take out a neatly ironed handkerchief and wrap the leaf. Picking up the leaf on own his plate, Yokoishi, who was around the same age as these women, was surprised to see that such a leaf could attract the hearts of young women. For him, these leaves were found everywhere in Kamikatsu. Then, he thought, "We have plenty in Kamikatsu. We have leaves to sell!" (Yoshioshi 2007, 52). His heart beat faster with the idea. He asked the restaurant where it purchased the leaves, and was told they were handpicked in the mountains by the cooks. It seemed the leaves were not sold at the wholesale market. He also learned the leaves decorating the plates were called "*tsumamono*," meaning a small decoration representing the beauty of the changing seasons (see Fig. 7.2). Yokoishi felt confident this was a market opportunity.

As soon as he returned to Kamikatsu, he explained his leaf-selling idea to the *Nokyo* but nobody really listened to him. Frustrated, he explained his idea to the farmers, but again no one listened. Even worse, Yokoishi was ridiculed: "Sell leaves and make money? What a fairy tale! Don't waste your time thinking such foolish things, work hard instead" (Yoshioshi 2007, 54–55). Some even got angry at Yokoishi. "We have our pride. Selling something already out there in the mountains, that's what only really poor people would do. Poor I may be, but I'm not down and out" (Katsumi 2008, 45).

But still believing in his idea, Yokoishi enquired with wholesale markets around Japan and found there were a few flower products available for tsumamono, such as Japanese apricot, Japanese peach, and cherry blossoms. So Yokoishi visited the farmers who were cultivating flowers and trees for flower arrangements and asked for their cooperation. Finally, four farmers agreed to try.

Fig. 7.2   Example of *tsumamono. Source* Yokoishi, T. (2007: 169)

Learning about Leaves, with Pocket Money

Four farmers, all women, collected natural leaves from the mountains and packaged them nicely. Yokoishi branded the product "Irodori (in colors)" and took them to a wholesale market in Osaka. Assuming that "natural" leaves would sell well, they packaged leaves of various sizes, even those with worm bites. But the leaves did not sell at all. Disappointed because there were no other *irodori* products, or *tsumamono*, in the market, they had to ask themselves what was wrong. How could they sell the leaves? But they were unable to find any answers.

Struggling through trial and error, one day a cook approached Yokoishi and said: "I can't use any of these leaves on my plates. Do you know anything about the leaves for decoration?" (Yokoishi 2007, 60). This opened his eyes; Yokoishi realized that he knew nothing about *tsumamono* or the customs of traditional Japanese cuisine. He had never experienced actual Japanese dishes at a high-class Japanese restaurant. He was ashamed to have tried out his idea without first experiencing the real thing. So he went to a traditional Japanese restaurant and asked for advice, but the cook threw him out. One of the customs of traditional Japanese cuisine is "to steal the techniques and know-how from veteran cooks." But because Yokoishi was not a cook, there was no way he could glean such information from the veterans. All he could do was to become one of their customers.

So he started visiting famous high-class traditional Japanese restaurants, spending his own pocket money, whenever on a business trip in Kyoto or Osaka. He sometimes spent his entire salary (150,000 yen per month) to pay for dinners costing 20,000–30,000 yen. Each time he jotted down what kind of leaves were used on which type of plate while the server was not looking, and whenever he had a chance, he asked the server about *tsumamono*. The more he visited, the more the servers became cautious and suspicious that Yokoishi might be a cook trying to steal their techniques.

About 2 years after repeatedly visiting a traditional Japanese restaurant, the server finally asked Yokoishi whether he was trying to steal their techniques. Yokoishi answered that he was a *Nokyo* employee trying to sell leaves. The server recognized Yokoishi's enthusiasm and passion and took him back to the cook in the kitchen. In the custom of traditional Japanese cuisine, a non-cook being invited to the kitchen is a sign of trust and respect. Yokoishi was deeply impressed when he stood next to the cook in the kitchen.

The cook taught him about the traditions, know-how, techniques, and needs related to *tsumamono*. *Tsumamono* must present the ideal form of truth, goodness, and beauty. For example, leaves are used not simply for their beauty but rather to present the approaching seasonal atmosphere. Accordingly, the leaves must decorate the dish a little earlier than their natural high season, say, about 45 days earlier. In the case of red maple leaves, selling them in mid- to late fall is too late; they need to be sold from late summer to early fall. Also, the size of the leaves matters because they have to fit to the size of the designated plate. Leaves must not have any worm bites, as beauty is the most important value. Such know-how was finally made available to him.

In the end, Yokoishi gained weight and suffered from attacks of gout, but he was also able to gather knowledge on how each leaf was used in the actual situations.

Getting the Business on Track

Gaining confidence in the ability to sell leaves, Yokoishi started to visit the wholesale markets around Japan as well as open new markets and set up distribution channels for *tsumamono*. He often discussed the business aspects with buyers in the wholesale markets and listened to the needs and wants in the particular markets.

In parallel, to convince Kamikatsu's farmers of his plan, he shared what he had learned from the cooks and the buyers. He even took the farmers (most of them elderly women) to traditional Japanese restaurants to actually see with their own eyes how the leaves were used to decorate the plates (see Fig. 7.2). Yokoishi invited chefs and cooks to Kamikatsu to give lectures on *tsumamono*. Along with these efforts, the products were refined and the selling prices and volumes increased.

These trends encouraged other farmers to join the rodori business. Some farmers started cultivating the leaves to give them better control over the product, rather than picking them from natural trees in the mountains. In addition to the existing know-how on planting trees, elderly female farmers accumulated knowledge and wisdom on how and where to plant specific trees, avoid worms, and harvest earlier than the natural high season and produce beautiful leaves (see Fig. 7.3). Gradually, the irodori business attracted attention around Japan as a

Fig. 7.3   Examples of Irodori Products. *Source* Yokoishi, T. (2007: 169)

unique business model, and in 1991, the irodori business won the prestigious "Asahi Agriculture Award" from Asahi Newspaper, which generated a lot of excitement and nurtured a sense of pride in the people of Kamikatsu. Sales revenue from the irodori business grew from 1.16 million yen in 1986 to 57 million in 1991, with the number of collaborating farmers increasing from just 4 to 160.

GROWING THE LEAF-SELLING BUSINESS

Since he had begun to work in Kamikatsu, Yokoishi had always kept in mind how women and the elderly could live more happily with a greater sense of achievement and fulfillment, rather than complain all day or drink from the morning. Leaves were beautiful, lightweight, and easy to handle, but required patience; this made them a perfect match for women and the elderly to work with. But the issues were how to inform them of the market demands, how to place purchase orders, and how to coordinate between the *Nokyo* and the farmers.

In the beginning, the *Nokyo* used the town's outdoor broadcasting system to loudly announce the market demands to the village. But people not involved in the irodori business complained that the loud voice woke their babies. Moreover, the voice echoed and could not be heard clearly by the elderly. So Yokoishi and the *Nokyo* staff came up with the idea to utilize wireless fax machines.

One advantage of using the wireless fax network was that it was already in place in Kamikatsu for use during disasters and emergencies. Other advantages included the capability to send faxes simultaneously to various locations, even during electricity black outs. The disadvantages included the high cost of fax machines at that time and issues over legal regulations. It took Yokoishi and the staff 2 years of experimentation to overcome these problems. In September 1992, the wireless fax network was launched with a few collaborating farmers. Seeing how easy and useful the fax network was, other farmers began using it and soon the number of farmers increased to 136.

After the introduction of the wireless fax network, the ordering routine changed dramatically. Now every morning, the *Nokyo* combined the purchase orders from the wholesale markets and sent the order list to each farmer by wireless fax by 11:00 am. Each farmer then looked at the list and decided on which order to take. The taking of orders was first come first served, so a sense of competition was created as a side effect. This meant every farmer had to call the *Nokyo* as soon as they decided on which order to take, and to make such a timely decision the farmers had to know precisely what products were available on their farms.

This process enthused the hearts and minds of the farmers, especially the elderly women. The elderly women competed with each other, and the competitive atmosphere stimulated their willingness to do more and better. The more they took orders and produced, the more they accumulated know-how on cultivating leaves and the ways of shipping them in a timely manner in each particular situation. Yokoishi felt the irodori business was growing steadily.

To Leave or to Stay

By 1994, the irodori business was generating annual sales of 100 million yen and still growing. In 1996, the now 37-year-old Yokoishi felt it was time for a career change. Almost 20 years had passed since he first came to Kamikatsu. Achieving the success of the irodori business, he felt he had done enough to revive the town and his enthusiasm was waning. In addition, his financial status was not improving; he received less than 200,000 yen per month, a salary hardly changed over the years while the farmers were making much more. He also had three sons to care for and felt guilty for neglecting his family over the years. So in 1996, he handed in his resignation to the *Nokyo* and planned to leave town. The *Nokyo* did not force him to stay.

However, the news spread like wildfire and hit all the farmers in Kamikatsu. Letters and phone calls poured into his home, the *Nokyo*, and the town office, all asking him to stay. Yokoishi shed tears of gratitude and was thankful to the townspeople for caring so much, but he did not alter his decision to leave. Just when he was about to leave town, Mikie Shimosaka, a leader of the elderly women, stepped in front of his car and said, "If you're going to leave, you'll have to run over me first." This forced Yokoishi to rethink his decision to leave. Everyone in town tried to stop him from leaving, but the last push came from his wife, who said: "The final decision is yours, but I think you should stay because everyone thinks so much of you" (Yokoishi 2007, 121). With this, he withdrew his decision to leave Kamikatsu.

Taking the situation seriously, Mayor Yamada and members of the Kamikatsu town office offered Yokoishi another special arrangement: a transfer to the town office from the *Nokyo* and a salary increase of 100,000 yen per month. With this arrangement, Yokoishi made up his mind to stay in Kamikatsu as a town office employee. Yokoishi, who up until then had always spent his salary on work-related activities (such as eating at prestigious restaurants), could finally bring home his salary to his wife.

But after Yokoishi left the *Nokyo* and the irodori business, sales plummeted immediately. Sales revenue in 1996 was 150 million yen, but decreased to 140 million in 1997, to 120 million in 1998, and to 80 million in 1999. Even with the economic downturn at that time, this drop seemed unusual. With the sudden sales drop, people realized the success of the *Nokyo* and the irodori business owed much to the leadership of Yokoishi, who motivated the farmers and expanded the relationship with the wholesale markets.

To once again revive the irodori business, and without Yokoishi's knowledge, people began discussing and planning the details of incorporating a new company. In 1999, Irodori Company was established with 70% of its capital coming from Kamikatsu. Yokoishi was invited to be the CEO, with the mayor of Kamikatsu appointed president of the company. Yokoishi gratefully accepted the offer and became the company's first CEO.

Founding of "Irodori Company"

The first thing Yokoishi did after taking the CEO position was to introduce easy-to-use PCs to support efficiency and competition, getting a hint from Seven-Eleven Japan's POS system. It was a method of managing every single item to realize timely deliveries to stores to minimize what is called the "opportunity-loss" of selling the products. Yokoishi's idea was to develop a new PC equipped with an easy-to-use trackball and simple keyboard, with software that utilized barcodes to manage inventory and shipments and analyzed sales data to match the market demands. By introducing PCs to each farmer, Yokoishi's aim was to have farmers manage their own production and shipments. In return, the system provided a breakdown of daily sales revenue and ranking of each farmer, which Yokoishi expected to stimulate the feeling of competition among the farmers and increase their sense of achievement.

In 1998, he persuaded the national government to support this idea and obtained funding to the amount of 16 million yen as a government-led "experiment." He worked closely with the PC vendors to create a PC system with a large trackball, a keyboard with a few keys to send and receive information, and easy to understand menus. During the first phase, he introduced 40 units to 40 farmers according to the sales results of the previous year. Yokoishi visited each farmer and encouraged them to use the units, even holding seminars on how to use them effectively. Eventually, even the elderly grew accustomed to using PCs to check the best-selling items or sales ranking. They gradually learned how to read trends from the data and started to enjoy projecting the future. It was similar to the excitement of trading stocks, and their minds and bodies were greatly stimulated.

Another stimulus was intentionally designing the ranking system so that farmers would not know each farmer's specific rank, but would know where they ranked among the other farmers. This lit the fire in the hearts of the elderly: "I will do better the next time," "Tell me who did better than me. I'll do my best to beat them," "I was planning on a trip, but decided to postpone it until sure o`f my results" (Yokoishi 2007, 137–138). The elderly started predicting which leaves would sell and by when through their understanding of the seasonal changes and the reading of market demand trends and past sales results. The more they competed, the more activated and energized they became. Yokoishi felt happy to see such changes. In 2000, the irodori business turned around and sales revenue started to grow once again.

Changing How Yokoishi Works

Seeing the elderly gain greater autonomy, Yokoishi realized it was time to change how he worked with the farmers. Until then he had been a distinctive leader; he taught, persuaded, and managed the farmers while gathering demands by visiting wholesale markets and traditional Japanese restaurants throughout Japan. This style matched the founding phase of the business, but as the business model of irodori became established, he also realized the style had to change. He then changed his role from "leading" to "producing" to motivate people and facilitate relationships.

As an example, to back up the PC system, Yokoishi sent a handwritten letter to the farmers every day via the wireless fax network (see Fig. 7.4). He wrote about what was happening in the wholesale market, or what was selling most at restaurants, and encouraged them with notes such as "we can do more!" or "let's go for it!" Elderly women called it "a love

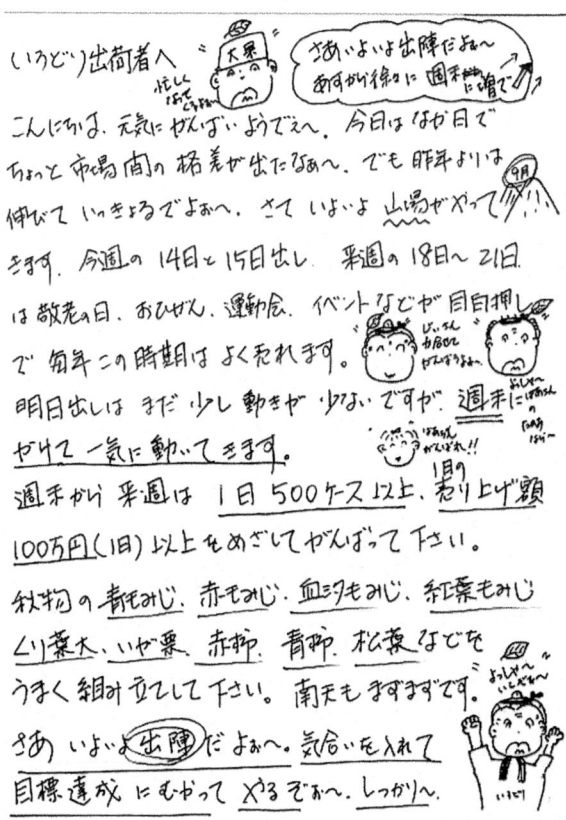

Fig. 7.4 Example of a Fax from Yokoishi. *Source* Yokoishi, T. (2007: 169)

letter from Yokoishi," appreciating that it motivated them to work "a bit more" (Yokoishi 2007, 168–169).

THE FUTURE OF IRODORI AND KAMIKATSU TOWN

In addition to the irodori business, Kamikatsu declared "zero-waste" as a town policy, which was to reduce, reuse, and recycle all the waste generated by the town. As a result, collaboration and competition among the townspeople were further stimulated.

TOWN OF ZERO-WASTE

With Kamikatsu remotely located in the mountains with a declining population, the town did not have its own waste treatment facility or incinerator. Instead, the town burned its waste on open land. Knowing this measure was not sustainable and would produce toxic substances like dioxin, the mayor and town office staff discussed what to do about the waste (Ministry of Internal Affairs and Communications 2009).

The first thing they did was to investigate the contents of the waste. It turned out that around 30% of the waste was kitchen garbage, so the town decided to promote the use of composting equipment. They searched for a compost equipment vendor, and by collaborating with the vendor on its R&D activities, the town managed to purchase the equipment at a reasonable price. As a result, almost 100% of the kitchen garbage is now recycled as compost, which improves sanitation and benefits the farmers.

At the same time, along with the new recycling regulations implemented in 1995, the town started to recycle plastics and glass. Viewing this as an opportunity, the town examined the possibility of recycling other waste. Once they knew the kinds of waste, they searched for vendors who could recycle it. As a result, by 2002, the town was separating 34 kinds of waste with 34 vendors recycling it. The waste for which vendors could not be found was disposed in landfills outside the town. So the town was declared "the town of zero-waste," and in the future, no waste will come out of Kamikatsu.

One unique part of this system is the lack of centralized garbage collection. Each resident brings their own garbage to the recycling station and the place where the town used to burn its waste was turned into a recycling station. Thirty-four specific types of waste are clearly indicated at the station, so all residents know where to dispose of their waste. For the elderly who cannot go to the station, a volunteer support group takes it for them. At the station, because almost every resident comes, people meet and chat. The staff at the station repair some items that can be reused within the town, like clothes, furniture, electric products, and others, and the station shop (called a "shop" though the recycled items are free of charge) is another social meeting space.

Another unique element of this system is that the "zero-waste" declaration caused people to start thinking from the viewpoint of production instead of consumption: If a product contains no unrecyclable materials, then everything can be recycled. This thinking led the people of Kamikatsu to meet and collaborate with manufacturers. The town even founded an NPO called "Zero-Waste Academy" to research, promote, and collaborate on how to make zero-waste products.

Relentless Pursuit of a Sustainable Town

The success of the Irodori business and zero-waste activities has attracted media attention not only from Japan but also from around the world. The number of visitors to the town is around 4500 annually. With JICA's support, visitors from the Philippines, Thailand, Myanmar, and more than 20 other countries have come to Kamikatsu to learn from the success of the Irodori business and zero-waste activities and also to learn how local and natural resources can be utilized to revitalize the local community.

Kamikatsu Town used to reject outsiders, but the more visitors came from the outside, the more the people of Kamikatsu began to welcome them. The more the elderly women became used to interviews, being videoed, and having their pictures taken, the more they became positive and active. Elderly women started to wear makeup and to dress neatly. They were proud of themselves and the town. Irodori Company received several awards, and Yokoishi himself was recognized as one of the top 100 social entrepreneurs in the world in 2007 by Newsweek Japan. But Yokoishi, having been taught by his father about the dangers of complacency and arrogance, made sure that he remained humble and honest.

One benefit of the elderly becoming more active and energetic was the need for less healthcare support. As a result, the facility for the aged was actually closed down in Kamikatsu. All of the elderly in town had work to do, something that gave them the sense of achievement and the joy of satisfaction. They had pride and believed in themselves. Another benefit was that with the money earned, the elderly could now encourage their sons and daughters to return to Kamikatsu. Now there is an active and lively network of people.

Yokoishi knew he had finally answered the question, "Why are the elderly always talking ill of other people?" "It's because they have nothing else to do. Being busy is good for both the pocket book and the mind." Managing the Irodori business, Yokoishi formed a vision: "Women and the elderly are the leaders. Unless women and the elderly change, the local community will never change. Let's realize a society where these people can enjoy their work" (Yokoishi 2007, 160, 192–193).

One last episode is worth recounting: One day while strolling about town as usual, Yokoishi saw an elderly woman planting tree seeds that would take at least 30 years before being able to harvest the leaves. When asked why, she replied, "Maybe I can't harvest the leaves myself, but if I don't plant the seeds now, there won't be any chance to harvest leaves in the future. It's not the trees but my dream that I am planting" (Yokoishi 2007, 207–208).

LESSONS TO BE LEARNED

In Japan, it is recently said that town revitalization is often led by "out-of-towners" (*yoso-mono*), "young people" (*waka-mono*), or "foolish people" (*baka-mono*). Foolish people here refers to those who are open-minded and willing to take risks. Tomoji Yokoishi, who came to Kamikatsu as a young man, nicely fits all of these descriptions. These descriptions suggest that town revitalization needs physical and mental toughness—it needs a vision and new ideas, and it needs people to gather for one purpose and to get things done, even if new or unexpected situations unfold. In terms of organizational knowledge creation theory, this is the ability of wise leadership that promotes the SECI process to co-create social value.

What then are the lessons to be learned from the case of Kamikatsu and from Yokoishi himself? To repeat, we do not want to over-generalize, but at the same time, we do not want it said that this success was possible only because of Yokoishi and because it occurred in Kamikatsu. So we will list some of the key episodes relating to the theory of knowledge creation that may be applied in different contexts.

1. SECI and *Ba*

The first step of the process of knowledge creation in the SECI process is socialization, where people share their tacit knowledge while interacting with each other through direct experiences. When creating new knowledge, both the quality and amount of socialization matter in the way they affect each of the following steps of the SECI model: externalization, combination, and internalization. We can see from this case that Yokoishi promoted socialization on various occasions.

For example, the first thing Yokoishi did when he came to Kamikatsu was to build trust with local people by walking around the town. After the mandarin orange crop was destroyed by the unseasonably cold weather, he proposed the cultivation of vegetables that could generate income with a quick turnaround. However, with other issues at hand, socialization on its own might not have been enough. After a visit to a sushi restaurant in Osaka, where he watched and listened to a group of young women, Yokoishi had the idea of selling leaves. However, almost all the elderly townspeople opposed his idea, except for four elderly women who agreed to cooperate. Yokoishi then invited the women to high-class Japanese restaurants so they could actually see how the leaves were used in the presentation of traditional dishes.

Yokoishi also set up various *ba* for socialization. One example of building actual *ba* was visiting traditional Japanese restaurants to learn about *tsumamono*. Seeking advice from chefs and market wholesalers and inviting them to Kamikatsu was another example. Yokoishi tried out the idea first and then thought about what to do and how to do it. The use of fax machines and personal computers was a way to establish virtual *ba* that promoted a better understanding of what to do and how to do it. With faxes and PCs, the elderly could actually feel the impact of their business and begin to compete and collaborate. Yokoishi facilitated these *ba* both actually and virtually, by walking around the community and by sending out handwritten fax messages.

2. Yokoishi's Leadership

Leaders in the social context need to be recognized as leaders by their communities, because they are usually not appointed as leaders because of their social position or role. They must have personal magnetism to gather, facilitate, lead, and guide people in the community. This is not an easy task for people who use either hard power (reward power, coercive power, legitimate power) or soft power (expert power, informational power), or both, rather than referent power (French and Raven 1959; Raven 1965). Referent power is based on the identification of one with the other, or attitudes such as "I would like to be like her/him," or "I would like to do something for her/him." In the case of Yokoishi, his referent power evolved over time.

When he came to Kamikatsu, he was a mere youthful outsider and as a result, the townspeople virtually ignored him. To establish a trust relationship, Yokoishi had to prove that he was willing and capable of doing something good for the town. Accordingly, he did what he could for the town during the time of crisis: He proposed new products and helped the farmers cultivate these products and promoted sales. Even so, his idea to sell leaves was beyond the common understanding of most elderly people, except for four women who listened and offered to try. This was the first turning point. If Yokoishi had still been regarded as an outsider, no one would have offered a helping hand—but because he was trusted, these four women offered their support.

The initial success of selling leaves was based on an understanding of the needs of customers, persuading farmers to produce based on these needs, and by cultivating the markets for irodori products. Once the initial success had been achieved, Yokoishi planned to leave Kamikatsu, which was another turning point. However, because he had earned the trust of the irodori farmers, he was asked to stay, and their passion and commitment moved the town administration and the town mayor. Another turning point here was, that once Yokoishi decided to stay, he changed his role from a leader to a producer. This was evidence that Yokoishi also trusted the farmers to think and pursue the business on their own. Yokoishi's role was to maintain good *ba* for producing and selling leaves.

Now the mission of Yokoishi is to cultivate his successor, and his plan is to sow the seeds of a dream. The aging of the townspeople makes it difficult to nurture the next generation of leaders and producers inside the town. But a greater number of younger people are now residing in Kamikatsu, and people who empathized with the irodori business have also begun moving into the town. Other "out-of-towners" (yoso-mono), "young people" (waka-mono), or "foolish people" (baka-mono) may come and succeed Yokoishi. A sprout may rise up, and the story will continue.

REFERENCES

French, John R. P, Bertram Raven., and D. Cartwright. 1959. The bases of social power. *Classics of Organization Theory 7*.
Katsumi, A. 2008. *Seikou no Honshitsu: Irodori* [The essence of success: Irodori]. Works, Apr–May, 45. Tokyo: Recruit Works.
Ministry of Internal Affairs and Communications. 2009. Chikihatsu Zero: Waste Suishin Katsudou [Local Development: Implementing Zero Waste Activities]. Tokyo: Ministry of Internal Affairs and Communications. http://www.soumu. go.jp/main_content/000063256.pdf.
Nakajima, J. 2008. Irodori. *Weekly Toyo Keizai*, April 26, 121. Tokyo: Toyokeizai.
Raven, B. H. 1965. Social influence and power. In *Current Studies in Social Psychology*, eds. I. D. Steiner and M. Fishbein, 371–382. New York: Holt, Rinehart, Winston.
Yokoishi, T. 2007. *Souda, Happa wo Urou!* [Yes, let's sell leaves!]. Tokyo: SB Creative Corp.

AUTHOR BIOGRAPHY

Ayano Hirose Nishihara is an Assistant Professor, Department of Global Business, College of Business, Rikkyo University, and a research collaborator to Professor Emeritus Ikujiro Nonaka. She received her B.A. (Law) from Nagoya University, MBA in 2005 and DBA in 2011 from The Graduate School of International Corporate Strategy, Hitotsubashi University. Prior to her academic track, she worked as an assistant manager at NEC Corporation. Her research topics include knowledge creation at public and private organizations and communities, knowledge-creating leadership, and social innovation. Her recent publications include Nonaka, I., Hirose, A., & Takeda, Y. (2016). "Meso"-Foundations of Dynamic Capabilities: Team-Level Synthesis and Distributed Leadership as the Source of Dynamic Creativity. *Global Strategy Journal, 6*(3), 168–182.

"It Can Be Done": Economic Forests and Social Entrepreneurship in Doi Tung, Thailand

Mae Fah Luang Foundation under Royal Patronage

Pimpan Diskul na Ayudhya

INTRODUCTION

In 1988, the Mae Fah Luang Foundation under Royal Patronage (MFLF) started the Doi Tung Development Project (DTDP) on the initiative of HRH Princess Srinagarindra, late mother of HM the King of Thailand. Mom Rajawongse Disnadda Diskul, better known as Khun Chai, Secretary-General of MFLF, was given responsibility for planning and implementing

The author would like to acknowledge the contributions of staff of the Mae Fah Luang Foundation—too many to name personally—in assisting with this paper.

P. Diskul na Ayudhya (✉)
Mae Fah Luang Foundation under Royal Patronage,
Pathumwon, Bangkok, Thailand
e-mail: pimpan@doitung.org
URL: http://www.maefahluang.org

A. Hirose Nishihara et al. (eds.), *Knowledge Creation in Community Development*, DOI 10.1007/978-3-319-57481-3_8

DTDP. As part of an innovative economic forest program under the project, Khun Chai was the architect behind the creation of the Navuti Company, which was among the first social enterprises in Thailand.

Founded in 1989, Navuti established coffee and macadamia plantations to combine reforestation with sustainable livelihoods. Navuti was key to DTDP applying sound business practices to transform opium fields and denuded hillsides into lush forests and self-reliant communities with licit livelihoods. The economic forests under Navuti were part of the broader innovative development implemented under DTDP, which included health, livelihoods, and education, together with environmental management and social enterprises established under several business units. This case centers on the role of economic forests and Navuti Company within the broader context of DTDP.

BACKGROUND

Located in a mountainous area in Chiang Rai province in Northernmost Thailand, DTDP covers 14,962 ha along the Thai–Myanmar border. Before 1987, illegal logging and slash-and-burn agriculture destroyed nearly 55% of the forests in the Doi Tung watershed area. As part of the Golden Triangle, the source of most illegal opium at that time, Doi Tung was a drug-trafficking route—remote, dangerous, and lawless, controlled by warlords and their armed militias. Many villagers grew opium; some served in militias or drug caravans. The 10,359 people in the first census of Doi Tung were all ethnic minorities, with most having migrated into this border region from Myanmar and Yunnan, China, in recent decades. Nearly, all of the 29 villages were high in the hills, with the population predominantly comprised of Akha or Lahu, with some Thai Lue and Lawa among them. One large settlement at the foot of the hills was Tai Yai (Shan), and another large community was Chinese, settled by remnants of the Nationalist 4th Army in the Chinese Civil War.

Few government services reached what was then a remote and contested area. There were no schools or health centers—even security forces rarely ventured in. People traveled on trails by foot or on horseback. The nearest market towns and government offices were at least several hours away. Most people lacked the documents needed for citizenship showing proof of birth or long-term residence in the country; nor could most speak Thai. In 1987, only 30% of Doi Tung residents were Thai citizens. The rest were stateless and considered illegal migrants. Even their agricultural activities were considered illegal because they had cleared forests in protected watersheds for traditional shifting cultivation. After a few years, as soil nutrients were depleted, yields shrank; they no longer grew enough to eat, but had no new land to clear. Opium was their main source of cash income, with traders coming to buy the raw opium. Some families even had to sell their daughters to the sex industry to survive. When these young women returned home, some unknowingly were infected with HIV/AIDS. Trapped in a vicious cycle of sickness, poverty, and ignorance, they were unsure of what tomorrow might hold: a lack of food for their next meal, arrest for being an illegal migrant or using forest land illegally, or death from HIV/AIDS.

THE DOI TUNG DEVELOPMENT PROJECT

In 1988, the Princess Mother, late mother of His Majesty King Bhumibol of Thailand, initiated DTDP under the management of MFLF to empower the people of Doi Tung to escape the vicious cycle of poverty, sickness, and lack of knowledge, and to build new lives in harmony with their environment. She realized that the root cause of the problems in Doi Tung was poverty. The Princess Mother believed that, "No one wants to be bad but they just don't have the opportunity to be good" and that man and nature should be able to coexist. She said,

> Every person should develop toward the essential truth of his or her being, and not be trapped in the cloak of ignorance. The capacities and gifts that each are born with should be used to the best of each one's ability.

DTDP embodies many of the concepts that the Princess Mother developed throughout her life from her childhood as a commoner, to her experiences as the young widow of a prince raising three young children (two of whom were to become kings), and as a development practitioner traveling throughout the country to help those in remote areas starting when she was in her 60s. She was a humanist who believed people are born with equal potential, though their opportunities may differ.

Khun Chai was appointed Private Secretary to the Princess Mother by HM the King in 1967. He served her for 28 years until her passing in 1995, regarding her as his mentor and role model. Throughout almost three decades of following, observing, and listening to the Princess Mother, Khun Chai adopted many of her traits, among them a mind open to different viewpoints, sensitivity to others, and their situations—and most importantly, a relentless pursuit of excellence for the common good. His own characteristics also contributed to his leadership style, among them attention to detail, insistence on accurate information, need for hands-on involvement at all stages, and a firm belief that anything is possible.

Before MFLF started to work in Doi Tung, a few NGOs had worked there and occasional government projects had reached the area, but they tended to be project-based, focusing only on particular issues. DTDP brought in a new, more holistic, integrated area-based approach. DTDP wanted to fill the gaps in economic and social services until the government agencies could become established in this remote border region.

"QUICK HIT": REFORESTATION AND JOB CREATION

In the first years of DTDP, development priorities were directed toward reforestation and job creation. The Princess Mother envisioned a future where the people of Doi Tung would flourish in revitalized forests. At the request of the Royal Forest Department (the legal owner of the area), DTDP planned to rehabilitate the vast denuded lands with several types of forests appropriate to eco-zones ranging in altitude from 450 to 1500 m above sea level.

Khun Chai and his team, including forestry experts, realized it would take significant initial investment to reforest effectively. Government funding was only sufficient to reforest small patches. MFLF was a small foundation with only limited resources of its own. With the Princess Mother in her late 80s, Khun Chai did not want to wait long to realize her vision. Wanting to act quickly and effectively, he came up with an idea to raise the funds to reforest a large portion of Doi Tung.

As the Princess Mother approached her 90th birthday in 1990, Khun Chai took this opportunity to invite all the provinces of the country along with all government ministries and branches of the security forces to participate in Doi Tung's reforestation program. As the number nine is considered auspicious in Thailand, he devised a project to reforest 9900 rai (1584 ha)[1] divided into 99 plots of 100 rai (16 ha) each. He and his forestry advisors estimated it would cost 300,000 baht, or US$11,675[2] to reforest each plot. He then sold his idea to the governors of all 73 provinces, the prime minister and government ministers, and the heads of the police and armed forces. MFLF received sponsors for 96 plots. Khun Chai asked the Princess Mother, her daughter Princess Galyani Vadhana and her son King Bhumibol Adulyadej each to sponsor one of the remaining three plots. Through these donations, the entire country joined to commemorate the 90th anniversary of the Princess Mother's birth by reviving a significant portion of Doi Tung's critical watershed forests.

The residents of Doi Tung were hired to plant and care for the trees. This was a "quick hit" to provide the people of Doi Tung with steady incomes for the first 3 years. As that work progressed, Khun Chai began to take the next steps: DTDP had to plan for the longer term future of the people. With slightly more than 10,000 people living in 29 villages, based on economic and demographic data of a census taken by the project, Khun Chai calculated that on average one person had to feed 10 family members and that DTDP had to create jobs for about 900 people so everyone would have enough to eat for the entire year. Medium- and long-term plans to generate steady incomes had to be considered.

ECONOMIC FORESTS

Planting the watershed forests was necessary to bring back the water and soil fertility, but this reduced the land area available for shifting cultivation plots by half. More sustainable farming and higher value crops could help generate more income while also stopping further encroachment. DTDP mapped land use in the project area, clearly delineating residential areas, cultivation lands, watershed forests, and a new innovation—economic forests. Khun Chai asked for permission from the government to provide people with land-use certificates for home plots and cultivation areas. Though all the land at Doi Tung was still officially forest under the Royal Forest Department and the certificates did not provide legal ownership, recognition of their usage rights backed by DTDP gave people greater security than before.

Creating economic forests in plots throughout the project area, in addition to the watershed forests, was seen as an answer to provide long-term incomes while encouraging the Doi Tung people to help protect the forests. Several tree crops were explored. Tea was considered but rejected because it needs to be trimmed to waist level, countering its value as a forest tree. A better alternative was Arabica coffee, because it grows well at the same altitudes where opium is planted and produces high-quality beans when taller trees provide it with shade. Growing coffee trees under forest cover would give people a livelihood while also looking after the forest. Man and forest could coexist, each dependent on the other, echoing the aim of the Princess Mother.

Khun Chai also asked forestry experts about indigenous trees at Doi Tung: One they told him about was a type of chestnut. Further study showed various nut trees could grow well in the area as an economic crop. Khun Chai studied global market trends of high-value nuts and found that macadamias were the most expensive and had the highest demand. In 1989, they were mainly grown in just two countries, Australia and the U.S.A. (in Hawaii), with a total production of about 8000 tons—this seemed to be appropriate for the environment of Doi Tung.

Therefore, Arabica coffee and macadamias were selected. Even if they did not thrive, Khun Chai felt that planting them would not be a waste. If the macadamia trees did not produce many nuts, they would still be healthy evergreen trees lasting for generations; and if the coffee did not prove to be commercially viable, its berries would still provide food for birds and animals without harming the forest.

Supporting Economic Forests: Founding Navuti

With its firm belief in economic forestry, DTDP started to work on a business plan. The project was facing three major issues: the need for significant initial investment, the ability to weather the risks of an agro-forestry business, and the need to operate as a sustainable business, earning enough to support 900 workers and their families. In any agro-forestry business, the return on investment is slow. Trees take several years before they fruit (coffee about 3 years and macadamias at least seven when grown from seedlings), and several more years to reach their full potential. Production depends on the uncertainties of weather and other natural conditions, while commodity prices fluctuate greatly. Investors in economic forests had to have firm financial standing and be able and willing to support the project over the long run. Arabica coffee and macadamia plantations were both new to Thailand, neither having been grown yet on a commercial scale (unlike lower quality Robusta coffee). An innovative approach was therefore needed to make the economic forests a reality.

MFLF was a small not-for-profit organization, with neither the capital nor the ability to withstand the risks of such a large undertaking. As Secretary-General of MFLF, Khun Chai was key in orchestrating the collaboration of all sectors that enabled the establishment of Navuti. He worked with government agencies, local government, the community of Doi Tung, and the private sector. He communicated with all parties until they reached a common understanding of the goals of creating economic forests and the company. This followed the development approach of

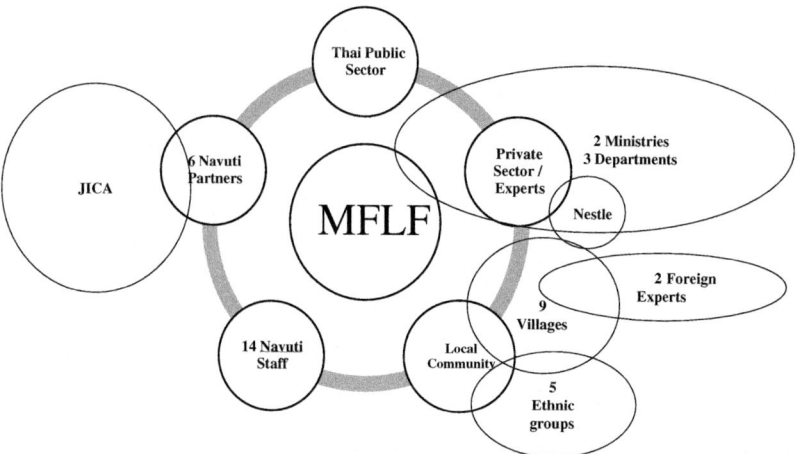

Fig. 8.1 Schematic of stakeholders in Navuti and DTDP's economic forests. *Source* Mae Fah Luang Foundation and the author

MFLF of seeking cooperation and commitment from three levels: central government, local government, and the community. At first, working with the communities was the most challenging. Though they were the intended recipients of the development, they had many doubts and concerns.

From these efforts grew a web of stakeholders, each playing a key role in the social enterprise that developed Doi Tung's economic forests (Fig 8.1).

Developing Collaboration with the Private Sector

Khun Chai studied potential investors among Thai as well as foreign companies in Thailand. He presented a new concept for a company in Thailand, investing for a social cause rather than financial profits. He found six prominent investors both financially strong and able to provide support in business expertise, marketing, and technology. They were the Crown Property Bureau, the Siam Commercial Bank, the Euarchukiati Company, the Bank of Asia (acquired by United Overseas Bank in 2005), the Sumitomo Mitsui Banking Corporation, and Mitsui Company (Thailand) Ltd., each with extensive global networks to

help Navuti tap into additional resources for funding, expertise, and
agro-forestry markets.

In 1989, the Navuti Company was established with three objectives:

1. To revive the environment and develop economic crops on Doi
   Tung and to instill a sense of environmental preservation;
2. To create jobs and generate long-term incomes and to build agricultural skills for the people of Doi Tung; and
3. To set an example in livelihood development.

LOAN FROM JICA

Navuti Co., Ltd., was registered with initial capital of about
US$1.16 million (30 million baht),[3] paid in full by the investors in 1991.
Total investment required at start-up was estimated at twice that amount
or US$2.33 million (60 million baht). The other half was to come
from loans. Thai banks then lent at rates of 12–15%. The investors recommended that a much lower rate could be obtained from the Japan
International Cooperation Agency (JICA), a Japanese government international development organization.

Mitsui (Thailand) Co., Ltd., applied for the loan and in 1992 was
able to secure 128 million yen, or slightly more than US$1 million (then
about 26 million baht).[4] The interest rate was 0.72% plus carrying costs,
or 1.3%. The loan was long-term, for 20 years with a 5-year grace period,
and installment payments thereafter until 2011. The Crown Property
Bureau and the Siam Commercial Bank guaranteed the loan.

The Navuti Board agreed that dividends would not be returned to the
shareholders, but instead donated fully to DTDP and MFLF for social
and environmental development once the loan from JICA had been paid
back. Navuti was thus one of the first and still one of the few authentic
social enterprises in Thailand.

TECHNICAL COLLABORATION WITH NESTLÉ COMPANY

Navuti started planting coffee seedlings provided by the agriculture
department of varieties developed for conditions in north Thailand. Doi
Tung had to ensure they were sufficiently hardy, resistant to disease,
and provided a high yield. On one of her returns to Switzerland, her
home for many years, the Princess Mother told Khun Chai she would
meet with the President of Nestlé S.A. and asked whether there might

be anything Nestlé could do to help DTDP. Khun Chai requested R&D assistance from Nestlé to find suitable, high-yield varieties of Arabica coffee for Doi Tung. Soon after in 1989, Nestlé (Thailand) Co. set up an office at Doi Tung. DTDP allotted a 24-ha demonstration plot at 1200 m above sea level, with the slope facing the northeast where it would be fully exposed to half a day of sun, considered ideal for coffee cultivation.

Nestlé brought 27 Arabica varieties from throughout the world with goal of planting and cross-breeding them with those already in Thailand. Nestlé was able to provide new varieties to Navuti and local farmers, improving the quality of Doi Tung coffee. Nestlé also provided Navuti with technical advice on coffee growing and processing. The Nestlé R&D unit hired about a hundred local residents from two nearby villages in Doi Tung. With on-the-job training in coffee growing, harvesting, and post-harvest processes, many participants became independent coffee farmers, producing good-quality coffee and selling green beans and even roasting coffee for the market. Coffee became their main source of income: In 1988, coffee provided an average of US$547.4 per household each year; by 2012, these villagers earned an average per annum of US$15,751.8 per household from coffee.

Technical Collaboration with Governmental Agencies

When MFLF started implementing DTDP, government agencies contributed by developing infrastructure: roads, electricity, and the water supply. At first, each worked independently, according to the plans and budgets of each agency. In other projects with several government agencies, their work overlapped or was at cross-purposes, with considerable effort and expenses wasted. Khun Chai strove to assure the efforts of all stakeholders would be coordinated. He established a coordinating committee of those working with DTDP, to coordinate overall planning for the project and assure collaboration among the stakeholders, including the villagers. He held meetings almost daily for people to update others on their work, make plans, discuss, and solve problems together. To make sure they worked as efficiently and effectively as possible, Khun Chai often posed the question, "If it were your own money, how would you do this?" This helped the agencies and groups consider what would be the most appropriate solutions, and how best to coordinate their efforts to avoid waste, contradictory efforts, or duplication.

Several government agencies provided technical and in-kind contributions for the economic forests. Navuti purchased 736,000 coffee saplings, 83,200 macadamia seedlings, and 14,000 chestnut trees from the Department of Agriculture to be planted on 582 ha. To help assure the trees survived, the department sent personnel to live and work at DTDP for about a year, providing advice and supervising the care of the trees. The department later donated small coffee roasters and a drying silo and gave training on coffee processing.

Other government agencies that aided the economic forests were the Royal Forest Department, whose officials helped delineate the economic forest plantation areas, and the Land Development Department, which conducted soil surveys to assist in land-use planning. The Highland Agriculture Research Station gave technical training and advice to local people and project staff.

COMMUNITY COLLABORATION AND EMPOWERMENT

The most important group of stakeholders at DTDP was the local people. No matter how much the private sector might contribute or government agencies might assist, Khun Chai realized the work of DTDP would succeed only with the understanding, strong support, and involvement of local residents. When DTDP started, Khun Chai recruited young people from among the villagers and new graduates able to speak the local languages. These young people (known as volunteers) lived in the villages and serve as liaisons between the villagers and the project. They understood the lives, traditions, and needs of the people and were able to collect accurate information and communicate it to DTDP. They played an important role in setting up Navuti, helping to explain the concept and objectives of the company and the benefits that the local people were expected to gain.

MFLF learned from the volunteers that most local people were skeptical about DTDP and plans for Navuti and the economic forests. Though the land they had used for their traditional agriculture was officially illegally encroached forestland, it was still their main source of livelihood and they saw it being taken away for the forests. They did not believe the economic forests could provide a sustainable living. Too often, government agencies had provided training and implemented development projects in Doi Tung, including the introduction of coffee trees; but these earlier efforts failed, leaving the people with no confidence in development projects. A major challenge of MFLF was to gain the commitment of the local people to DTDP.

Khun Chai recognized that close communication and timely action with tangible results were essential to earn the trust of the local community. He singled out one of the most respected local leaders, a village shaman, to explain the objectives of the economic forests. Khun Chai explained how the founding of Navuti Co., Ltd., and the establishment of economic forests could provide sustainable long-term livelihoods for the people of Doi Tung and that villagers would be hired and trained by Navuti to grow high-value crops. The village leader was convinced, and he offered his own cultivation land to Navuti to grow coffee and macadamia trees. Together with the volunteers, he helped to recruit hundreds of local people to work for Navuti.

This was how Khun Chai began to turn around the fortunes of the poor subsistence farmers of Doi Tung, first giving them wages for sufficient income. Workers at Navuti earned US$1.50 (about 40 baht) a day, consistent with rates then elsewhere in rural Thailand. This immediately raised their average income from US$106 per person per year (much of this as cash earned from opium) to US$380. They now had steady and legal work and income throughout the year and, for the first time, could enjoy some security in their lives. With this immediate increase in income and secure jobs, trust was earned from the communities, and they began to cooperate and participate in the project's activities. Just as important was the on-the-job training the villagers received in basic procedures of planting and caring for coffee and macadamia trees, and in harvesting methods, by Thai and foreign experts. These were basic skills used for their own coffee farms in later years.

A key objective was to provide work for as many people as possible. Navuti set up six plantations scattered over the project area, to be accessible to as many of the 29 villages as possible and provide work and transfer skills to people throughout DTDP. The company engaged whoever needed work, including older schoolchildren wanting to work on weekends, holidays, and school breaks.

Difficult Times: Low Productivity and Financial Crisis

By 1991, Doi Tung had planted all its economic forests and started caring for the trees. According to the Navuti business plan, the coffee trees were expected to yield about 1 kg of cherries per year. This was a conservative estimate, as Arabica often produced 2–3 kg of cherries annually after

3–4 years. The macadamia trees were expected to start fruiting after 7 years. These yields even before the trees reached full maturity were expected to provide enough green coffee beans and macadamia nuts for commercial sale, giving Navuti sufficient cash flow to begin repaying its loan to JICA.

However, Navuti and its partners faced two crises—one after the other—that nearly doomed the economic forests of DTDP. The first was much lower productivity than expected. The second was the financial crisis of 1997. Coffee yields were half of what was forecast for the first years and the quality was below standard. After 5 years, the macadamia started bearing nuts, but by year seven, the yield had not increased. This was a result of several factors. As this was the first attempt in Thailand to grow Arabica coffee and macadamias on a commercial scale, the country had no practical experts in establishing either crop. There were only researchers and lecturers whose knowledge, skills, and techniques came from research or from books, not from experience in environments similar to Doi Tung. Some of the training and information provided to the foremen as well as the growers was thus not practical or helpful in addressing problems in this particular location. Furthermore, the foremen and growers themselves lacked discipline and sufficient attention to the importance of proper procedures. This led to several problems: not using fertilizer when appropriate, or not pruning the trees at the right time.

Just as bad for quality, instead of picking only the ripe, red cherries as instructed, the workers picked all the cherries together, whether ripe or green, to finish work quickly. They were paid by the day, so they did not care about the quality of the beans. Navuti lacked strict quality control in processing, using all the cherries, whether ripe or not, to make the green beans. New directions were needed, to improve the yields and quality of the coffee and macadamia and improve the capacity of the Navuti staff as well as the growers. Khun Chai needed to take decisive action.

With the much lower than expected yields and quality in the first years, Navuti struggled with cash flow. Just as production started to improve, for reasons described in the next section, the 1997 Asian Economic Crisis hit. Like other companies that borrowed from overseas, Navuti was badly affected by the baht being devalued more than 100% in just a few months.[5] Navuti's 128 million yen loan doubled from about 27 million to nearly 55 million baht. The Board of Directors of Navuti believed the company could not survive. They wanted to inject the additional funds needed to pay back the JICA loan and then close down the company.

Khun Chai resisted. He believed the social consequences of shutting down Navuti and ending the economic forest program would be dire. Thousands of Doi Tung residents who relied on the economic forests would be without incomes. This would defeat the purpose of DTDP, as they might need to return to drug smuggling, selling their daughters, and other illicit activities to make a living. Besides, yields were just beginning to improve. The people of Doi Tung were just starting to believe in their future. Closing Navuti and ending the economic forests would dash their hopes and damage the trust built up over the years between DTDP and the communities.

Empowering the People and Building Value

Starting the social enterprise Navuti was an innovation for Thailand. Facing the dual crises required even newer and more innovative approaches. Khun Chai identified a key cause of the low coffee and macadamia yields: the lack of ownership and incentives for the workers and foremen. They lacked interest and had an inadequate sense of responsibility, because whatever happened they still received their wages. Most urgent was the need to find practical experts on coffee and macadamias who could help solve the problems of productivity and quality control, and train the staff to understand the importance of proper procedures and how to solve problems themselves.

Learning from Doers

- **Coffee Expert**

In 1994, Khun Chai was introduced to Mr. Andy Roy from Kona, Hawaii, a region renowned for its high-quality Arabica coffee. Mr. Roy's Bay View Farm was the largest Arabica coffee farm in Hawaii and ranked second best. DTDP invited him to visit and provide advice on Navuti operations. He took considerable time to study the Navuti coffee farms and procedures. During several visits to Doi Tung, he changed techniques and provided on-site training to staff and workers on basic methods to improve the condition of the trees.

Khun Chai then sent the Navuti General Manager and supervisors to Mr. Roy's farm for 1 month of on-the-job training. They worked full time, 15 h a day, to understand coffee at all stages, and learn techniques for the entire process—from seed to cup—of producing quality coffee: from tending the trees, to harvest, post-harvest processes, roasting, and cupping.

- **Macadamia Expert**

Australia, as one of two countries dominating the world macadamia market, was quite advanced in macadamia research and development. In 1995, Khun Chai asked an Australian friend with good connections to the agricultural sector to introduce him to macadamia growers who could help provide practical expertise to Navuti. Two growers were recommended for their high-quality product. Khun Chai decided to visit the smaller farm, that of Mr. Ron Barnett. Mr. Barnett started his farm in 1989, the same year Navuti first planted macadamias. His farm had about 6000 trees, was clean and well kept, and had the highest recovery percentage in the country. Only two people operated the farm, Mr. Barnett and his wife, using a small tractor. When Khun Chai visited them, he knew he had come to the right place. He invited Mr. Barnett to become an advisor to Navuti.

After visiting the economic forests, Mr. Barnett advised the staff that their method of pruning the macadamia trees was damaging the trees. Pruning macadamia trees were unlike pruning other fruit trees. Branches that could bear the most nuts were being cut, an important reason why productivity was low. Navuti's General Manager was sent to work on Mr. Barnett's farm for 1 month, to learn the entire process of growing and harvesting macadamias. Mr. Barnett also took him to other farms and processing plants to broaden his experience. Mr. Barnett continues to assist Doi Tung to improve the macadamia plantations, restore, and maintain the trees, and train staff in post-harvest technologies and processing macadamia into various snacks.

Learning from Mistakes

At the start of the economic forests, Navuti planted coffee and macadamia trees together on each site, with macadamias to be the cover crop for the coffee. This turned out to be a costly mistake. Both experts suggested the two crops be separated, as each needed different conditions and nutrients. Although Arabica coffee grows best with some shade, the macadamia trees provided too much cover for the coffee to get enough sun, leaving the coffee trees unhealthy and susceptible to disease. Macadamias require a clear and clean ground so when fully mature nuts fall they can be easily harvested. With coffee undergrowth, fallen nuts were damaged and easily eaten by rats and squirrels. As a result of these realizations, DTDP and Navuti decided to allot three of their six sites for coffee and the other three for macadamias. The other trees in each plot, though already mature, were removed. The total overhaul of the economic forest crops took 3 years to complete.

By 1997, the economic forest crops were rearranged. It was now time to consider how to improve the commitment and involvement of the workers. Khun Chai recognized they needed more incentives than just being wage laborers. He proposed to the Navuti Board of Directors that the company should change its policy from hiring labor to renting coffee trees to workers who were interested and had the skills to care for the trees. This would give them a sense of ownership, and responsibility for the entire process from growing and tending the trees to harvesting the ripe cherries, allowing them to improve the farms, the quality of their crop, and increase their incomes. It would also be an important incentive for the farmers' self-development, as Navuti would select and purchase only ripe coffee cherries to assure quality and guarantee the purchase price. Navuti in turn would support the farmers with technical and practical knowledge. Navuti was to provide the fertilizer and equipment at the start of the season, the costs of which would then be deducted from the sale of the cherries. This was to encourage the farmers to become micro-entrepreneurs, learning to work more efficiently, reducing costs where possible, and increasing the quality of their crop.

The board approved the proposal, and the trees changed hands. Navuti set the rental rate at US$0.04 (one baht) per tree, with the farmers paying half and DTDP subsidizing the other half. Though the rental rate was low, it was highly symbolic to the farmers, encouraging them to continue with coffee rather than cut down the trees to switch to other crops. The farmers could not rent the land as it was legally under the Royal Forest Department, but by renting the trees, they were given a sense of security and continuity they had not had before, as long as they continued growing coffee.

Khun Chai consulted with Navuti staff, those working directly with the coffee and the farmers, on how to divide the plots. They assumed one family could tend about 3000 trees, producing at least 3000 kilograms of cherries, earning US$900–$1000. Where the condition of the trees was below average, more would be provided to assure sufficient yield and income. Seventy-five hard-working local farmers were among the first to accept the challenge. Plots were selected at random near their homes to avoid claims of favoritism. After the first group showed their choice had paid off and they enjoyed much higher incomes, other families quickly took the remaining plots in the next 2 years.

Within just 1 year, the farmers took better care of the trees, worked longer hours, followed proper procedures using correct techniques, and worked on schedule. The trees were much healthier, and yields improved from 0.5 to 1.61 kg per tree. Because Navuti only purchased ripe red cherries, farmers now picked the cherries one by one, only when ripe, to earn the guaranteed price. With better quality cherries, the quality of green beans also greatly improved. This initiative turned into a win-win situation for all, reducing Navuti's costs and burden of quality control and increasing the quality of the product, while improving villagers' incomes, raising them to a new level of economic production, and improving their livelihoods. Macadamia plantations, by contrast, still had to be operated directly by Navuti. Experience in Australia and Hawaii had shown that slight variations in weather could lead to significant fluctuations in yield. Navuti and MFLF still needed to bear the risks of this tree crop. In 1997, yields started to improve somewhat, and skills of the staff and workers in production and processing were progressively improving.

Overcoming the Economic Downturn: Convincing the Partners and Building Value

Khun Chai believed in the people of Doi Tung and their ability to grow good-quality coffee and macadamias if given ownership and sufficient incentives. He convinced the partners to continue supporting Navuti, asking the board to give MFLF another year to get Navuti back on target. The board eventually complied and agreed to pool their resources to save the company. Three of the largest shareholders, Mitsui Company (Thailand), Siam Commercial Bank, and the Crown Property Bureau, increased the capital by another 10 million baht (US$232,500)[6] immediately, an additional 15 million baht (US$386,100)[7] in 1999, and finally 5 million baht (US$116,000)[8] in 2000. The Crown Property Bureau took responsibility for increasing the capital of the other founding companies, thus becoming Navuti's largest shareholder.

When the coffee and macadamia plants began to bear fruit in 1994, attention turned to post-harvest processing. Coffee cherries had to be processed into green beans and macadamia nuts into kernels for sale. A small processing plant was built in 1994 to handle the increased volume of coffee cherries. The staff that had receiving training from the Agricultural Engineering Research Institute in Thailand and Mr. Andy Roy in Kona, Hawaii, was able to manage the post-harvest processes, using the small dryer and coffee roaster contributed by the Department of Agriculture. With its roasting facility to add value to the coffee beans, DTDP first sold its roasted coffee to local shops and later packaged the roasted beans for sale under MFLF's DoiTung brand. Each step added more value to the product. By the early 2000s, MFLF had opened its own Cafés DoiTung in Bangkok, at Doi Tung, and in selected Northern Thai cities.

MFLF started purchasing macadamia-processing equipment in 1995, following the advice and with the assistance of Mr. Ron Barnett. Staff who trained at his farm and on-site in Doi Tung now carried out post-harvest processing of the macadamia nuts.

MFLF began earning income from sales of these value-added coffee and macadamia products, using this money to share Navuti's burden of repaying the JICA loan. MFLF bought coffee cherries and macadamia nuts from Navuti at a price that allowed Navuti to pay JICA US$200,000 annually. Final repayment of the loan was made in 2011. While this meant MFLF had to buy the product at higher-than-market prices, MFLF could make up for this higher price by selling the higher value-added goods. By 2000, packaged roasted coffee under the DoiTung brand sold for five times the value of green beans. When sold at the Cafés DoiTung, the value of coffee in cups rose to US$177 per kg, nearly 300 times the price of green beans(Table 8.1).

With value-added processing, income earned by MFLF from macadamia nuts also increased considerably. Nuts that sold as raw kernels for US$13 per kg could fetch US$30 sold as roasted, flavored, and packaged nuts under the DoiTung brand. Even more value was added—up to US$55 per kg—when the nuts were used in macadamia cookies, and up to US$140 per kg when sold as chocolate-coated macadamia.

Even more important were the benefits derived by the people of Doi Tung. The social businesses of coffee and macadamias provided incomes totaling 150 million baht (more than US$4 million)[9] to many of the

Table 8.1 Coffee Yield and Income, 1994–2000

Year	Yield/Tree (kg)	Yield/Year (kg)	Sales ($US)
1994	0.80	35,469	145,260
1995	1.00	44,339	230,251
1996	1.43	60,245	444,033
1997	1.63	65,827	552,663
1998	1.63	58,696	640,144
1999	1.75	60,466	693,078
2000	1.88	65,802	702,272

Source Mae Fah Luang Foundation and the author

nearly 10,000 residents of Doi Tung. Together with the development of high-value handicrafts, horticulture, and support of tourism services by DTDP, the social businesses based on the economic forests were crucial to improving the incomes and lives of the people of Doi Tung, raising their average household income from less than US$3000 per year in 2006, only half the average household income in Chiang Rai Province that year, to nearly US$13,000 per year, over a third higher than the provincial average(Fig. 8.2).

This partnership of stakeholders from all sectors—private companies, government, local authorities, and communities—in creating the successful economic forests of Doi Tung, the social enterprises of Navuti and DTDP, and the value-added businesses of MFLF, was possible under the leadership of Khun Chai. His charisma and energy built faith and trust among the stakeholders and staff. His "it can be done" attitude became infectious, spurring on the efforts of Navuti and DTDP staff and leaders of Doi Tung villages. By always going into the field himself, checking what actually was happening, talking with villagers, his commitment also encouraged the commitment of all partners in the enterprises. His measurement "What do the people get out of it?" led everyone toward the common good, and his exhortation "What would you do if it was your own money?" made sure everyone worked efficiently and effectively.

FUTURE CHALLENGES

In 2002, the organizational structure of DTDP changed. Much of the outside support of the first years ended and the project could fund itself. The decision to support Navuti proved right. DTDP and Navuti

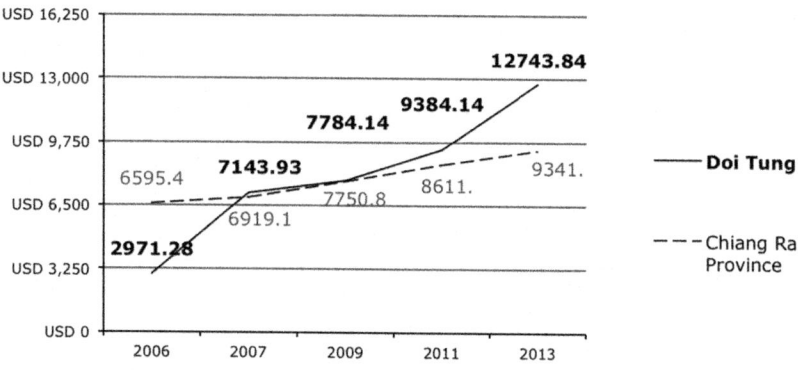

Fig. 8.2 Average Income per Household: Doi Tung Compared to Chiang Rai, 2006–2013. *Source* Mae Fah Luang Foundation and the author

were now on a firm enough foundation. With production from the coffee farms and macadamia plantations steady and the income consistent, establishing the DoiTung brand in the market now became a priority in order to maintain the incomes of coffee farmers and macadamia workers, and provide revenue for DTDP's social and environmental programs. Some Doi Tung residents even became coffee entrepreneurs themselves, establishing local coffee businesses handling the entire coffee value chain, from growing to processing and selling to cafés.

Along with these new conditions, new challenges also arose. Khun Chai turned leadership of DTDP over to others; at the same time, the business environment for macadamias and especially coffee changed dramatically.

Grooming the Next Generation of Leaders

Khun Chai believed in working himself out of his job to develop the next generation of leaders. He always believed and wanted to prove that DTDP's success was due to effective management that could be applied by others, and not due to the Princess Mother or him. He often said, "If I dropped dead tomorrow, would you be able to continue? It's time for you to get up and take control of your own destiny." For his succession, he groomed three tiers of leadership.

Khunying Puangroi Diskul na Ayudhya[10] was designated as leader of the first tier. Serving for years as the Princess Mother's lady-in-waiting, she learned firsthand from the Princess Mother and had observed DTDP since its inception. Khun Chai took on a new role as CEO, responsible for policy and overall supervision of the project, turning management of daily operations and the business units over to the first tier team.

The leader of the second tier was Mom Luang Dispanadda Diskul, or Duke, Khun Chai's son. As a teenager, he helped plant coffee trees in the economic forest. After working several years in the private sector, Duke formally joined MFLF in 2004, setting up the first Café DoiTung in Bangkok. In 2007, he was asked to be Operations Director at the Centre for Social Entrepreneurship, a new unit set up to extend MFLF's development work elsewhere in Thailand and overseas. He is now Deputy CEO overseeing the development and social business of DTDP.

Khun Chai saw the third-tier leaders as those who would take DTDP and MFLF into the next generation. He built a first-class team highly skilled at grassroots interventions. Many were young volunteers and Navuti staff who had started to work with DTDP or the company in their early years. Among them was the General Manager of Navuti, who trained in Hawaii and Australia, and later assigned to lead MFLF's first development project in Myanmar. He was appointed Director of Field Operations in 2002 and is now leading a 35-member development team, many from the Doi Tung community. Two key members of this development team, the middle managers, were an early Navuti employee who worked with villagers as plantation officer, and the former foreman at the Nestlé plantation. They now apply their experience of working with local communities to helping MFLF projects elsewhere in Thailand, and in Myanmar, Afghanistan, and Aceh, Indonesia.

One early staff member who was assigned to train in Hawaii has since became integral to DTDP coffee business as master roaster and manager of the entire coffee supply chain from trees to cups. Another who first joined Navuti as a plantation officer now oversees all macadamia farming at Doi Tung, supervising a team of seven full-time employees and hundreds of local workers. Yet, another early DTDP worker, who first helped supervise reforestation then joined Navuti to oversee coffee plantations and work with local farmers, was recently appointed head of the Coffee Research Farm of Navuti.

Many of the third-tier leaders from the economic forests, and from DTDP's other business units and administration, are from the local communities and grew up with the project. Khun Chai has succeeded in fostering a new generation of leaders.

COFFEE AND MACADAMIAS UNDER TRANSITION

Despite its many achievements, the future of DTDP, Navuti, and its economic forests remains uncertain, in part because of DTDP's own success. Coffee farmers who rent the coffee trees are now in their late 40s and older. Many are spending less time and effort maintaining their coffee, while others have stopped working altogether. Their children received an education and have grown up; they now have Thai citizenship and new opportunities to pursue different aspirations than their parents. Only a few see a future in agriculture and continuing the traditional way of life. Most prefer less strenuous, better-paid work and opportunities in the wider world. Some coffee farmers have also tried to earn more money by planting more trees in their plots, hoping to increase their yield; instead, this reduced productivity, producing lower yields, and poorer quality coffee.

Changing weather patterns has also affected yields. Longer rainy seasons seriously damaged both coffee and macadamia harvests. The amount of coffee cherries sold to Navuti has declined since 2010, reducing the company's income and that of DTDP and the farmers as well. The coffee shop business has also faced increasing competition. Well-known international brands came to dominate the Thai market, and new ones have tried to secure a place. Many small Thai coffee shops proliferated, competing in price though not in quality. With the opening of the ASEAN Economic Community in 2015, coffee tariffs were lifted, and Thai coffee will face increasing competition from neighboring countries. Cafés DoiTung has to find a new strategy while maintaining the concept of a social business in which benefits to people are more important than profits. While the existing model of the Cafés DoiTung is still thriving in some locations, others are facing faltering sales. Eight Cafés DoiTung have closed since 2010.

NEW VISION FOR THE FUTURE

In 2012, Duke established a task force to address the new challenges. Some were assigned to solving production problems, while others were asked to reassess the market niche for DoiTung roasted coffee and Café DoiTung. Instead of competing with major international brands, DoiTung has to identify its target customers and meet their needs. The concepts behind the DoiTung coffee and Café DoiTung have to change to survive.

Duke and his team believe that DoiTung coffee and macadamia nuts stand out because of their origin, high quality and total control of quality from tree to cups and snacks. They assembled new teams of world-class experts in coffee, to teach, train, and improve work, from the field to processing the value-added products, marketing, and sales. This should also help the people of Doi Tung acquire new skills and techniques to sustain their livelihood and the environment. But development takes time, good management, and capable leaders. With the inherited DNA of "it can be done", Duke and his task force can drive the change, learning from DTDP's history, and innovating to develop new approaches, with one thing remaining the same: everything is being done for the common good of the Doi Tung people.

For the past 3 years, Navuti has set up model coffee plots to strengthen coffee cultivation. They work with the most successful farmers to identify best practices, intending to convince their peers to learn and take better care of their plantations. Navuti has sought Japanese experts to develop new coffee varieties with a unique character most suitable for Doi Tung.

DTDP has created new collaborations with Japanese coffee importers, roasters, and retailers, sourcing coffee directly from farmers to penetrate the Japanese market. Navuti, DTDP, and MFLF are coming full circle with Japanese partners: They had not only provided Navuti with assistance ever since its establishment but also maintained good relationships over the years. DoiTung coffee has always been well received in Japan. Kaldi, for example, buys 50–70 tons of DoiTung coffee each year.

MFLF and DTDP now plan to work with a social enterprise in the Japanese coffee business, setting up coffee shops in Japan—currently in Muji Café and Tokyo University—to create jobs for local underprivileged people, especially the elderly, the unemployed, and women who need to work outside their homes. The main objective is to return pride and dignity to the people. Duke believes that these Japanese baristas, trained with good knowledge and skills, can effectively represent DoiTung coffee. They can be the future ambassadors of DoiTung or even entrepreneurs to share Doi Tung stories and expertise with their communities. What the Japanese companies have given to MFLF since the beginning of DTDP and founding of Navuti are now allowing MFLF to give back to Japan.

LESSONS LEARNED

One of the key factors of DTDP is its people-centric leadership, as shown in the following examples:

- HRH said, "No one wants to be bad but they just do not have the opportunity to be good."
- HRH also believed that all people can develop to realize their full potential, become self-reliant, and coexist with nature if their basic needs are fulfilled.
- Khun Chai continued HRH's legacy by empowering the local people and his staff to realize their full capacity.
- People-centric leaders empathize with people's situation, problems, needs and wants, and put themselves in other people's shoes.
- Khun Chai came up with a plan that would absorb risks for the local people who were reluctant to join Navuti due to bad experiences with earlier projects that failed.
- Khun Chai realized that giving Navuti farmers a sense of ownership and the prospect of earning more would provide the best incentive.
- There was a willingness and ability to talk to and convince people at all levels.
- Efforts were made to inspire others to work to achieve common goals.
- Perseverance & continuity were important.
- Timeliness was an important consideration. Knowing the appropriate stage of action.
- Understanding the interconnected consequences of action was key to success.

Khun Chai fostered the new generation of leaders at Doi Tung to sustain its achievement. This was done through:

- learning by doing and from their mistakes, as in the three rounds of surveys of the economic forests;
- believing in accurate first-hand information and data and the reality they experience on the ground;
- on-the-ground training from expert practitioners (i.e., Mr. Ron Barnett and Mr. Andy Roy), and
- leading by example, committed attitude.

Going forward, Duke's special task force considered how to best analyze, plan, and implement measures to revitalize Doi Tung coffee and macadamia nut farming and marketing:

- Assess what the actual conditions are acquire first-hand information and data.
- Analyze past social and financial trends to project future goals.
- Keep the goals grounded in the people's abilities and aspirations.
- Maximize the lessons learned from past experience to expand benefits further.
- Form a team and acquire necessary partnerships.

EPILOGUE

The team believes the recent downturn in Navuti's fortunes is that the farmers are losing faith and interest in coffee farming. To address this, Navuti has developed new planning incentive schemes to encourage the younger generation to work on the farms in order to address the problems of an aging labor force and low productivity.

Navuti set up model coffee plots to identify best practices with the successful entrepreneur farmers. The coffee growers still have the right to use the land and ownership of the trees, and all the yields still belong to them. Under the proposal, however, there has been a change in payment schemes. Navuti has turned the farm owners back into wage earners to arm them with new knowledge and practices; once improved practices have been introduced and assured, the coffee trees, and the risks, will be transferred back to the local farmers.

The next phase of responsibility for DTDP involves upgrading roasting, processing, and marketing, thereby moving toward the premium coffee market and away from the price-competitive Thai market. "Business as usual" is shifting to become a social enterprise with a focus on empowering people. The trained baristas with good knowledge and skills will be the future ambassadors of DoiTung or entrepreneurs to share Doi Tung stories and expertise with their communities. At the same time, some people in Doi Tung, especially in Akha Pha Hee village, are seeking to build their own community enterprises. In order to strike a balance between economic, social, and environmental aspects, DTDP has sought experts to prepare practical business models for future community coffee businesses. Macadamias are in a better position than coffee in terms of productivity and income. Navuti has prepared incentive schemes to encourage the younger generation to work on the macadamia plantations and factories, to address the problem of an aging labor force while also increasing productivity.

Navuti, DTDP, and MFLF are coming full circle with Japanese partners, not just because they have provided Navuti assistance from its establishment—but because they have always had good relationships and an exchangeof knowledge

NOTES

1. A *rai* is a Thai measure of area equal to 1600 m^2 or 0.16 ha.
2. 1 US Dollar = 25.7 baht in 1989.
3. From 1989 to 1991, the average exchange rate of US$1 to Thai baht fluctuated between 25.4 and 25.8, usually hovering around 25.7, the rate used here (Data obtained from the Exchange Rates Archive of the Titi Tudorancea Bulletin website: http://www.tititudorancea.com/z/exchange_rates.htm).
4. Yen to US$ rates were around 125 yen to US$1 for much of 1992, and yen to Thai baht rates averaged around 4.9 yen to 1 Thai baht during the year (Data obtained from the Exchange Rates Archive of the Titi Tudorancea Bulletin website: http://www.tititudorancea.com/z/exchange_rates.htm).
5. The exchange rate dropped from 21.3 baht per 100 yen in early July 1997 to 42.7 baht per 100 yen in late January 1998. Data obtained from the Exchange Rates Archive of the Titi Tudorancea Bulletin website: http://www.tititudorancea.com/z/exchange_rates.htm. In the same period the exchange rate of the baht to US dollar went from baht 24.5 to US$ 1.00 to baht 54.1 to US$ 1.00.
6. By March 1998, the exchange rate had stabilized at about baht 43 to US$1.00. Data obtained from the historical foreign exchange records of the Federal Reserve Bank of New York website: http://www.ny.frb.org/markets/fxrates/historical/home.cfm.
7. In 1999 the exchange rate fluctuated between nearly baht 37 and up to baht 41 per US$1.00, with the average for the year around baht 38.5. Data obtained from the historical foreign exchange records of the Federal Reserve Bank of New York website.
8. The exchange rate again went up to about baht 43 to US$1.00 for much of 2000. Data obtained from the historical foreign exchange records of the Federal Reserve Bank of New York website.
9. Exchange rates from the mid to late 2000s ranged from about 32 baht up to nearly 40 baht per US$1.00. An average rate of about baht 35–36 to US$1.00 was used. Data obtained from the historical foreign exchange records of the Federal Reserve Bank of New York website.
10. "Khunying" is the Thai equivalent of "Lady".

AUTHOR BIOGRAPHY

Ayano Hirose Nishihara is an Assistant Professor, Department of Global Business, College of Business, Rikkyo University, and a research collaborator to Professor Emeritus Ikujiro Nonaka. She received her B.A. (Law) from Nagoya University, MBA in 2005 and DBA in 2011 from The Graduate School of International Corporate Strategy, Hitotsubashi University. Prior to her academic track, she worked as an assistant manager at NEC Corporation. Her research topics include knowledge creation at public and private organizations and communities, knowledge-creating leadership, and social innovation. Her recent publications include: Nonaka, I., Hirose, A., & Takeda, Y. (2016). "Meso"-Foundations of Dynamic Capabilities: Team-Level Synthesis and Distributed Leadership as the Source of Dynamic Creativity. *Global Strategy Journal,* 6(3), 168–182.

CHAPTER 9

Transformation and Innovation: People-Centric Leadership and Management to Tackle Social Issues

Woothisarn Tanchai and Kittima Bunnag

INTRODUCTION: KEY CHALLENGES FOR LEADERS

This chapter presents an overview of innovative approaches undertaken to solve social issues and develop communities in Thailand, connecting them to hypotheses on management factors and the development of leadership necessary to facilitate transition and innovation. This chapter builds on the Thailand contexts presented in Chaps. 3 and 8, synthesizing the practice and theory, the particular and universal, and subjectivity with objectivity. In other words, it provides a bridge between case studies (Chaps. 2–8) and theory verification (Chap. 10).

There is widespread awareness of the global uncertainties and challenges we face today, which leads us to consider what capabilities strong

W. Tanchai (✉)
Department of Community Development, Faculty of Social Administration, Thammasat University, Bangkok, Thailand
e-mail: woothisarn@gmail.com

K. Bunnag
King Prajadhipok's Institute, Bangkok, Thailand
e-mail: kbun88@gmail.com

© The Author(s) 2018   175
A. Hirose Nishihara et al. (eds.), *Knowledge Creation in Community Development*, DOI 10.1007/978-3-319-57481-3_9

leaders require. As a result of global uncertainty, deepening financial and economic crises and unprecedented challenges, today's leaders face a new set of challenges and changes that are rapidly transforming both the public and private sectors. Even leaders with the ability to adapt their strategies are only just keeping pace with change. In creating solutions for complex issues and driving change in a rapidly fluctuating world, leaders need to be both strategic and agile, possess collaboration skills and leadership resilience as well as a strong capacity to appraise uncertainty. The traditional expectation is that leadership is created and delivered by one person—a leader. As the complexity of organizations and the rapid pace of change are becoming too great for any one person to cope with, more organizations see leadership as a function of a group working collaboratively. To derive the greatest benefits from expertise, we need different leadership skills and behaviors than before.

We are also facing a paradigm shift, which leads us to consider the meaning of good governance and good growth. Government and public sector leaders need to play key roles in the shift toward increasing uncertainty by refocusing their organizations on the changing environment and projecting a clear vision for the future, while at the same time delivering affordable services. Moreover, to ensure that public services reach the best possible standards, governments need to find the right balance between managing internal organizational efficiency and the effectiveness of external delivery. A key challenge in public administration is to achieve a balance between the materialization of good governance and good growth in a context that is customer driven and characterized by fierce competition and change at both regional and global levels.

To address these changing demands in today's world, we therefore need public sector leaders that possess the skills to survive in this uncertain world. They need to be able to rethink the role of government, develop policies to achieve good growth, and tackle deficits by doing things very differently. Public sector leaders need to think of different target groups/stakeholders, the most important of which is citizens. Leaders need to keep citizens at the very center, meeting their needs effectively. In connection with this, the new public management (NPM) approach attaches importance to civil participation, which is the foundation of democratic principles focused on public needs. As a key factor at the heart of administration, the citizen is the government's partner in various activities. Therefore, administration requires participation, consultation, transparency, and systematic working approaches.

If we focus on Thailand, we can see growing social and economic issues, namely poverty and disparities. The effects of globalization on Thailand's political, economic, and social realms are ever increasing. On the political front, decentralization has taken center stage and now encompasses the strengthening of local administrations via delegation of powers and duties of the central and provincial administrations. In addition, decentralization involves a new model of area management that does not conform to a traditional administrative structure (e.g., Changwat (province), Amphoe (district), Tambon (subdistrict), or Muban (village)). Instead, decentralization attaches greater importance to stakeholders, including participation of local administrations, the private sector, and civil society. These approaches—good governance and a people-centric approach—are embedded in the Royal Decree on Principle and Procedure for Good Public Governance, B.E. 2546 (2003), which proclaims that public administration must maximize public welfare and cater to popular demands.

Economically, Thailand's continual development has paradoxically widened the country's wealth gap. The majority of people, therefore, still depend on the government for necessities such as health care and education. Inevitably, restructuring the allocation of resources and economic interests is on the agenda, as access by the poor to resources and government services is essential. With this in mind, the new challenge facing public administration is to find ways of dealing with ongoing issues of poverty and disparities. According to the Office of the National Economic and Social Development Board (NESDB), Thailand's highly unequal income distribution persists. In 2011, 20% of the country's richest people earned as much as 54.38% of the total income, while 20% of the country's poorest people earned just 4.91%. Of the total 21,821,000 households, poor households in both urban and rural areas accounted for 2,344,000, or 10.74%.

Advocating for a reduction in inequalities—politically, economically, and socially—is imperative in tackling poverty, as opposed to adhering to the traditional dependency concept of relying on support from wealthier philanthropists or the public sector. In the country's strategic plan for 2013–2018, the government and related agencies were assigned to address the following issues: increasing the country's competitiveness, escaping the middle-income trap, reducing disparities, embracing environmentally friendly practices, striving for balance, integrating public administration, and preparing for the ASEAN community. A government resolution on November 2, 2012, required all related agencies to adhere to inclusive growth policies in accordance with the seven facets of the country's strategic plan. They include (1) improving the quality of education, (2) improving the quality and standards of healthcare services, (3) assisting the elderly, children, women, and underprivileged, (4) creating opportunities and income for small- and medium-sized enterprises and economic communities, (5) labor, (6) court systems to reduce disparity, and (7) materialization of anti-corruption mechanisms, good governance, and transparency. Therefore, inequality reduction and poverty eradication have steadily become part of the country's national agenda.

Ongoing disparities, inequality, crime, and conflict require tangible structural changes to achieve sustainable reform. Unraveling disparities and conflicts, as well as promoting people's well-being, should be the foremost obligation of both central and local administrations. A stable and self-reliant country hinges on the adherence of leaders to a people-centric approach that provides convenient and easy accessibility to services, while at the same time promoting self-reliance, social participation, and social integration without government assistance. Initiatives for social innovation therefore need to be activated in every corner of the society, thus mobilizing untapped knowledge resources to solve societal problems.

This overview reveals the challenges faced by many organizations amid the current global situation of uncertainty and change, as well as efforts by the government/public sector to mobilize people-centered services in accordance with new public management approaches. Thus, leadership and management can play an integral part in an organization's success or failure, which affects the dynamism of social innovation in the domain that is administered by an organization.

WHAT GUIDES AND SHAPES THE FUTURE PUBLIC SECTOR?

In seeking to promote structural change, the public sector faces several dilemmas, including global uncertainty and ongoing economic and social issues, as well as the difficulties involved in introducing a new approach that emphasizes public sector management. To achieve the goal of citizen-centered advocacy, maximum resource allocation, and the ability to adapt to new challenges, the public sector must take into account the following strategic enablers (see Box 9.1). By institutionalizing these effectively, a public organization can become a potent social innovator that can efficiently cope with the mounting societal challenges through innovative solutions. The following sections discuss each of these strategic enablers in turn.

Box 9.1
Strategic enablers for citizen-centered advocacy

- *Understand and reflect current issues and future realities through people's insights*
- *Involvement of stakeholders inside and outside the organization*
- *Centered around the citizens/people*
- *Achieving sustainable outcomes*

---

(1) Understand and reflect on current issues and future realities through people's insights

The foremost step in prioritizing the people's well-being is problem identification: knowing the needs of the people. The ability of related agencies and local administrations to foresee the hardships of the local people, even before complaints or resentment can emerge, is of paramount importance, and necessary in providing a foundation for further action.

In addition, local administrations are encouraged to implement policy initiatives that cater for people's needs. Effective public sector management is built on the goal of improving the quality of life for citizens, maximizing resource allocation, and a profound understanding of current issues and future realities through people's insights. The public sector must give priority to engagement with citizens, openness, empathy, and consideration of governing for and with citizens.

(2) Involvement of stakeholders in and outside the public sector

Stakeholder participation is another key component of an effective decision-making process based on creating a psychological sense of belonging. Successful policy initiative and implementation occurs as the brainchild of a consensus on demands and direction, and thus, participation, of citizens and stakeholders can contribute to a more comprehensive policymaking process. The materialization of stakeholder participation hinges on emphasis on cooperation, integration, and decentralization, among the public sector-related agencies, including community and international organizations.

Decentralization and local governance are key elements in the public administration's engagement of local administrations. The core principles of decentralization rest upon the need to address the following issues: the local government as a responsive public service workforce, representative democracy, direct democracy, autonomy, and self-determination. With this in mind, Thailand's public administration incorporates an approach to decentralization and local governance that has become a feature of modern democracies. The Constitution of the Kingdom of Thailand, B.E. 2550 (2007), delineated authority and obligations between central and local governments. It clarified local government duties to ensure self-reliance, autonomy, decision-making involvement, and the delivery of public services that includes strengthening local economies, infrastructure, and facility development.

In addition, the Constitution states that additional laws regarding the framework for decentralization must be enacted, further delineating authority between central and local administrations, public service provision, budget allocation, and appointment of decentralization committees. Local government is authorized as a responsive public service workforce to comprehensively conduct area/issues-based management by disregarding the rule-bound rigidity of the traditional administrative structure (ministries, departments, or provinces). However, these are just guidelines issued to local governments, given their proximity to communities. The real question is how to maximize the delegated authority and promote citizen participation and cooperation between local/central administrations that contribute responsive policy making/implementation and highly efficient public administration.

(3) Centering on the citizens/people

The people-centered approach in Thailand was initially stated in The Eighth National Economic and Social Development Plan (1997–2001), which attached importance to civil society advocacy, public sector efficiency, capacity building, cooperation among citizens/local governments, citizen/people participation advocacy, and self-reliance. The crux of the people-centered approach includes responsiveness to people's demands, bureaucratic integration among the administrative structure in policymaking and public services delivery, and the availability of evaluation processes. Successful citizen participation stems from leaders' and the public sector's insightful understanding of the people's demands, as well as their ability to involve people in the policymaking process of the public and private sectors. In cases of social innovation, the role of public administration must shift from the mentality of "citizen/people under control" to "citizen/people in control" to ensure that the authorized policy and public services delivery is working in the best interests of the people.

In a public administration context, legitimate decisions are made with reference to citizen participation in the decision-making process. Should stakeholders' interests be compromised, public hearings, or consultations must be conducted to foster cooperation, acceptance, compliance, and ownership among related parties, and to achieve sustainable solutions to manage changing momentum. Participation in policy initiative and implementation involves acknowledging effective data collection mechanisms that can capture the real situations of stakeholders, as well as their perceived issues and demands.

(4) Achieving sustainable outcomes

The challenges facing NPM in a globalized world lie in determining how to successfully promote community capacity building to ensure cooperation, provision of continuous support, building of effective intra-organizational networks, and creation of strong communities via integration to successfully carry out the activities according to the objectives. Achieving sustainable development can be attained by changing the mentality of leaders and government officials to work in the best interests of the people in the short/long term, creating and cementing a sense of belonging, and achieving a sustainable community and society (from government ownership of inputs and processes to government and citizen ownership of the outcomes).

By Whom? the Bottom Line: "Leadership"

Thailand is observing the emergence of a new type of governance anchored in the concept of social innovation. Seemingly, intractable societal problems are being successfully tackled by society with innovative solutions that unleash citizens' potential. In this process, society is gradually transforming itself into an innovative society that can cope with challenges by utilizing its own knowledge resources. At the center of these cases, there are always exemplary leaders who strongly cherish Thai values. Regardless of their position, either in local government or in social enterprise, they share many common features that enable them to effectively facilitate public organizations and citizens in the society in generating social innovation. In this section, we review the case study from Chap. 3 of Mr. Pongsak Yingchoncharoen, the mayor of Yala Municipality, to clarify the significance of social innovation and its expediting factors in the Thai context.

(1) Mr. Pongsak Yingchoncharoen's role in the Yala crisis

Mr. Pongsak Yingchoncharoen, the mayor of Yala Municipality, has been in office since 1994, working for the interests of local people amid an ongoing crisis. Yala, one of Thailand's southernmost provinces, was formerly a major financial and commercial center and was one of the most well organized examples of city planning. People of different religions and races (Buddhist, Muslim and Chinese) lived harmoniously, and the Muslim and Buddhist populations had equal social status. But over the past year, people have fled the city due to violence—recurrent incidents of mass shootings and bombing attacks on houses, business centers, and government offices. Irreconcilable differences, intense distrust and a lack of interaction have become commonplace between Muslims and Buddhists. Fears over safety have pushed people out of Yala, bringing economic growth to a halt and making people afraid to visit the city.

Pongsak's outstanding contribution to the local administration and responsiveness to people of different races, religions, and cultures have earned him significant respect. His innovative vision and perseverance have helped to rebrand Yala from being a city of violence to one full of innovative learning projects. The role and nature of local administrative leadership is the key to providing effective administration in Yala Municipality amid the context of ethnic diversity, intense distrust, and social conflict. Such approaches are indicative of the generation of new policy initiatives, followed by implementation in ways that promote reconciliation and development of local innovations to address the ongoing issues.

The mayor's main slogan for Yala, "Gratitude for Homeland," has underpinned his wish to work in the best interests of the people to foster peace and reconciliation and designates Yala as a place of respectful coexistence of people of different religions and cultures. His blueprint bridges the gap of cultural differences, stimulates conflict prevention, and creates joint activities, embedding a sense of community and promoting a positive image through these projects. Despite the fragmented purposes, disparate content and people involved, such projects represent integrated management in which solving political unrest, encouraging peaceful coexistence between people of different religions, and fixing the economic downturn outweigh the issues of authority, knowledge, and budget constraints. This exemplifies the mayor's commitment to peace and people's well-being. Consequently, Yala Municipality's innovative projects have earned it numerous awards over the past decade. They include the UN Peace Award, the King Prajadhipok Award for Transparency and Civil Participation, and the Outstanding Achievement in Good Governance Award from the Department of Local Administration, Ministry of Interior, among others.

(2) Social enterprise: The Mae Fah Luang Foundation

The Mae Fah Luang Foundation provides a model for a people-centric approach to alleviating poverty. Poverty lies at the root of other social issues including drug trafficking, deforestation, environmental degradation, and even vulnerability to psychological problems. Formerly, Doi Tung, situated in the Golden Triangle, was notorious for illicit opium production and drug trafficking. The local people faced a lack of government support and complex social problems: no citizenship, extreme poverty, lack of basic education, poor healthcare access, and infrastructure, as well as deforestation through slash-and-burn farming. In realizing that poverty and lack of opportunity caused socioeconomic and environmental problems, HRH Princess Srinagarindra, the Princess Mother, was determined to revive Doi Tung through forest restoration, socioeconomic development, and land rehabilitation, according to Her Royal Highness's "Improving Quality Of Life" mantra. This program provided hope and opportunities to ethnic minorities and local residents regardless of race, religion, or nationality and promoted sustainable coexistence between people and nature.

Mom Rajawongse Disnadda Diskul (Khun Chai) continues his predecessor's legacy of tackling poverty and inequality. His plan for Doi Tung's development builds on the Princess Mother's project to incorporate legitimate job opportunities, sufficient income, education opportunities, and sustainable alternative livelihood development. His belief is based on the goodness of human nature, the value of giving people opportunities, self-reliance, and perseverance. Consequently, it took just a few decades to change Doi Tung from an area of slash-and-burn farming to an educational site and a model for sustainable economic and community development.

The initial concept of the Doi Tung Development Project (DTDP) rests upon human and economic coexistence in harmony with nature. This is exemplified by the success of shifting from slash-and-burn farming and opium cultivation to economic forest sustainability, in which forest-related income and economic well-being are sustained without deforestation or environmental degradation. Despite the initial challenges of unexpectedly low yields, earning trust and acceptance from residents, embedding ownership value, coordination with public and private sectors, and an economic downturn, Khun Chai's perseverance kept his momentum going. He had the best interests of the local people in mind and was successful in planning the following:

- offering education opportunities and capability building for local people and stakeholders,
- promoting development to enhance the quality of life,
- creating value-added products,
- building the Doi Tung brand to generate more revenue from local products, and
- preparing new leaders for management of business development.

With this in mind, perseverance and sacrifice enabled Mom Rajawongse Disnadda to succeed. He is known not only as a pioneer and developer of Doi Tung but also as a key agent in improving the livelihoods of ethnic minorities, who now have sustainable socioeconomic security. For its accomplishments, the Mae Fah Luang Foundation's Development Project has been widely recognized and replicated domestically and internationally. It provides an education center for the general public and organizations. The following are examples of recognition bestowed on the project for its outstanding achievements:

- In 2002, the DTDP received permission to use the United Nations Office on Drugs and Crime (UNODC) logo on its products in recognition of the project's role in providing sustainable alternative livelihood development (SALD) for societies in areas of drug production.
- In 2003, UNODC recognized the DTDP, especially its coffee and macadamia growing activities, as a model for sustainable alternative livelihood development through a multisectoral participatory rural economy.
- In 2006, the foundation registered geographical indication (GI) for coffee grown at Doi Tung to prepare for the brand's sustainability. The people of Doi Tung now owned both the coffee trees and the Doi Tung name.
- In 2009, Khun Chai was named Social Entrepreneur of the Year 2009 for the East Asian region by the Schwab Foundation at the World Economic Forum for his innovative and replicable social business plan that proved successful in addressing the problems of opium growing, drug trafficking, deforestation, and border issues.

How—The New Paradigm of Thai Public Management

Formerly, the public sector administration was policy-driven or decentralized by the national government. It was divided into management steps, each with preset attributable goals, eventually delivering services to the public. The new paradigm for bureaucratic reform and the future of the public sector administration focuses on re-examining leaders' roles and responsibilities by viewing them through a different "lens." This approach is citizen/people-centric, allowing them to contribute to the policy initiation and implementation process by setting the objectives. It involves revamping from "Policy/Purpose–Process–People" to "People–Policy/Purpose–Process." Most importantly, it is aimed at achieving sustainable outcomes. In this regard, the public sector must conduct a thorough evaluation and take into account long-term advantages and disadvantages.

The two cases cited above show typical examples of a people-centric leadership and management style, which is different from the former public sector management process. That is, it infuses citizen perspectives into the process to ensure that societal issues, public requests, and feedback are expediently addressed by government. The former approach used a top-down model for the government to exercise power. It shifted to a more bottom-up approach with the relevant parties engaged in the policymaking process with the best interest of people in mind, to achieve the same goals on the following:

- Narrowing sociocultural, economic and political gaps,
- Creating opportunities to access government services,
- Empowering people, and
- Sustainability

The leaders in both cases have a good understanding of the historical, social, cultural, and geo-social aspects of their communities. Their hands-on experience and compilation of knowledge have contributed to insightful understanding of the policy initiative/implementation process. They have incorporated their understanding of ongoing problems and empathy into rendering comprehensive policy initiatives and creating blueprints that contribute to the well-being and sustainable growth of the community. In this regard, some of the ongoing issues that the leaders must take into account include community violence due to race and religious diversity in Yala (Pongsak) as well as issues of poverty, sickness, and ignorance of the community in the Doi Tung area (Khun Chai).

(1) Right process–right abilities–right values

With the public administration's paradigm shift from the central administration to citizen-centric public management, policy, working processes, and goals must also shift to cater to the people's demands. The former top-down control mentality, in which policies were set up freely by public entities, must be now be integrated by various parties in the public sector, and is outweighed by the need for leaders to take into account the opinions/demands of the public. Embedding values of participation in the decision-making process is also crucial. In this regard, knowledge creation and management are vital to achieving citizen-centric public management. It is the driving force for successful policy implementation, working processes, and development. Nonaka and Takeuchi (1995) explained in *The Knowledge-Creating Company* the difference between knowledge and information. They defined knowledge as "a dynamic human process of justifying personal belief toward the 'truth'" (p. 58). Thus, the public sector, acting as a dominant information center, must change to acquire knowledge of facts and truths as they apply in each specific context. Consequently, this can contribute to rational policy initiative processes and goals.

The case studies show the typical characteristics of wise leaders in the "knowledge creation process" and "knowledge-based management." Their knowledge originated from hands-on experience, which brings in-depth or tacit knowledge, and is derived from socialization and the process of transposing it to the externalization of policymaking and implementation. Moreover, the leaders showed that they have the ability to judge goodness by making decisions based on virtues, not on profitable benefits to themselves or competitive advantages. Wise leaders must decide on what is right for their organizations and society as a whole. They must understand the core context of each matter and be able to build mechanisms to transform/communicate their experiences. In addition, great leaders process the ability to unify people with diversified objectives (in the case of conflicts of interest) to be able to work together. In addition, they can foster phronesis in others to build resilient organizations.

Box 9.2
Dharmmaraja: The Ten Royal Virtues

1. *Dana (generosity or charity)—being prepared to sacrifice one's own pleasure for the wellbeing of the public, such as by giving away one's belongings or other things to support or assist others, including giving knowledge and serving public interest*
2. *Sila (high moral character)—maintaining a high moral order in one's personal conduct and being a good example for others*
3. *Pariccaga (sacrifice for the good of the people)—being generous towards the people, avoiding selfishness*
4. *Ajjava (honesty and integrity)—being honest and sincere towards others, performing one's duties with loyalty and sincerity to others*
5. *Maddava (kindness or gentleness)—having gentle temperament, being kind and gentle, never arrogant*
6. *Tapa (austerity in habits)—self-controlling, destroying passion and performing duties without indolence*
7. *Akkhoda (non-anger, freedom from hatred or enmity)—remaining calm in the midst of confusion.*

8. *Avihimsa (non-violence)—being non-violent, not persecuting the people*
9. *Khanti (patience and tolerance)—practicing patience to serve public interests*
10. *Avirodhana (non-opposition ruling in harmony with the people)—respecting public opinion, promoting harmony, avoiding prejudice and promoting public peace and order.*

Each society needs the right culture, values, and behavior to survive and grow in uncertain and challenging environments. In Thai society, core values are important and are the key driving force toward controlling and developing great leaders. This is because leaders must take people's demands into account; this is the core concept of the people-centric approach. The core value in Thai society is the of *Dharmmaraja*, which is centered on sacrifice, and outweighs profit, numbers of votes, or fighting for influential positions. According to this concept, a king or a leader who can unite people must have good principles and virtues to follow, so that he can serve as a good example and be relied upon by his people. The royal virtues are followed not only by a monarch but also government figures, bureaucrats, or any ordinary citizen.

The concept of *Dharmmaraja* is a key characteristic of Thai public leaders. Leaders are required to govern themselves, society and the country with affection, care, discipline, and responsibility. *Dharmmaraja* is a system of virtue ethics that has had a profound impact on Thai leaders since ancient times, and comprises numerous principles. The next section will examine how these cases embody important characteristics that kings or leaders have practiced—the ten royal virtues (see Box 9.2)—and consider how such virtues can be applicable to all leaders in society. The core values focus on generosity, abstaining from bad deeds, high morals, and sacrifice for the good of the people. The paradigm shift for Thai public management is not an easy process but must be accomplished through a spiral of knowledge creation processes over time, with both tacit and explicit knowledge. In the sense of tacit knowledge, the core values in evaluating and generating public policy are beliefs, perspectives, and mental models.

Lessons Learned

The case of Yala Municipality clearly shows how a public organization under effective leadership can transform a society. In the following sections, the dynamism and expediting factors in the cases are analyzed by focusing on the three stages of policy processes and final outcomes.

(1) Problem identification: Connection and clarity of thought and purpose

In today's world, the challenges for a bureaucracy that focuses on a people-centric approach include determining how to meet people's needs and be responsive to public concerns. Identifying public issues/problems provides an initial step in the public policymaking process. Diversified structural problems that may receive the attention of leaders can range from deforestation, rebellion against authority, conflict between groups, inequality of opportunity, and lack of well-being. Public issues/problems may derive from political demands that are further incorporated into the decision-making process on many levels. Leaders of local/regional or central administrations will formulate policies to address particular issues through the appropriate agencies. If people face a lack of information, or are ignorant, or are unaware of their rights, relevant governmental entities must be responsive in identifying any problems involved and initiate public policy accordingly. Responsible agencies are more likely to have a direct understanding of the issues/problems due to their proximity to their communities. Once a problem is identified, objectives in problem-solving should be issued in accordance with the local context of the problems.

In the case studies, leaders play important roles in understanding the core issues and related parties and are able to grasp the essence of problems before contemplating and initiating policies and strategic planning to solve such problems. "Yala: Gratitude for Homeland" is the essence of Mr. Pongsak Yingchoncharoen's ambition to serve his community. Pongsak attaches importance to acquiring knowledge, defining stakeholders' demands, and analyzing the possibility of each project before initiating it. Mr. Pongsak Yingchoncharoen appears to provide help to all members of the community regardless of whether this will further his own political ambitions and agendas or not. Mr. Pongsak resides in

Yala and despite the ongoing unrest, interacts with the local people on a daily basis, and renders moral support. As both a citizen and mayor of Yala Municipality, he understands the ongoing intense distrust and divided opinions among different factions. By acknowledging this, he understands the relevant issues and specific target groups that need to be addressed.

For the Mae Fah Luang Foundation, poverty alleviation and improving the quality of life were the initial objectives. Khun Chai's success in the Doi Tung development project rests upon in-depth research and direct experience in the socioeconomic and environmental aspects. In realizing that poverty and lack of opportunities were behind Doi Tung's problems, Khun Chai followed HRH Princess Srinagarindra's plan to revive Doi Tung through forest restoration, socioeconomic development, and land rehabilitation. Consequently, the project has tried to provide opportunities to ethnic minorities and local residents regardless of race or religion and promotes sustainable coexistence of people and nature.

In summary, accessibility of facts, subject matter, people, and relevant issues are the key factors in ensuring that leaders have a thorough understanding of the situation and the development of their approach in each community. In both of the case studies, local leaders play important roles in understanding the core issues. They work to ensure that they have good information flows to and from the community, and they do not favor one community over another, but regularly meet with all parties.

(2) Policy formulation: Social innovation and kindness with wisdom

formulation is an important part of the policymaking process because it underpins political behavior and other managerial matters. At present, policy formulation does not rest in the hands of only the state. Good public policy is not only a vital tool in the development of strategic planning in many ways—it can help to restore peace, order, and stability. It can also provide a mechanism for handling emergencies, meeting people's demands, and promoting equality in society. In the policy formulation process, responsible agencies at the national and local levels should attach importance to the citizen/people-centric approach and use it to prioritize resource allocation and income distribution the public interest.

Similar social challenges exist across many areas of Thailand, with many pressing problems that need to be solved for the common social good. This becomes particularly important when the central government or traditional governance model does not satisfy the needs of society or address societal issues, promote social innovation processes, or ensure leadership that facilitates social innovation. In the aforementioned cases, leaders facilitate the process of policies as movers and shakers. The leaders are pioneers in conducting the interaction between tacit and explicit knowledge, in which practical wisdom comes from socialization with many related parties on different levels. Subsequently, it propels people toward consensus to initiate new policies or create new working guidelines.

In the case of Yala, although Mayor Pongsak is very keen and well aware of focusing on living together amid diversity for peace and order within Yala Municipality, he does not rely only on his own judgment but coordinates with other municipalities. He also seeks advice from other experts and relevant communities by disseminating knowledge through meetings, exchanging ideas, and providing opportunities for his team to express their ideas. He used some of these projects as a political campaign slogan and initiated other innovative projects such as the youth orchestra, Gratitude for Homeland Youth Camp, and Yala Bird City to demonstrate that transforming potential ideas into practice is possible.

As for the Mae Fah Luang Foundation, with a basic belief in human goodness and offering people opportunities, Khun Chai's Doi Tung development plan is aimed at offering local residents legitimate job and education opportunities, a stable income and sustainable alternative livelihood development. He has shown that this alternative method can be successful in alleviating poverty and enhancing the quality of life. Although DTDP has not been implemented at a major national policy level, it consists of projects in various fields—namely health, education, agriculture, and environment—that involve multidimensional realms of development. In addition, the project covers a considerable period of time: 1989 to the present. The process consists of offering educational opportunities, basic health care knowledge, opportunities to become financially stable and improve the quality of life, as well as strengthening of Doi Tung's business unit to achieve sustainability. The concept of sustainable alternative livelihood development has been thoroughly analyzed in the private and public sectors domestically and internationally to provide useful information necessary for establishing development plans.

Mom Rajawongse Disnadda Diskul has been the main driving force for the past three decades.

With this in mind, the intertwining process used by leaders exemplifies an ongoing learning process that starts with an insightful understanding of the subject matter and context to further initiate a blueprint. As for the Yala and Mae Fah Luang Foundation cases, they exemplify the initiation of local policy and integrated development projects that require originality and defining direction, process and target groups to achieve the goals.

The other key factor that has contributed to the generation of policy and various projects is the willingness of leaders to help people make a good living. This is also referred to as "Kindness with Wisdom," a concept that embodies the leaders' knowledge, willingness to assist, and ability to transform ideas into organizational blueprints for change. Pongsak and Khun Chai play a critical role by supporting people's participation, empowering people to contribute to social challenges, enhancing social relations to increase the quality of social services, reducing poverty, and improving fairness. New and small projects are key drivers not just as knowledge sources but also as knowledge exploiters, playing a fundamental role in breakthrough innovations. In these cases, the leaders are key factors in the success of social innovation by creating social value and introducing new ways of achieving goals, bringing new patterns and new combinations or hybrids of elements for social innovation.

(3) Policy implementation: Communication, alignment, and agility

Public policymaking does not end with the legislative process. It requires implementation of new policy initiatives by bureaucracy and other organizations, delegated by heads of state (Dye 2014). The challenges in successful policy implementation are aligning all the necessary components, including reforming organization management, establishing new agencies or organizations, reforming public administration, cooperation between public/private sectors and civil society, becoming participation-oriented, and building strong networks. At this implementation stage, leadership takes center stage to translate strategy into operational terms in the context of large- rather than small-scale change. The following are important for leaders to carry out change of management strategies:

- Strategic alignment of the organization's structure, values, culture, information technology, body of knowledge, and personnel competency with the policy/strategy.
- The ability to create shared contexts (both formal and informal) and communicate/deliver to related parties.
- With such diversified and external variables related to policy implementation, leaders must cultivate traits of flexibility and adaptability to make timely adjustments without compromising on set goals.

In the above cases, the significance of the Yala projects has been the integration of diversified sources and a body of knowledge conducive to developing innovative projects, public services provision, and acceptance of differences. Subsequently, these projects have been incorporated into the community. Each project has different objectives and involves a variety of parties—community, residents, students, youths, and supporters, both local and abroad—contributing to the establishment of agencies with different methods of operation in accordance with different set goals. With the ability of Pongsak and his team in regard to communicating and coordinating skills, flexibility, and creating consensus, these diversified projects resemble a jigsaw puzzle that signifies peaceful coexistence.

There is no quick fix or one-size-fits-all solution for Mae Fah Luang. The DTDP began with the acknowledgment that poverty is the root cause of other social issues such as drug trafficking, environmental degradation, and weak social structure coupled with lack of educational opportunities and basic services from the government. Khun Chai has initiated many diversified projects to tackle each issue in accordance with the local context. These projects range from offering job opportunities, education, and practical experience to fostering people's participation: "Each problem was thoroughly examined through hands-on experience. If a question is wrong, we change it so a new set of solutions can be obtained." DTDP is divided into three phases, in which residents are on track to become financially sustainable. They progress from (1) financially independent to (2) financially stable and (3) financially sustainable. Mae Fah Luang also uses this model to develop other projects. These stages have been thoroughly examined according to variables such as economic downturns or unexpectedly low yields. Khun Chai draws on traits of flexibility and adaptability to tackle unprecedented issues by adapting new strategies. He is well liked and has been successful in developing Doi Tung.

(4) Policy outcome: Sustainability

Policy evaluation is conducted to evaluate the effects of the policies of respective agencies. It involves policy monitoring, efficiency measurement, and effectiveness evaluation. In addition, it provides a means of checking policies in terms of their efficiency and validity and to suggest solutions to achieve sustainable outcomes. Thus, in terms of policy outcomes, a multilevel analysis of the cases can be summarized as follows.

- Yala faces continuing violence, casualties, vandalism, and feelings of alienation. It requires leadership competency in terms of goodness and the capability to ensure outstanding performance in running Yala Municipality. Politicians there must practice selfless devotion and have a strong work ethic. Mr. Pongsak has successfully transformed Yala by attaching importance to peace building, promoting harmonious coexistence between different people, offering education opportunities, building leadership among children, keeping the municipality clean, supporting economic growth, and enhancing the people's well-being. The success of Yala Municipality derives from residents' cooperation and participation in various activities initiated by the municipality. The local people are part of the policy initiatives and implementation, as well as being involved in procedures for dealing with wrongdoing by public officials. Through integration of such diversified sources and knowledge, the Yala innovative projects referred to below have consequently been incorporated into the community: The Gratitude for Homeland Youth Camp emphasizes conducting joint activities to bridge cultural gaps and develop Yala's youth leaders. There is a tangible work structure, participation, and input from various groups in terms of content, activities, and the work process.
- The Yala TK Park is the epitome of knowledge management, offering new learning technologies and activities conducive to coexisting in harmony.

- Recognized both domestically and internationally, the Yala Municipality Youth Orchestra offers young musicians an experience to work together through classical music.
- Yala Province, which was selected as one of ten pilot cities by the Ministry of Commerce, is renowned for holding the world's biggest Red-whiskered Bulbul traditional bird-calling competition. This exemplifies using indigenous knowledge as an integral part of the development process of local communities and economies.

Every project is an integration of such a uniquely diversified body of knowledge, sources, and indigenous communities for innovation, public services provision, community participation, and acceptance of differences and equality, with the common goal of peace building. Yala Municipality is thus a strong and vibrant civil society with continuing development projects amid ongoing unrest. Pongsak has cultivated a sense of joint ownership through various activities in a bid to see peace in Thailand's three southernmost provinces that have been continuously plagued by insurgent attacks. Yala hopes to pursue its formerly designated name of the "Second Singapore" by fostering peace building, ensuring a stable and harmonious society, and promoting economic growth.

Making a profit is seen as the main objective of any business unit, but the Doi Tung development project attaches importance to enhancing local well-being. With its financial success, the business is now expanding its contributions to society. The new paradigm shift includes expanding beyond the current concept of sustainable coexistence between humans and the environment to redefining new business in terms of its socioeconomic and environmental benefits. In addition to the Mae Fah Luang Foundation's typical evaluation process in terms of measuring successful outcomes and changes, the success of the DTDP is exemplified by awards, which ensures that it remains the epitome of sustainable development and an education center for community development and economic growth. The DTDP project also incorporates expansion into other areas including Doi Tung coffee, which was granted a GI, and a cotton factory that involves three generations of a family. They combine the indigenous knowledge of ethnic minorities with a modern twist that contributes to successful brand building and is internationally recognized.

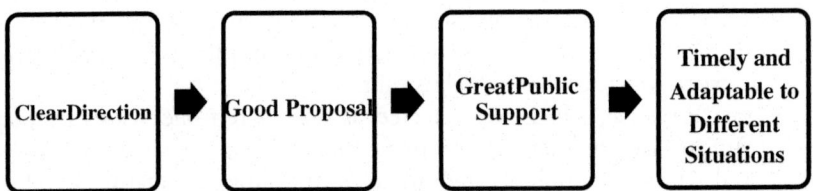

Fig. 9.1   Factors affect the effectiveness of a policy

In terms of attempting to evaluate the success of projects, the criteria should involve both the output from Doi Tung and local wellbeing/quality of life. The residents are a strong community, and have substantial income and safe and secure lives. The latter intangible criteria represent a valuable outcome that contributes to changing people's lives to create a sufficient economy and sustainable development. (Piyani Rungratthawatchai 2012)

WHAT'S NEXT? AGENDA FOR ACTION

In reference to the case in Thailand, three factors can be seen to promote the effectiveness of a policy that is designed by a public organization to solve societal issues. Those factors define the intensity of citizens' activities that will substantiate social innovation for a seemingly unsolvable societal problem (Fig. 9.1).

(1) Clear direction

Clear direction in public policymaking is a priority as it helps to provide continuity and clarity in terms of goals. The direction of Thailand's current public policy is set in accordance with the country's strategic plan (2013–2018). All previous National Economic and Social Development Plans have similar objectives in exemplifying clear directions for public policy initiatives. However, the overall view of Thailand's public policy still lacks clear direction, resulting in insignificant effects on policy initiative and projects. Hence, implementation of these policies and projects has failed to coincide with the country's strategy and the National Economic and Social Development Plan. Therefore, integration between country's strategic plan and the public policymaking process is of paramount importance.

(2) Good proposals

Good proposals provide essential conduits to beneficial policy initiatives and practical implementation. Based on the following criteria, a good proposal should

- be in accordance with the country's strategic plan;
- be practical and predictable, with a well-planned resources management scheme;
- promote innovative use of public services;
- be supported by the government in terms of resources and instruments for policy implementation; and
- draw from a people-centric approach, and should be in compliance with people's demands.

In this regard, the success of public policies results from encompassing all the necessary criteria for comprehensive public policymaking. For example, Yala and the Mae Fah Luang Foundation's policies initiative process coincides with the country's strategic plan, which strives to increase people's well-being. The leaders initiate new and small projects to solve societal issues and offer people opportunities. These people-centric leaders try to understand the viewpoints of the affected people and empathize with people's situations, needs, problems, and wants. The spiral effect of the SECI process of knowledge creation is manifested in the way that leaders and the people they work with continuously learn and come up with ideas on how to improve their strategies or initiate new services. In the process, they are able to reform their organizations, applying a push-and-pull approach between people and other stakeholders as well as managing multidimensional goals for the common good in collaboration with other affected projects.

(3) Strong public support

Public support provides an essential conduit to the materialization of public policy. However, previous policies gave priority to leveraging the public sector's status and failed to address people's demands. Therefore, the focus of the Thai public administration on a citizen-centric approach is significant. The bottom-up approach currently plays a pivotal role in a democratic society that attaches importance to citizen participation.

Policies initiated by people have rarely resulted in the development of national-level policy, but tangible examples of people's demands and policy implementation at the local administration level do exist. The administration of Yala Municipality during its ongoing crisis and the Gratitude for Homeland Youth Camp are components of public policy derived from bottom-up approaches and local support.

(4) Capacity of public organizations

As stated above, governing successfully in the best interests of the people may depend on a number of factors, including comprehensive public policy initiatives, as well as management and implementation. It may also require public organization reform to ensure that it is responsive to citizens' needs. The challenges faced by the Thai bureaucratic system according to many studies include meeting the demands of the people through a people-centric approach. This includes

- providing more public services amid budget constraints and taxation dilemmas by increasing productivity;
- effectively responding to people's needs by promoting decentralization and citizen participation;
- initiating promises and taking responsibility for failures by ensuring responsibility for job assignments;
- promoting credibility and earning people's trust by fostering morality, transparency, accountability and responsibility; and
- reforming bureaucratic processes through professional leadership and management.

These challenges are directly related to bureaucratic administration and public services delivery. They are indicators of successful public administration. In developing a new paradigm that focuses on a people-centered approach, other important considerations might include being aware of differences in characteristics between public organizations and the need to generate future leaders and create a new culture.

With this in mind, public organizations need effective and efficient internal management capabilities. These have to be redesigned to offer responsive public services, providing citizens with easy accessibility and smooth delegation of standardized public services to other agencies. Therefore, strategic decision-making is necessary to determine whether activities should be undertaken in-house or outsourced to the private sector or other enterprises. Furthermore, public organizations have to decide which functions are critical to perform or too risky to outsource. The role of the public sector needs to shift from service provision to service facilitation or service brokering, which requires different skills and a new set of capabilities to set up, monitor, and assess outcomes.

To manage and lead effectively in a challenging environment and make a real difference, leadership must be integrated and situation-based. The success of public management hinges on leadership, an integral factor that contributes to comprehensive policy implementation and propels an organization forward. Good leaders and performance of public service delivery are related to levels of citizen trust. The process and solution of a policy issue may require a long, complex process in which public sector leaders need sufficient capabilities to lead within their own organizations or in society. To make this happen naturally, future leadership requirements in terms of abilities, the process of policy innovation and its critical factors, or values required have to be identified and adopted as the new norm. A potential leader needs various experiences through both formal and informal schemes.

(5) Leadership and management

Success in the case studies shows that a change in mindset at all levels in an organization (both leaders and operational levels) can be conducive to solving dilemmas and initiating innovative policies. Unconventional leadership based on a pragmatic people-centric approach would demonstrate a tremendous change in the policymaking process. The above-mentioned public policies originated in the leaders' values of prioritizing a people-centered agenda and being sensitive to socio-geographical contexts: the mayor of Yala municipality's enthusiastic attitude and determination to use unconventional techniques to run a local administration by responding to local problems; the Mae Fah Luang Foundation's unique goal of enhancing local people's well-being based on H.M. the King's principle of "Understand, Reach out and Develop." These approaches highlight the critical roles played by the leaders as the key "drivers and connectors" in transformation and innovation in the public sector. The entrepreneurs and institutions that link together people, ideas, power, and money can contribute by creating, designing, and changing common social goods and solving local problems. For Thai leadership development, the ability to judge goodness is more significant than other skills. Therefore, it is important to transform leaders' mindsets and inculcate core values of dedication to helping others without expecting anything in terms of profit or votes, or using the practice of favoritism to assume positions. This can be a step toward initiating comprehensive public policies and obtaining sustainable outcomes.

CONCLUSION

Given the need for more agility and flexibility in response to socio-economic and political complexity, the public administration needs to undergo a restructuring phase that emphasizes decentralization, modernization, law/regulation renewal, and increasing the country's competitiveness. In such an enabling environment, public organizations, whether they are local governments or social enterprises, can demonstrate potential as social innovators in solving societal problems by activating citizens' untapped potential. Within this context, leadership can provide a critical component in the successful realization of this goal. Leaders of public organizations face a future of dealing with uncertainty, changing environments, growing citizen demands, and multiple challenges on several fronts. While leadership styles can vary, all such leaders must have a clear vision of the future that incorporates a renewed focus on people's needs. To create future public organization leaders, we believe it is necessary to focus on key abilities and core values. The role of leadership training and development programs has to be designed and developed in an innovative way. Our new public organization leaders will need to think, act, and behave differently if the public is to see and believe in a trusted and collaborating to create greater public values.

REFERENCES

Dye, Thomas R. 2014. *Understanding public policy.* New York: Pearson New International Edition.
Nonaka, I., and H. Takeuchi. 1995. *The knowledge-creating company.* New York: Oxford University Press.
Rungratthawatchai, Piyani. 2012.

Authors' Biography

Tanchai Woothisarn is the Secretary General of the King Prajadhipok's Institute and Associate Professor at the Department of Community Development, Faculty of Social Administration, Thammasat University. He is also a qualified committee member of the Ministry of Culture, a sub-committee of the Office of the Public Sector Development Commission (OPDC), and a sub-committee of the National Anti-Corruption Commission (NACC). His master's degrees were in Public Administration from the National Institute of Development Administration, Bangkok and in Policy Science (International Program) from Saitama University, Japan. His research interests include decentralization, local governance, and citizenship. He served as a member of the Constitution Drafting Assembly in 2007, as a Constitution Drafting Committee member between 2014 and 2015, and as an advisor to the second Constitution Drafting Committee in 2015 and 2016. His recent publications are "Special City: Concept and Possibility" and "Research Project on National Reconciliation Promotion" in 2012.

Kittima Bunnag currently serves as an independent Human Capital professional, at King Prajadhipok's Institute with directive responsibility for Human Resource consultant and curriculum design of Curriculum academic Board. She was previously Human Resource Director at PricewaterhouseCooper Thailand (pwc). Kittima is a versatile Human Capital professional with hands-on corporate and consulting experience through change and challenge by implementing Human Capital strategic planning, establishing direction, and executing initiatives in support of business objectives and corporate goals. Specialties: Human Resource Management, Human Resource Development, Leadership Effectiveness and Development.

CHAPTER 10

Unleashing the Knowledge Potential of the Community for Co-creation of Values in Society

Ikujiro Nonaka, Kiyotaka Yokomichi
and Ayano Hirose Nishihara

The leaders who work most effectively, it seems to me, never say "I." And that's not because they have trained themselves not to say "I." They don't think "I." They think "we," they think "team." They understand their job to be to make the team function. They accept responsibility and don't sidestep it, but "we" gets the credit. This is what creates trust, what enables you to get the task done.
—Peter F. Drucker, 1990

I. Nonaka (✉)
Hitotsubashi University, Tokyo, Japan
e-mail: inonaka@ics.hit-u.ac.jp

K. Yokomichi
National Graduate Institute for Policy Studies, Tokyo, Japan
e-mail: yokomiti@grips.ac.jp

A. Hirose Nishihara
Department of Global Business, College of Business,
Rikkyo University, Tokyo, Japan
e-mail: ayano.nishihara@rikkyo.ac.jp

© The Author(s) 2018   203
A. Hirose Nishihara et al. (eds.), *Knowledge Creation in Community Development*, DOI 10.1007/978-3-319-57481-3_10

204 I. NONAKA ET AL.

INTRODUCTION

Each of the seven case studies shared in Chaps. 2–8 showed steps taken by leaders to solve social issues and eventually co-create new social values in community. Throughout the process, the activities and mindsets of the people were transformed and new ways of doing things were developed, a process we referred to as "social innovation." In other words, community development and social innovation are about co-creating social values by changing the way people think and act by establishing new relationships among multiple stakeholders. The key here is the transformation of people's activities and mindsets.

In this chapter, building on the case studies presented in Chaps. 2–8 as well as the review of the Thai case studies in Chap. 9, we would like to, firstly, summarize the key findings from the case by grounding them in knowledge creation theory to explain the process of community development; and secondly, present the implications of the research and public sector practice grounded in knowledge creation in management. By grounding the cases in knowledge creation theory in management, we are able to explain the process and the key drivers in transforming the people's activities and mindsets. These points complement the theory and the practice of new public management (NPM), especially in the space of social innovation.

1. Vision and commitment to the goals

It is clear from each of the case studies that citizens, political leaders, and members of local governments always had a set vision and goals. They showed a clear a commitment to improving the quality of life of citizens and did all they could to realize this. They involved people around them, inspiring and motivating them to embrace the same vision, which sometimes compelled them to go beyond their daily tasks to achieve their goals. Thus, all of the leaders in the cases presented in Chaps. 2–8 had strong beliefs and commitments in terms of their visions and goals.

At the same time, the leaders were open to making changes by listening to their staff and/or citizens. Charismatic leaders, committed to their own vision, sometimes ignored the significance of doing this. This leads to the question of how the leaders in the case studies were able to be so open. We think it is because the leaders had deep and wide historical imagination over the time-space nexus, a consideration explored later in this chapter, and they were able to obtain their vision and goals from that source. We believe that *vision and goals are dreams with a deadline*. Vision and goals need to stem from the accumulation of high-quality tacit knowledge gained from a variety of experiences in the past if they are to be practical. At the same time, those with the vision and goals need to aim for the ideal. In order to synthesize the practical and the ideal, leaders need to be flexible in integrating and reconciling contradictions. This is what we call professionalism or artisanship—the relentless pursuit of excellence.

2. Knowledge-creating processes in transformational management

Among the four steps of the SECI model we presented in Chap. 1, the Socialization step is the foundation and the most essential of all the SECI processes. From the case studies, we can see that the Socialization step plays a central role in each case study—that is, sharing direct experiences and building up tacit knowledge through empathizing with others and the environment. It is important to note that Socialization is not just about sharing time and space together, but emphasizing, synchronizing, and resonating with each other physically and psychologically. Through such actions, tacit knowledge can be obtained from actual situations through mutual experiences. With the accumulation of tacit knowledge embedded in each individual, in the Externalization step, individual tacit knowledge can be transformed through dialogue transformed into explicit knowledge, concentrated into concepts, and shared with others. We call this approach inductive, as well as abductive.[1]

In this sense, the SECI process is different from the *plan-do-check-action* (PDCA) cycle, which is often deployed in both public and private sectors, because PDCA is a deductive process. For example, political leaders and administrative officials make a plan and disseminate it from the top down. There is no room for citizens to participate or collaborate in the planning phase, and all too often, the plan is based on an armchair theory. In each case, there were PDCA cycles, but at the same time, they were integrated with high-quality Socialization processes before and/or during the planning phase. We think that deployment of the SECI process before the PDCA cycle provided one of the triggers for the development of innovative processes to address social issues, thus moving from an armchair PDCA cycle to SECI+PDCA cycle.

Another difference between SECI and PDCA is that the SECI process promotes what we call "middle-up-down" management, rather than a merely top-down or bottom-up process often seen in PDCA cycles. According to Nonaka and Takeuchi (1995, 127), middle-up-down presents a continuous iterative process by which knowledge is created by middle managers who are often leaders of a team or task force, through a spiral conversion process involving both the top and the frontline.

Middle-up-down management is situated in the *ba*, in which tacit, explicit, and practical knowledge are synthesized. *Ba*, defined in Chap. 1 as "context in-motion," is a time-space nexus formed between people and the environment in a "here-and-now" relationship. In *ba*, meaning is created from the interactions of people and the environment. Accordingly, *ba* and the environment constantly change over time, affecting each other to adopt and act with the changes. In other words, synthesis and convergence occur between people, the environment based on their knowledge and the meanings they generate (Nonaka et al. 2014).

In the municipal transformation, middle managers—or a middle person who connects multiple *ba*—can play a key role in co-creating new knowledge and new values for society. Those people at the intersection of multiple *ba* become the very center of knowledge management, at the intersection of the vertical and horizontal flows of communication (Nonaka and Takeuchi 1995). This middle-up-down management process that is installed in organizations, or shared among multiple *ba* in communities, is something we call "*kata*" or "creative routines."[2] A creative routine is a routine to create a new routine. With good creative routines, the organization or multiple *ba* should become more resilient, because the middle person will work autonomously to realize the vision and achieve the goals in a here-and-now situation.

3. Exercising political power and distributing wise leadership

We have presented the abilities of wise leadership in Chap. 1 that are essential in driving the SECI process and promoting innovation: (1) the ability to set a good goal, (2) the ability to grasp the essence, (3) the ability to create *ba*, (4) the ability to narrate the essence, (5) the ability to exercise political power to realize story, and (6) the ability to foster phronesis in others. From the case studies, among the six abilities, we observed that abilities 5 and 6 are closely related to undertaking the steps necessary to achieve the goal.

The ability to exercise political power is closely related to theories of power. French and Raven presented six kinds of power bases: reward power, coercive power, legitimate power, referent power, expert power, and informational power (French and Raven 1959; Raven 1965).[3] Of the six, the strongest one is referent power, a point that is sometimes misunderstood by leaders in bureaucratic organizations, because they think the position itself will give them power. In such situation, leaders will use only hard power, reward power, coercive power, and legitimate power, which will only result in forcing their staff members to do as they are told. Such members may be motivated to carry out routine tasks but they are seldom inspired to make improvements or undertake innovations.

In communities, people often become leaders because people around them empathize and resonate with them, and they are inspired and become motivated to collaborate with them. It does not matter too much if the leaders hold the position officially or formally. Real leaders need to present their vision and goals, commitment, passion, and beliefs in order to obtain empathy and trust from those around them. If they are successful in doing this, they can co-create social values. As shown previously, referent power is the key.

Ensuring the best mix of hard and soft power depending on the context—i.e., smart power—is critical for leaders (Nye 2011). Nye presented two categories, hard power and soft power, which he defines as follows: hard power is physical, direct, and imperative power (e.g., military power, police power, financial power, and the power to hire and fire personnel), as well as manipulating others through material incentives based on inducements (carrot) and threats (stick), while soft power refers to the ability to gain the desired result by capturing people's hearts. The power to shape the preferences of others and attract their attention is often an intangible asset through, for example, personality, culture, political values, appeal of a political system, legitimacy, or ethical policies. Nye then describes the ability to know when to use hard power or soft power, and how to combine the two, as "smart power." This is close to the concept of phronesis (wisdom, practical wisdom, and practical reason) (Nye 2013).

The ability to foster phronesis in others is about cultivating the leaders of a community. In the case studies we examined, we could see that there were a few key people who formed a new *ba* and connected it to other *ba*, by identifying or nurturing leaders who were also able to form *ba*. These leaders introduced new knowledge as well as values and beliefs, and with these, they reshaped the existing relationships between organizations and local communities, and such changes and values are induced in society. Driven by these leaders, *ba* expands into multi-layered relationships with universities, companies, and various other organizations in society, and they form a knowledge ecosystem by permeating each other through loose boundaries.

In addition, all *ba* manifest in similar forms—dynamic knowledge triads comprised of a synthesis of tacit knowledge, explicit knowledge, and practical wisdom. Multiple configurations of such *ba* create fractal organizations in which the parts represent the whole, and the whole is embedded in each part. We can see varieties of such *ba* in fractal configurations, in the case studies, and these are autonomously formed and change over time.

In the knowledge ecosystem, leaders are distributed everywhere but share the same purpose or direction so that each of them is able to co-create a narrative or an open-ended story of their own as well as of society at large. To create a narrative, as first suggested in Chap. 1, leaders should project the ideal of the common good for society and perceive reality as it is (abilities 1 and 2 of practical wisdom leadership, respectively), draw out empathy and resonance between people at the tacit knowledge level (Socialization), and enable the SECI spiral. Some of those people who resonate and empathize with leaders will eventually become leaders through a learning process like an apprenticeship, or resulting from the effective use of referent power.

SHORTAGES, CHALLENGES, AND IMPLICATIONS

1. Shortages and challenges

From the case studies, some common issues can be discerned: (1) neglect of tacit knowledge, (2) neglect of the role of front and middle managers, and (3) neglect of processes for new value creation. These points appear in the case studies both explicitly and implicitly. These issues are the reasons for, as well as the consequences of, bureaucracy, elitism, and paternalism in national/regional/local governmental organizations. Consequently, these issues lead political leaders and administrative officers to become detached from the actual situation, which then leads to superficial solutions. One of the root causes is low attention and/or lack of know-how on the part of political or elected leaders as well as top administrative officers on how to realize innovation. As a result, innovation never happens—or even if it does, it does not last for long even though there is a high demand for, and interest in, innovative solutions.

The Western approach to management—of which the application of NPM is one example—emphasizes management by quantitative, sometimes financial, key performance indicators (KPI). Political leaders and administrative officers are no exception. To meet the KPI, they are inclined to avoid risks. Consequently, middle and frontline managers also become risk-averse. Once a risk-averse syndrome spreads across an organization, it becomes homogeneous and the vitality to innovate is lost.

In such organizations—both in Asia and around the world—three major phenomena can be seen: over-analysis, over-planning, and over-compliance. These three points are not only the results but also the drivers of a negative spiral in which organizations and their members become detached from the actuality of society, middle, and frontline managers become occupied by administrative work, flexible contextual judgments are lost, they are not able to create new knowledge, and the organization cannot realize improvements in the quality of life of citizens. Political leaders and administrative officers are trapped by shortsightedness, preventing them from acting based on the vision and mission of the organization or society at large. In the end, everyone becomes exhausted but nothing creative or innovative happens.

Management should be subjective and practical. This is a fundamental view that we have stressed throughout this book. Of course, being objective and theoretical is equally important. However, from the perspective of knowledge creation theory on management, we emphasize the importance of subjectivity and practicality as the primary elements, meaning that management has to base itself on the beliefs of individuals, leaders, and members of an organization. We also stress that management is a synthesis of subjectivity and objectivity, practice and theory, emotions and logic, based on one's belief about resolving contradictions. In other words, management should transcend the dichotomy and the dualism to dynamic monism. However, in Western management theories, oftentimes only objectivity, theory, and logic are considered, while subjectivity, experience, and ethics and beliefs are neglected. This is the case in both the public and the private sector.

In the public sector, the most influential theory today is new public management theory (NPM), which emerged in the 1980s under the influence of theories on business management such as positioning theory, transaction cost theory, and game theory. Accordingly, NPM and business management theory share the same standpoints in that both seek to eliminate subjectivity while promoting efficiency and effectiveness—elements lacking in traditional public management theory and practice. On this point, for example, Hood (1991, 4–5) presented the seven doctrinal components of NPM: (1) hands-on professional management, (2) explicit standards and measures of performance, (3) greater emphasis on output controls, (4) disaggregation of units in the public sector, (5) greater competition in the public sector, (6) private sector styles of management, and (7) greater discipline and parsimony in resource use. We may assume that in both the private and public sectors, there was the same historical background of paradigm shifts: from welfare state to limited government, from Keynesian economics to neo-classical economics, and from communitarianism to neoliberalism.

What is interesting is that NPM has been a target of criticism and debate for quite some time. In the early 1990s, Hood (1991, 15) pointed out that NPM mainly works "in the direction of cutting costs and doing more for less as a result of better-quality management and different structural design." More recently, in 2005, Dunleavy et al. (2006) argued that NPM is dead. He stated that, despite the application of NPM in developed countries, it has now largely stalled or has been reversed in some key *leading-edge* countries. de Vries (2010) presented a counter-argument in 2010, stating that NPM is in trouble, but it is not really dead, and that NPM is an abstraction of the unity of ideas but in practice there is great variety in its implementation, and there are some new avenues of thought.

In the private sector, one of the most influential management theories is the positioning theory proposed by Michael Porter in 1985, which influenced the development of NPM. Porter is an economist rooted in neo-classical economics; therefore, his approach is scientific and objective, eliminating subjectivity as much as possible. He is best known for his development of the five forces framework, which determines the attractiveness of an industry and evaluates a firm's strategic positioning (Porter 1985).[4] Porter also presented cost-leadership or differentiation as two key concepts of a strategy to realize a sustainable competitive advantage. His view of strategy was that it involved outperforming the competition by focusing on efficiency rather than effectiveness and maximizing return on invested capital.

Porter considered not only the competitiveness of firms but also of nations, leading in 1990 to the development of the diamond model (Porter 1990).[5] The diamond model was intended to capture and analyze the capabilities, situations, and environment of a nation as determinant factors for a nation's competitiveness. In sum, Porter presented micro and macroviews to explain the sustainable competitive advantage of a firm and a nation. However, as he based his theory on neo-classical economics, he was always locked into a deductive way of thinking that theory is the absolute truth. This approach has clear limitations, because one of the factors that led to the global financial crisis in the 2007 was in fact computational finance, which neglected human subjectivity—especially its ethical and moral dimensions.

What is interesting about Porter's recent research is his attention to corporate social responsibility (CSR). CSR has gained increasing attention in the business management field since the early 2000s in reaction to the Enron and WorldCom accounting scandals. As a result of the global financial crisis, attention to CSR further increased after 2007, because for-profit organizations needed to react and respond to a social and ecological agenda to regain society's trust. Porter, who had originally excluded society as an externality in his theory of competitiveness, proposed the concept of Strategic CSR in 2006 and Creating Shared Value in 2011 (Porter and Kramer 2006, 2011). Porter and Kramer (2011) view society as one component in realizing a sustainable competitive advantage that firms should connect business goals and social benefits, and prioritize social issues that are closely related to the competitiveness and sustainability of the firm. However, even though this approach incorporates society, it is still employed as a way of maximizing the ROIC (return on invested capital) of the specific company.

In sum, we may say that there is a shift from an objective, logical, and scientific approach to a subjective and ethical, and practical approach to management. Henry Mintzberg (2004, 1) states that, "management is a practice that has to blend a good deal of craft (experience) with a certain amount of art (insight) and some science (analysis)." His statement perfectly echoes our approach that we need to synthesize science and art. As presented in Chap. 1, the concept of the dynamic knowledge triad synthesizes tacit knowledge and explicit knowledge with practical wisdom.

IMPLICATIONS AND FUTURE CHALLENGES

1. Historical imagination as basis of common good

When we think about co-creating social values, we have to make a value judgment on what is good for the community, or simply, what is common good. One critical thing here is that common good is subjective, and each individual good has its own value issues. This way of thinking may lead to egocentric individualism. To avoid this trap, we need to have a universal intent toward common good. In other words, we must think deeply and widely within the time-space nexus by sharing our subjectivity and justifying our personal beliefs within social contexts. This, in fact, embodies the knowledge creation process itself, and through the process, we are able to co-create strategic narratives toward the common good.

When we think about common good, we need to be aware that there are various perspectives and standpoints regarding the priority of individual—or private—justice and societal public good. These perspectives can be condensed into traditional conflicts between libertarianism and communitarianism. Libertarianism envisions a rational, free, and accountable individual, who prioritizes individual justice including ownership and property rights, over the common good of the community. Communitarianism is based on Aristotle's teleological perspective and concept of "fraternity," prioritizing the good and solidarity of the community over justice and the rights of each individual community member.

Libertarianism asserts that justice is derived abstractly and deductively and that people should unconditionally obey justice, as with Immanuel Kant's "categorical imperatives" (Kant 1785). John Rawls's theory of justice states that the universal rule is that which is ultimately agreed on by every member of society, based on the premise that everyone is subject to the same conditions behind the veil of ignorance (Rawls 2009). In contrast, Michael Sandel (2010) and other advocates of communitarianism believe that the common good is pursued while coexisting with specific and historical linguistic, religious, and cultural contexts of the community, and that it is agreed on and formed inductively by aiming for something better out of real practice, rather than being a universal principle. Communitarianism does not base its thoughts on abstract principles of justice, but rather on the practical values of the good in each member of the community.

History can be perceived as a self-organizing system that weaves relationships and structures from a complex mutual connection of events. The events etched in history or historical facts can only exist once in the here-and-now seconds of each moment. However, these countless events do not exist independently. They connect to each other in incidental fluctuations so as to weave new relationships and structures. Therefore, to apply the principle of causality (which asserts that a specific cause produces a single result) in a static environment does not allow us to see the true reality of nation management, in an attempt to analytically identify their rules or causes.

This is why historical imagination becomes critical. History consists of relations between numerous events. However, we need our subjectivity—historical perspectives—to choose important events, relate them, and create history. History is a narrative that many people would accept and agree as being past events. "History, consciously or unconsciously, reflects our position in time," and informs the view we take of the society in which we live (Carr 1961, 2).

Consequently, a social wise leader must, first of all, ask a very fundamental question: "what kind of future would you like to create?" The future reflects the past and the present. The leader picks up specific facts to justify a specific future vision. We have to be humble to the nature of reality and facts. We cannot create facts in the past. However, we can choose facts to create or justify our vision. That is what history is about: the making of the story.

An important point that wise leaders need to keep in mind is sensitivity to initial conditions, also known as the *butterfly effect*. Small differences at the beginning may broaden as time goes by. Therefore, a social wise leader needs to make timely and precise judgments—for this, we have to perceive reality as it is. The truth is in the details, so we must always stick to the ground.

Socially wise leaders must collect the knowledge of experience shared by people in an appropriate manner, and connect, interpret, and systemize past events through the prism of a nation's history, traditions, culture, and other knowledge assets. They must then build up an image of how society should be in future. As we discussed in reference to "tacit knowing," a minute detail can build up into a whole. Socially wise leaders should continue to expand and extend the width and depth of their historical imagination. To understand a society's history, tradition, and culture, they must visit actual places, feel the atmosphere with their five physical senses, and hone their sense of empathy. At the same time, to grasp the larger picture, they must also venture outside of their country, incorporate knowledge of the surrounding regions, and accept multiple histories and values. By doing so, their historical imagination can increase in breadth and depth.

2. Idealistic pragmatism: Relentless pursuit of excellence

Another ability or mental model of socially wise leadership can be characterized as "idealistic pragmatism." Socially wise leaders need to present their own ideals, positioning them as they exist within the social reality. By presenting ideals, making "better" assessments and taking "better" actions according to the real context, they approach their ideal. If we base the approach on idealistic pragmatism, we may be able to solve the contradictions between ideals and reality through trial and error.

Just as Aristotle (2004) argued, we see that human beings have a natural propensity to pursue the good of society. Such common good does not emerge deductively from a majority vote or the greatest common denominator of a particular community. It emerges from a relentless pursuit of excellence in our daily lives, through dialogue and practice in interactions with others and the environment. We must set the common good as an ideal and attempt to reach the ideal in practice.

Idealistic pragmatism is a dialectical approach used to synthesize contradictions between the ideal and reality by practicing trial and error. The point is that idealism and realism are in a dialectical relationship, not a compromise. Pragmatism is concerned with ways of developing a creative balance between idealism and realism. Extreme idealism is on one pole and reality on the other. Reality is always a gray in between those two poles. An idealistic pragmatist thus pursues excellence relentlessly on the basis of reality as it is and aims to achieve the ideal in the reality. The "just-right" judgment will be the key.

The basic idea of pragmatism is that, out of knowledge gained from experiences, what is effective is the truth ("the truth is what works"). James (1995) says that when people make very important decisions, there is often an insufficient foundation for making the decision and as such, no clear answer, and one can only depend on one's own beliefs. If those beliefs are translated into actions and ex-post evaluation of their outcomes shows that the desired results were produced, this is tentatively deemed as the truth. If mistakes are made, they will constantly be amended. Dewey (1986) asserts that good things in daily life are morally good. It is the thought that the ideals of truth or good can only be reached through practices.

John McDowell (1996) is one of the advocates of neo-pragmatism that emerged in the second half of the twentieth century. He focuses on experience and asserts that it is impossible to make a clear division between experience and concept. He states that any concept is blind without experience, that intent without visible activities is meaningless, and that the motion of four limbs without concept is simply an event, far from being an expression of the actor. He argues that individuals and specific experiences include the implementation of concepts, and that Aristotle's "virtue" comprises a synthesis of the ability to take action and the cognitive ability (perceptual and sensitive capacity) of being able to read the context appropriately and timely. He describes this as phronesis, and that the values inherent in one's way of life lie at the foundation of pragmatism, as discussed in Chap. 1.

This way of thinking rejects the idealism represented by Plato's theory of ideas, instead adopting the kind of realism that leads to the lineage of British empiricism embodied in scientific methodologies. At the same time, it may be described as an attempt of a dynamic monistic approach that does not separate mind and body, beyond the dualistic approach of the subjective and objective, which has been a general Western philosophical tradition. It is also a way of thinking that is fundamentally connected to concepts from the philosophy of phenomenology; Maurice Merleau-Ponty's "intersubjectivity," Michael Polanyi's "tacit knowing," Kitaro Nishida's "pure experience," "unity of mind and body," Henri Bergson's "pure connection," and Alfred Whitehead's "actual entity."

In other words, idealistic pragmatism should encompass our attitude toward pursuing our "way of life." In idealistic pragmatism, humans are deemed as social beings through which ideals can be pursued in practice within specific, individual contexts. Questioning one's way of life determines the ideal or the direction to aim for. This process leads to the accumulation of actual practices, which eventually prompts changes. Without such embodied practices, ideals would be meaningless, no matter how wonderful they may superficially sound.

3. A new model of leadership and management grounded in knowledge creation theory

In order to illustrate the new model of leadership and management grounded in knowledge creation theory, we have combined the SECI process and the six abilities of wise leadership, as shown in Fig. 10.1. Our model of "leadership" is not limited to political leaders or government officials, but is aimed at all-inclusive leaders, and at anyone who purses the common good from the ground level.

Figure 10.1 shows the dynamic leadership process of nation management based on phronesis. The upper circle contains the six capabilities of phronesis that were previously explained in Chap. 1: (1) set a good goal; (2) observe reality; (3) create *ba*; (4) narrate the essence; (5) exercise political power; and (6) foster phronesis. With these six abilities, leaders will utilize the basic capacity of the national, political, economic, and social powers—as well as available resources—to solve social issues and increase social wealth. In the process, historical imagination and idealistic pragmatism comprise two additional capacities or mental models required by socially wise leaders. Historical imagination is the ability to

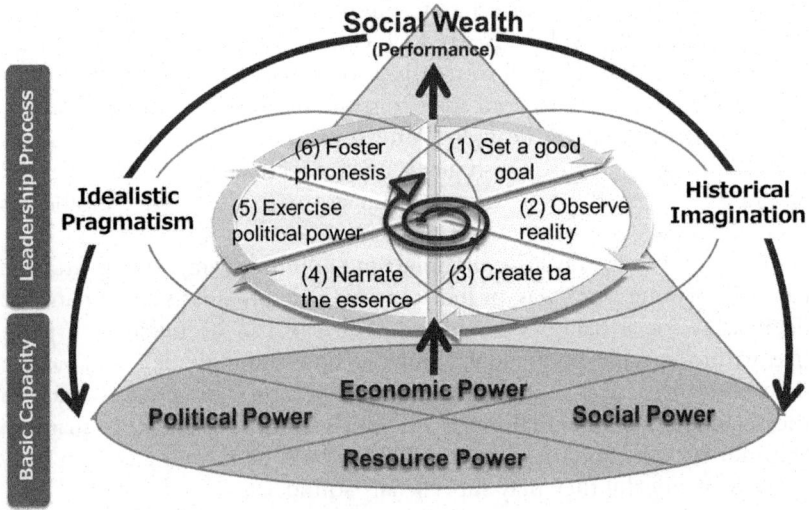

Fig. 10.1 Model of the Socially Wise Leaders. *Source* Nonaka (2014)

see a wide and deep time-space nexus, and idealistic pragmatism is an ability to synthesize idealism and pragmatism.

Furthermore, the leader needs to form teams connecting leaders at the national, regional, and community level, to form fractal organizations between all the levels, as shown in Fig. 10.2. This illustration is a simplified form of society, representing three layers from the community level to the regional and national level. This "distributed wise leadership" is critical in fostering an inclusive society at large, from the national level to the regional and community level.

Each fractal in each layer has autonomy and freedom to connect, relate, and interact with other fractal parts at any level. Therefore, it is inclusive and open, with permeable boundaries. If society is configured in such a way that it has such autonomous fractal organizations throughout, then it will be more broadly resilient—and not only able to quickly respond to risk and crisis but also to quickly achieve transformation and innovation. At the same time, actions taken in communities will be based on the actual situation grasped at the very front of the community fractal, effectively meeting people's needs and wants. This is why we emphasize the importance of distributed leadership and fractal organization in every part of society.

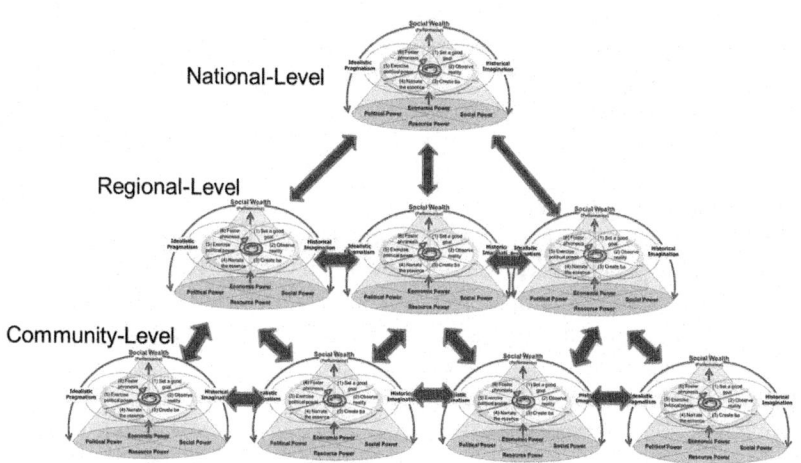

Fig. 10.2 Dynamic Fractal model of Society. *Source* Nonaka (2014)

FUTURE CHALLENGES

As our work comes to an end, we would like to present as a conclusion three propositions drawn from the seven case studies presented in this book, based on the theories and practices of public management and knowledge-based management on pursuing social innovation, or co-creating social values in communities toward the common good.

Proposition 1: A human-centric view is needed in promoting social innovation Social innovation is centered on human beings, and therefore, a human-centric view is needed in promoting social innovation. In particular, Socialization in the SECI process—empathizing reality through actual experiences, or in other words, *tacit knowing*—will be the key at the start of a social innovation process. Citizens should be at the center, because social innovation is about co-creating value for citizens and society. However, we tend to overlook important factors such as tacit knowledge and people's subjectivity. As pointed out in the case of Mitaka City, many citizens remain silent when it comes to city planning or city administration until such time as they are offered opportunities to present their opinions, a phenomenon that is likely to be commonplace in other communities and settings.

On the other hand, when taking a scientific approach to management, people are often measured by certain categories or demographics in terms of quantifiable data. According to WHO (1997), quality of life is defined as an individual's perception of their position in life in the context of the culture and value systems in which they live and in relation to their goals, expectations, standards, and concerns. It is a broad-ranging concept affected in a complex way by the person's physical health, psychological state, level of independence, social relationships, personal beliefs, and their relationship to salient features of their environment. However, even with these measurements, it is not easy to understand the reality of people's everyday lives. For one thing, the data only represent the average of people in a certain category, and for another, the situations and context people live in change every day while the data are merely information about the past.

We think that the ultimate goal of social innovation is to address problems, increase access to resources and decision-making processes, and improve skills and capacity, so that people can enhance the quality of their everyday lives. It is about each individual citizen, with their own identity and personality, and their own motivations and dreams, etcetera. We need to understand their lives, socialize with them, and feel their actual problems with all five senses before generalizing about issues. In other words, we must grasp the essence of actuality—first, by sharing people's tacit knowledge; and second, we must grasp the essence of actuality by gathering and mutually sharing tacit knowledge between community members, and with the leaders. The essence of actuality cannot be grasped by analysis. The analysis is only useful as a complementary tool for the Combination step, as means of relating and systemizing the concepts in the Socialization and Externalization steps.

There is considerable evidence from research in neuroscience that human beings are born to be social. A mind-body synthesis has been proposed by philosophers of phenomenology such as Merleau-Ponty (inter-corporality) and Francisco Valera (embodied mind) to name just two (Merleau-Ponty 1962; Valera 1991). More evidence comes from mirror neurons, which may explain how we understand the intentions of others (Iacoboni et al. 2005; Rizzolatti 2005). Another argument points out that in Maslow's hierarchy of needs, what should come at the bottom is not physiological needs but social needs (Lieberman 2013). One more interesting finding is that cognitive skills do not guarantee a child's success, but non-cognitive skills do (Tough 2013; Heckman 2013). Children's success over time comes as a result of non-cognitive skills (= personal skills) according to research done by James Heckman (see Tough 2013), Professor of Economics at the University of Chicago and 2000 Nobel Laureate in Economics.[6]

If we look back at the leaders that appeared in the case studies we examined, they do present these non-cognitive skills. Interestingly, Heckman and Tough pointed out that non-cognitive skills are only obtained through good habits of trial and error in our daily lives, learned under the influence of the mentoring and personalities of exemplars (Tough 2013; Heckman 2013). This point echoes with the sixth ability of wise leadership.

Proposition 2: Knowledge creation theory on management helps realize social innovation The knowledge creation theory on management can provide a practical theory and methodology for realizing social innovation. In this project, we looked at social innovation in ASEAN countries from the perspective of knowledge creation theory on management and concluded that this theory provides a good explanation of the process of social innovation, namely the spiral-up process of the SECI model, wise leadership (phronesis or practical wisdom), *ba*, fractal organization, and middle-up-down management. This theory can help to explain how social innovation can be achieved.

As we have already discussed, social innovation is different from innovation in the private sector (for-profit organizations) or the public sector (government organizations or not-for-profit organizations) as social innovation involves a variety of diverse stakeholders whose relationships are built voluntarily. This means it is not legitimacy but intimacy that connects the stakeholders. What connects them in the beginning is empathy and resonance in response to the purpose or the vision of the future and the leaders' phronesis or practical wisdom, rather than analysis or plans, which are often proposed by consultants. In short, unless we really think deeply—as a part of that society—it is unlikely that effective or creative solutions to local problems will be found. Not enough attention was paid to these points in the past, but we think their critical importance has become apparent from our case analysis. The theory is practical in that it presents the process of knowledge creation and the abilities of wise leadership.

Once we know that the knowledge creation theory on management is effective in explaining the social innovation process, then we may reverse the order: Knowledge creation theory on management may provide a practical framework for promoting social innovation. The next step is to increase the awareness and the application of knowledge-based management theory in social innovation processes. Generally, knowing the theory behind everyday work will promote better results by leading to creativity and innovation.

Proposition 3: Need to solve long-term and short-term problems simultaneously In solving long-term social problems and the day-to-day problems of citizens simultaneously, historical imagination and idealistic pragmatism are essential. In the case studies of social innovation, the wise leaders set out a common good that they aspire to, but this common good reflects their personal experiences within society. Through their experience, the leaders feel and understand the history and traditions that underpin the society in which they live and work, and in reflecting these in their own experiences, as well as the opinions of citizens, the leaders articulated a common goal that they believe is shared in society. In other words, the first ability of wise leadership—setting good goals—reflects the historical imagination of the leader. If the leader can imagine history and traditions in a deep and wide sense, they may be able to judge and act from a long-term and wide-ranging perspective.

Setting good goals also requires leaders to be idealistic pragmatists. Leaders should approach social issues with an image of what an ideal state would be like after all of its problems have been solved. However, at the same time, leaders need to be pragmatic when actually addressing issues. Discussing solutions to problems is usually much easier than implementing them and may require a huge amount of money or time. In these cases, leaders should look at the actuality of the current situation and make a pragmatic judgment based on their understanding. However, in order to avoid such judgments becoming a mere compromise, idealism is important. In other words, idealistic pragmatism provides a way of synthesizing long-term and short-term problems and the day-to-day problems of citizens.

Social leaders need to inspire and motivate various stakeholders with diverse backgrounds, beliefs, knowledge, and opinions, so that every stakeholder ends up moving in one direction. Telling a strategic narrative, or open-ended storytelling is a good way of sharing the leaders' beliefs, values, and directions and synthesizing the narrative of each stakeholder toward realizing the common good of society at large.[7]

MESSAGE TO ASEAN COUNTRIES AND THE WORLD

As a finally conclusion for this book, we would like to emphasize once again that management is a "way of life." In co-creating values for society, those who are involved in social innovation must always ask the question, "what do we want to achieve?"—the answer to which involves consideration of beliefs, vision, and values for the future, of leaders as well as citizens. We must acknowledge that we are in fact living in a world of many conflicts, crises, and uncertainties, but at the same time, we must believe in our own potential. Knowledge is an unlimited resource, and one that only human beings can create. In order to reach our ultimate ideal of the future, we must unleash our knowledge potential, and relentlessly pursue excellence in our daily practices.

Let us all together unleash the knowledge potential of people everywhere as we attempt to co-create values for society.

NOTES

1. Abduction, or often so called Inference to the Best Explanation (or sometimes called abductive reasoning, abductive inference or retroduction) is a form of logical inference that provides best explanation of what has been observed; simplest and most likely explanation. Source: Stanford Encyclopedia of Philosophy, retrieved from http://plato.stanford.edu/entries/abduction/.

2. Kata is a "way of doing things," which is "the core of ideal action." Good Kata functions as archetype that fosters creative routine but provides higher freedom. Shu 守 (learn), Ha 破 (break), and Ri 離 (create) steps are critical in continuous self-renewal processes (Nonaka 2006).

3. Of the following six power bases described by French and Raven (1959) and Raven (1965), a–c are considered to be hard power, e–f are soft power, and d is smart power.
   (a) Reward Power: Power based on one's ability to reward the other.
   (b) Coercive Power: Power based on one's ability to punish the other.
   (c) Legitimate Power: Power based on the perceptions that one has a legitimate right to determine other's behavior.
   (d) Referent Power: Power based on the identification of one with the other.
   (e) Expert Power: Power based on the perceptions that one has some special knowledge or experiences.
   (f) Informational Power: Power based on the perceived relevance and validity of one's information.

4. According to Porter, (1985), the five forces consist of (1) threat of new entrants, (2) threat of substitute products or services, (3) bargaining power of buyers, (4) bargaining power of suppliers, and (5) intensity of competitive rivalry.

5. The diamond model (Porter 1990) consists of (1) factor conditions on various resources, (2) demand conditions in home market, (3) related and supporting industries, (4) firm strategy, structure, and rivalry, (5) government policies that affect other conditions, and (6) chances which are outside the control of a firm. These six factors interact with each other to improve the competiveness of the cluster, which is an accumulation of related industries that affects the competitiveness of the nation.

6. Examples of non-cognitive skills according to Heckman (2013) are; (1) grit and perseverance, (2) self-control, (3) zest, (4) social intelligence (Ability to recognize the dynamics of human relations and to respond quickly to the changes in the social situation), (5) gratitude, (6) optimism, and (7) curiosity.

7. As stated in Chap. 1, we are talking about 'narrative' but not 'history.' The difference between a story and a narrative is that a story will have an end while a narrative is never-ending. It continues as new situation and context unfolds. If the context changes, we quickly change the plot and script.

REFERENCES

Aristotle. 2004. *The nicomachean ethics.* London: Penguin Books.

Carr, E. 1961. *What is history.* Harmondsworth, England: Penguin.

de Vries, J. 2010. Is new public management really dead? *OECD Journal on Budgeting 2010* 10 (1): 87–91.

Dewey, J. 1986. Experience and education. *The Educational Forum* 50 (3): 241–252.

Dunleavy, Patrick, et al. 2006. New public management is dead-long live digital-eragovernance. *Journal of Public Administration Research and Theory* 16 (3): 467–494.

French, J.R., and B. Raven. 1959. The bases of social power. In *Studies in social power*, ed. D. Cartwright, and A. Zander, 259–269. Ann Arbor MI: Research Center for Group Dynamics, Institute For Social Research, University of Michigan.

Heckman, J.J. 2013. *Giving kids a fair chance.* Cambridge, MA: MIT Press.

Hood, Christopher. 1991. A public management for all seasons? *Public Administration* 69 (1): 3–19.

Iacoboni, Marco, et al. 2005. Grasping the intentions of others with one's own mirror neuron system. *PLoS Biology* 3 (3): e79.

James, W. 1995. *Pragmatism.* New York: Dover Publications.

Kant, 1785/2002. *Groundwork for the Metaphysics of Morals*, Trans. and eds. A. Zweig. T.E. Hill, and A. Zweig. Oxford: Oxford.

Lieberman, Matthew D. 2013. *Social: Why our brains are wired to connect.* Oxford: OUP.

McDowell, John. 1996. *Mind and world.* Harvard University Press.

Merleau-Ponty, M. 1962. Phenomenology of perception, C. Smith trans. London: Routledge.

Nonaka, I. 2014. Knowledge creation of nations. Paper presented at the second workshop on leadership and management development in Asian countries, 29 Sep–1 Oct. Tokyo: National Graduate Institute for Policy Studies (GRIPS).

Nonaka, Ikujiro, and Hirotaka Takeuchi. 1995. *The knowledge-creating company: How Japanese companies create the dynamics of innovation.* Oxford University Press.

Nye, Joseph S. 2011. *The future of power.* PublicAffairs.

Nye, J.S. Jr. and D.A. Welch. 2013. *Kokusai Funso–Riron to Rekishi (Gensho dai yon Han)* [*Understanding international conflicts: An introduction to theory and history*], A. Tanaka trans., 9th edn. Yuhikaku Publishing.

Porter, M.E. 1985. *The competitive advantage: Creating and sustaining superior performance.* New York: Free Press.

Porter, M.E. 1990. *The competitive advantage of nations.* New York: Free Press.

Porter, M. E., and M. R. Kramer. 2006. Strategy and society: The link between corporate social responsibility and competitive advantage. *Harvard business review* 84 (12): 78–92.

Porter, Michael E., and Mark R. Kramer. 2011. The big idea: Creating shared value. *Harvard Business Review* 89 (1): 2.

Raven, B.H. 1965. Social influence and power. In *Current studies in social psychology*, eds. I.D. Steiner, and M. Fishbein, 371–382. New York: Holt, Rinehart, Winston.

Rawls, John. 2009. *A theory of justice.* Harvard University Press.

Rizzolatti, Giacomo. 2005. The mirror neuron system and its function in humans. *Anatomy and Embryology* 210 (5–6): 419–421.

Rosch, E., F. Varela, and E. Thompson. 1991. *The Embodied Mind: Cognitive Science and Human Experience.* Cambridge, MA: MIT Press.

Sandel, Michael J. 2010. *Justice: What's the right thing to do?* Macmillan.

Tough, P. 2013. *How children succeed.* London: Random House.

WHO. 1997. Measuring Quality of Life: The World Health Organization Quality of Life Instruments. WHO/MSA/MNH/PSF/97.4. Geneva, Switzerland: World Health Organization Division of Mental Health and Prevention of Substance Abuse. http://www.who.int/mental_health/media/en/68.pdf.

Authors' Biography

Ikujiro Nonaka is a Professor Emeritus, Hitotsubashi University, the world-renowned founder of the theory of knowledge-based management. He received his B.A. (Political Science) from Waseda University, MBA in 1968, and Ph.D. (Business Administration) in 1972 from the University of California, Berkeley. Prior to his academic track, he worked at Fuji Electric Corporation. He has won wide-ranging recognition for his work in developing the knowledge-based management theory and recently received the Lifetime Achievement Award by Thinkers50. His research interests are in the organizational knowledge creation and wise leadership in private, public, and social organizations. His recent publications include Nonaka, I., & Takeuchi, H. (2011), the wise leader, *Harvard business review*, 89(5), 58–67.

Kiyotaka Yokomichi is Vice President and Professor of National Graduate Institute for Policy Studies (GRIPS). He is a graduate of the University of Tokyo. After working for Japan's Ministry of Home Affairs, he joined the faculty of the Graduate School of Policy Science (GSPS), Saitama University in 1988. He is a leading expert on local administration and governance, with extensive research and practical experience in the area of local government reform in Japan. One of the founders of GRIPS, Professor Yokomichi now specializes in capacity development of government officials in Japan and other countries in Asia.

Ayano Hirose Nishihara is an Assistant Professor, Department of Global Business, College of Business, Rikkyo University, and a research collaborator to Professor Emeritus Ikujiro Nonaka. She received her B.A. (Law) from Nagoya University, MBA in 2005 and DBA in 2011 from the Graduate School of International Corporate Strategy, Hitotsubashi University. Prior to her academic track, she worked as an assistant manager at NEC Corporation. Her research topics include knowledge creation at public and private organizations and communities, knowledge-creating leadership, and social innovation. Her recent publications include Nonaka, I., Hirose, A., & Takeda, Y. (2016). "Meso"— Foundations of Dynamic Capabilities: Team-Level Synthesis and Distributed Leadership as the Source of Dynamic Creativity. *Global Strategy Journal, 6*(3), 168–182.

INDEX